D1560004

The Shakespeare Effect

The Shakespeare Effect
A History of Twentieth-Century Performance

Robert Shaughnessy

macmillan

First published 2002 by
PALGRAVE MACMILLAN
Houndmills, Basingstoke, Hampshire RG21 6XS and
175 Fifth Avenue, New York, N.Y. 10010
Companies and representatives throughout the world

PALGRAVE MACMILLAN is the new global academic imprint of the Palgave Macmillan division of St. Martin's Press, LLC and of Palgrave Macmillan Ltd Macmillan® is a registered trademark in the United States, United Kingdom and other countries. Palgrave is a registered trademark in the European Union and other countries.

ISBN 0–333–77937–1

A catalogue record for this book is available from the British Library.

Library of Congress Cataloging-in-Publication Data
Shaughnessy, Robert, 1962-
  The Shakespeare effect: a history of twentieth-century performance/
    Robert Shaughnessy. p. cm.
  Includes bibliographical references (p.) and index.
  ISBN 0-333-77937-1 (cloth)
  1. Shakespeare, William, 1564-1616--Stage history--1950-
  2. Shakespeare, William, 1564-1616--Stage history--1800-1950.
  3. Shakespeare, William, 1564-1616--Stage history--English-speaking
  countries. 4. Theater--English-speaking countries--History--
  20th century. I. Title.
  PR3100.S58 2002
  792.9'5'0904--dc21   2001050803

10   9   8   7   6   5   4   3   2   1
11   10   09   08   07   06   05   04   03   02

Transferred to digital printing 2005

For Caitlin, Nathaniel, Gabriel and Erina, with love

·

Contents

Acknowledgements

Parts of this book have previously appeared in print: an earlier version of Chapter 2 was published in *Theatre Notebook*, 51 (1997); parts of Chapters 1 and 3 in *Shakespeare Survey*, 53, edited by Peter Holland (Cambridge University Press, 2000). I am grateful to the editors and publishers for permission to reproduce this material. I also wish to acknowledge the support of the Arts and Humanities Research Board, the Society for Theatre Research, and the University of Surrey Roehampton. Thanks are due to Regina Doyle at the Tyrone Guthrie Centre, Annagh-ma-kerrig, Jane Edmonds and Trish Cuthbertson at the Stratford Festival, Christopher Robinson and Sarah Cuthill of the University of Bristol Theatre Collection, Sue Wiseman at the University of Kent Templeman Library, and the staff of the Birmingham Shakespeare Library, the Shakespeare Institute, the Shakespeare Centre Library, the Theatre Museum, Casarotto Ramsay Ltd, and the BBC Document Archive. Don Chapman shared with me his work on Terence Gray; Edward Bond responded helpfully to my questions; Tim Etchells generously supplied research material, answers and reflections on the Forced Entertainment *Lear*. Charmian Hearne initiated the project at Palgrave; thanks are also due to the anonymous reader and to Barbara Slater for superbly attentive copy-editing. The book has been expertly steered through the production process by Eleanor Birne and Becky Mashayekh.

During the period in which I have been working on this book, I have enjoyed and valued the many conversations that I have had with friends and colleagues, and with those who have witnessed its emergence in a variety of contexts. At the University of Surrey Roehampton I have benefited immensely from the company of Michael Dobson, Allen Fisher, Susanne Greenhalgh, Jen Harvie, Adrian Kear, Joe Kelleher and Susan Painter; Alan Read and Peter Reynolds have provided moral, intellectual and practical support by engineering the circumstances that enabled me to bring the book to completion. For creating opportunities for me to rehearse material in public, thanks to Richard Foulkes, Michael Shapiro, Peter J. Smith and Stanley Wells. For responses to these and other ventures, and for help, advice and support, thanks to Paul Allain, Claire Cochrane, Kate Fullbrook, Graham Holderness, Russell Jackson, Dennis Kennedy, Ania Loomba,

Christopher McCullough, Gordon McMullan, Marion O'Connor, Derek Paget, Liz Schafer, Ann Thompson and Peter Thomson. Very special thanks to Peter Holland, John Russell Brown and Barbara Hodgdon, whose candour, enthusiasm and generosity have been inspirational. My deepest thanks are to Nicola, who has lived with all this throughout a period of great change, and who remains the most patient and perceptive of readers, and to Caitlin, Nathaniel, Gabriel and Erina, each of whom arrived at a crucial moment in the book's development, and who have, I hope, taught me to keep it in perspective. It is you, above all, that have made it worth doing.

ROBERT SHAUGHNESSY

Introduction

The image on the cover of the theatre programme is an arresting one: the head and shoulders of a young man with close cropped dark hair, posed against a background of what looks like both finely scratched metal plate and a wall of television static. He wears an off-white T-shirt, his chin bears a shadowy trace of stubble, and his left ear and right nostril are pierced by rings. He faces the camera, but is unable to address us or even meet our gaze, for his eyes and mouth have been forced shut, held in place by crude but emphatically secure, thick black thread stitching running through the lips and eyelids. Since this is poster and programme image (borrowed from Amnesty International) for a production of *Hamlet*, we assume this to be the Prince of Denmark himself, but in this instance the relentlessly garrulous and observant protagonist is subdued to silence and blindness, a mute witness who can speak (and see) neither good nor evil. The pre-publicity for the production had prepared us for a 'fast-paced urban thriller' with its 'young prince at the centre of a paranoid world', envisaged as 'a Denmark in constant readiness for war' and 'a striking post-industrial landscape'; the programme announces that its aim is to link 'the public and the personal' and to expose the catastrophic consequences of 'a monarchy bent on survival at any cost'. It is evident, then, that Hamlet's exquisite mutilation is politically motivated, a violent act of corporeal censorship by a totalitarian regime which has both sufficient wit to grimly parody the Prince's own fashionable bodily ornamentation and a fetishistic ingenuity that would be at home in Kafka's penal colony.

It is a metaphor, of course, albeit one as telling as much of the visual iconography employed within the production itself; Hamlet's first appearance on stage confirms that while he still sports the T-shirt and

1

the earrings, he is as (un)free to see and speak as the rest of the cast (still, it might have made for an interestingly experimental reading of the play had the image been literalised). Nonetheless, London-based Red Shift Theatre Company's touring *Hamlet*, which visited medium-scale performance venues around the United Kingdom between Autumn 1999 and Spring 2000 (and which I saw, amidst a young, occasionally bemused but generally appreciative audience at the University of Kent's Gulbenkian Theatre on 14 March 2000) was an aggressively contemporary reading of the play. The vision of Danish power politics as a total stitch-up was confirmed in every detail of a production which was modern dress from head to foot. The *mise-en-scène* consisted of a set of tarnished metal coffin-like boxes, manipulated to suggest anything from castle ramparts to the Queen's bedchamber, and a few high-backed chairs. Searchlights swept the stage, sentries brandished rifles, and sound-effect jet planes swooped overhead. The action was punctuated by a cinematic soundtrack dominated by grunge and drum and bass: in the manner of the (probably apocryphal) 1950s instrumental, something was rockin' in the State of Denmark.[1] The wardrobe was provided by designer fashion label Red or Dead: Claudius and his court adhered to a rigid military dress code, while Hamlet's casually deconstructed jacket and soft shoes flouted protocol with style. The Prince himself (Peter Collins) was a genial, laddish figure, prone to the odd bout of drug use, and enjoying a matey rapport with the audience; a slacker with a copy of *The Outsider* peeping from his pocket. Of course, this was an idiom whose principles had been established in the 1920s, and revived wholesale by (among others) Michael Bogdanov and Michael Pennington with the English Shakespeare Company during the 1980s, and which is now the accepted mode for much small to medium-scale Shakespearean production, but it was employed here with verve and a keen sense of the production's target audience. A programme note indicated that the priority was accessibility: condemning a traditional Shakespearean theatre dominated by 'the dazzle of some theatrical Lord who is encouraged to interpose his idiosyncratic mannered style between the audience and the play', it laid claim to 'the guts of what Shakespeare means' and declared that 'people are entitled to have their artist made available'. Modern dress was the means to lug the guts of Shakespeare into the open, and onto the stage.

For audiences who might have been feeling jaded by yet another *Hamlet* (Matthew Warchus' RSC production ran in Stratford and London during 1997 and 1998, and it would be staged at both

Shakespeare's Globe and the Royal National Theatre in 2000), Red Shift's determinedly populist slant seemed a smart piece of niche marketing. But it made another claim to distinctiveness: the text used for the production was the 1603 Quarto, which had last been afforded a professional production in London in 1985. For director Jonathan Holloway, the First Quarto (billed in Red Shift's publicity as 'as close as we can get to the popular play seen on the Jacobean stage') was an acting version of the play ideally suited to the needs of a touring company. The pragmatic basis of this deployment of Q1 for a production dependent upon non-metropolitan audiences wary of public transport timetables (it ran for just over two hours, including interval), and carried by a cast of eight, was evident. The casting called for considerable ingenuity in places, such as in a play scene which set Pirandello against Hitchcock, inviting us to consider Hamlet watching Claudius (previously doubled with the Player King) facing us as a spectator of a performance of *The Mousetrap* which could be heard but not seen. Sidestepping the long-standing controversy over the text that had been revitalised by *The Tragicall Historie of Hamlet Prince of Denmark*'s publication in the much-debated Shakespearean Originals series in 1992,[2] Q1 was presented not just as an intrinsically more *theatrical* text but as one directly attuned to the radical and democratic spirit of the production as a whole. The production went by the title of *Hamlet: First Cut*, a designation which, as a number of commentators observed, invoked a filmic terminology which has been deployed in the past to restore to particular works the signature of the auteur, famously in the case of Ridley Scott's Director's Cut *Blade Runner* (and there was even a hint of Dekkard's final showdown with the replicant Roy in Hamlet's rooftop confrontation with the Ghost). If this was in keeping with the cinematic vocabulary which was one element of the production, it also connected with its musical register, with faintly archaic echoes of the technology of vinyl recording, and of cutting a track. The combination figured textual and theatrical authenticity simultaneously in terms of authorially-conferred legitimacy and as primitive, 'rough cut' spontaneity and immediacy.

The iconography prompts further reflection. If the image of sutured lips and eyelids depicted totalitarianism as a kind of violent writing upon the body of Hamlet himself, the idea of the 'first cut' also invoked (somewhat ambiguously) the familiar rhetoric of textual disfigurement which, as we shall see in the case of William Poel's own Q1 experiment, has shadowed the stage history of the play. As the ongoing, and acrimonious, debate about the good, bad or ugly status of Q1 as reported text, pirated text, first draft or mangled travesty of the play has demonstrated, employing it was a risky strategy, and not all of the production's reviewers were impressed (one described it as '*Hamlet* lite'[3]). It is easy to detect inconsistencies between Holloway's reiteration of the well-worn theory that Q1 was 'pirated ... dictated from memory ... and published without permission', his assumption that 'this text comes closer than the other longer versions do to actual stage practice', and his concern for 'the guts of what Shakespeare means'; as Ann Thompson records, Holloway 'seemed to oscillate between thinking of Q1 as a first draft which Shakespeare filled out to become the more elaborate Q2 and thinking of it as a "reported text", an abbreviated version of a longer play'.[4] For current purposes, however, the more interesting issue is not whether the scholarship deployed by the production is flawed or misleading, but the contradictory effect, within the overall production style, of its being there at all. Red Shift's rhetoric, in both the performance and its marketing materials, was that *Hamlet* is a thing of and for the people, a vital and visceral text urgently in need of liberation from the deadening clutches of a high cultural tradition: thus the modernity of the visual scene and soundtrack combine with Q1's estranging substitutions of text and character (Corambis for Polonius, 'I there's the point' for 'that is the question') to sustain a performance event which believed itself to be neither constrained nor mandated by its theatrical and literary inheritance.

At one level, then, the text's identity as a historical artefact is defiantly obliterated, the production's claim to theatrical and cultural authority rooted in its immersion in the condition of (post)modernity: severed from tradition, *Hamlet* is made to speak as a new play. But, just as the Ghost continues to cry for remembrance long after he has vanished from the theatrical field of vision, it seems that the authenticating presence of Shakespeare, as the ultimate arbiter of legitimacy, cannot be dispensed with. For all the apparent iconoclasm of the production's method, and employing a now-familiar modulation of traditional appeals to Shakespearean authority by citing the sanctioning force of performance, this *Hamlet*'s final defence is its presumed historical precedent: in an essentialising alignment of Jacobean and contemporary stage practice, the claim is that the needs and priorities of a touring company at the end of the twentieth century can be met by a text (apparently) tailored to those of a travelling company at the beginning of the seventeenth.

Red Shift's First Quarto *Hamlet* presents an unusually clear and focused example of a problem which is endemic to Shakespearean theatrical production, and which is one of the central concerns of this book: the deep, and possibly irreconcilable, tensions between the competing authorities of performance, the text, and the institutional apparatus of 'Shakespeare' (none of which are stable or homogeneous categories). To set these factors in a relation of opposition and conflict, however, might be seen as restarting an argument which many consider to have long been settled. The great achievement of performance-centred criticism has been to bequeath to Shakespeare studies in general its own faith in both the theatrical potentialities of the text and the contemporary theatre's capacity to realise them; as a consequence, the now-universal consensus that Shakespeare's plays were 'intended' for performance, and ideally should be experienced as such, has allowed the possibility of enactment virtually to become an imperative. On the face of it, the result has been a more congenial and mutually beneficial relationship between theatre and scholarship than ever before. The widely-accepted view that Shakespeare was no solitary literary genius but an active participant in a sharply entrepreneurial activity of theatre-making has legitimised a theatrically-aware approach to the plays at every level of pedagogy, scholarship and performance. Growing recognition of the mutability and adaptability of the texts within their originating theatrical contexts has been matched by greater tolerance of the contemporary theatre's ways with texts whose absolute integrity was in the past vociferously defended. The battle lines have been redrawn and old stereotypes have broken down: although the *idiot savant* literary scholar continues to appeal to many in the acting profession as an embodiment of pedantry and theatrical impracticality, actors and directors are no longer regarded as betrayers and violators of Shakespeare's sacred texts, but are treated with respect, even deference, by academics. Opinions about what Shakespearean performance is, and how it can be discussed, documented and analysed, have become more varied and more sophisticated. Just as the idea that Shakespeare is better read than said would nowadays be considered as heretical as the opposing position once was, few serious commentators would now advance the view that the business of Shakespearean production is, or should be, to deliver predetermined textual meanings. Few, I think, would object to the proposition that the task, and method, of performance criticism is not just to evaluate how 'successfully' a given production realises the potential of the text but to identify the complex logic of its alignments of performers, spectators, space and script, and that, in order to do this, it is necessary to locate these within the broader sphere of culture, politics and history. It goes without saying, I hope, that this critical enterprise has extended and enriched our appreciation of the manifold possibilities of performed Shakespeare, confirming, if confirmation were needed, the unrivalled richness of the plays' relation to their medium.

It is when more awkward questions are asked about Shakespearean performance, about the claims made for it, by it, and on its behalf, about what it is, what it does, and what it is for, that the relationship starts to look less harmonious. One of the consequences of the shift towards performance in editorial practice has been a renewed sense of the plurality and instability of the text itself: the evidence of the contingencies of script production, performance and publication reveals that placing Shakespeare in the realms of the theatrical rather than (or as well as) the literary tends to multiply indeterminacies, not contain them. The 'stage-centred' is not so centred after all. Moreover, the performance scholarship of the past decade which has taken on board the concerns of critical and cultural theory has extended and transformed the established commitment to detailed documentation of production histories by focusing attention upon the ways in which, for example, varieties of the 'authentic' are constituted within and around performance, and ideologies of class, race and gender are negotiated, reproduced or contested within theatre practice. This work has also involved a reconsideration of the ways in which performances negotiate the cultural positioning and authority of Shakespeare.

A key consideration here is that the *disciplinary* nature of Shakespearean textuality problematises the widely-held view that the collaborative partnership between Shakespeare and performance is conducted on equal terms. Within the dominant Anglo-American traditions of performance, certainly, the much-vaunted freedoms of performance have (under the auspices of a scrupulous regard for 'the text') remained strictly bounded and regulated, by the practitioners themselves, and by both popular and scholarly modes of criticism. Although the reanimation of Shakespeare's inherent and overriding theatricality has been widely welcomed as liberating, the performance of Shakespeare, as W.B. Worthen has argued, continues to be framed by questions of authority, authenticity and legitimacy: 'the sense that performance transmits Shakespearean authority remains very much in play, most strongly perhaps when the ostensibly free and disruptive activity of the stage is at hand'.[5] The 'authorising' presence of Shakespeare turns the production of the plays into a zone of performance activity unlike any other, while the script's theatrical origins are harnessed to the effort of regulating and validating its contemporary reproduction. According to Worthen, to think of performance as conveying authorised meanings of any kind, especially meanings authenticated in and by the text, is, finally, to tame 'the unruly ways of the stage'.[6]

A pessimistic extrapolation of this position would regard any theatrical appropriation of Shakespeare which retains an affiliation to the author as irrevocably compromised. In practice, as Worthen goes on to demonstrate, the making of meanings by performers and audiences is a rather more dynamic process than this initial formulation suggests. Although it would be an equally essentialist and ahistorical gesture to attempt to resist the taming powers of Shakespeare with an opposing insistence upon the liberty and licence of performance, a sense of the unruliness of the stage and its practices provides a useful point of departure for performance analysis, and it is a central preoccupation of this book. By 'unruliness' I mean the potential of performance to evade, exceed or rupture the impression of coherence that is conferred by the presence of Shakespeare, its capacity to work against the text, and against official structures and discourses of legitimation. This can operate at a number of levels, most obviously when a production consciously articulates a critical or resistant reading of a given play, and when a text (or group of texts) is actively reconstituted as adaptation in order to interrogate the source.[7] An increasing awareness of the intercultural context of current Shakespearean production has added fuel to the debates that have arisen around these modes of engagement, in that the severing of the automatic link between Shakespearean theatre and spoken English (and anglophone culture in general) has been accompanied by the partial and problematic incorporation of performance traditions and vocabularies which undermine the existing forms of dominant practice.[8] But it can also manifest itself through the more unexpected and, indeed, often unintended, forms of disruption and recalcitrance that inhabit Shakespearean performance.

Some of these are structural and contextual. Although Shakespeare in the theatre is promoted as the most natural thing in the world, it is deeply vulnerable and inherently unstable; it is becoming increasingly clear that the perpetuation of the practice relies upon a strenuous, and nowadays perhaps strained, suspension of cultural disbelief. Observing that 'Shakespeare's reputation peaked in the reign of Queen Victoria, and is now shrinking', Gary Taylor provocatively suggests a long-term 'decline in cultural authority',[9] among the consequences of which are a narrowing of the Shakespearean theatrical repertoire to a handful of more or less guaranteed or compulsory plays (*Romeo and Juliet, Hamlet, A Midsummer Night's Dream*), and a lowering of the boredom thresholds of both performers and audiences. While audiences were once persuaded by the gentle force of Shakespearean cultural authority to believe in fairies and in medieval conceptions of kingship, to laugh at the clowns and to feel moved by the tragedians, the fact that Shakespeare 'is now usually read without any other reason than the desire for a passing grade'[10] means that the theatre must resort to ever more drastic tactics to keep the work afloat, to make it seem relevant, compelling, or even comprehensible. Shakespeare has become an embarrassment in other ways: whereas the textual elements of racism, misogyny, xenophobia and class-consciousness that once won tacit or overt approval continue, like the outbursts of an elderly relative, to be grimly tolerated, what are to contemporary spectators the reactionary and offensive aspects of the work are less and less likely to receive the endorsement of performance (the recent stage history of *The Taming of the Shrew* is a case in point). In this respect, Red Shift's *Hamlet* is representative of a contemporary theatre practice which employs a battery of audience-friendly techniques less to revivify Shakespeare than to substitute for it, even displace it; and yet these seem daring only in relation to a medium which is deeply conservative.

Although the twentieth century has been widely viewed as the most radically experimental phase of Shakespearean theatre history, performers, audiences and commentators have, in the anglophone world especially, been prepared to put up with (indeed, have insisted upon) a pace of innovation and levels of excitement that in any other field of performance would seem antediluvian. Indeed, a brief survey of the history of Shakespearean performance in this period reveals a relationship with the avant-garde variously characterised by indifference, fierce isolationism and cautious and incremental assimilation. William Poel's experiments on mocked-up Elizabethan stages at the close of the nineteenth century provoked strong reactions, and he subsequently emphasised that he was a 'modernist', not an antiquarian;[11] across the Channel in Paris, meanwhile, the fist fights in the auditorium of the Théâtre de l'Oeuvre as it hosted the premiere of Jarry's *Ubu Roi* (which was, among other things, a reworking of Shakespeare) provide a reminder of how much further modernist provocation might go. In the Germany of the 1920s, Jessner's expressionist productions enlisted a Shakespeare who (like Wedekind and Schiller) 'must be thought of as the representatives of this generation as much as the youngest writers',[12] resulting in a scenography of extreme and violent distortion; in London, Barry Jackson famously caused uproar when he put Hamlet in plus-fours. In the Soviet Union during the same period, Meyerhold employed the technologies of biomechanics and constructivist stagecraft to dismantle and rebuild the classics for the post-Revolutionary machine age; when Terence Gray at the Cambridge Festival Theatre imported these techniques in a *Henry VIII* which used a steel revolve and playing-card costumes, he was denounced as a bolshevik. In the 1920s and 1930s Artaud imagined a theatre of cruelty which would combine the visceral and the oneiric, in which the tyranny of words would be overthrown by the terrifying power of the image, and in which masterpieces would be torn apart together with the rational sensibilities of the spectator; in the Shakespearean theatre of the 1960s Artaud was cited (along with Beckett and Brecht) in support of the baroque tortures of *The Wars of the Roses* and Peter Brook's *King Lear*. Brook himself is, of course, most often acclaimed as the pre-eminent Shakespearean *enfant terrible*, but his more iconoclastic treatments of Shakespeare rarely command the attention afforded to his celebrated 1970 *A Midsummer Night's Dream*, which, although it turned the stage of the Royal Shakespeare Theatre into a squash court populated by orientalised acrobats, nonetheless preserved every crisply-spoken word of the play intact. In 1977 Heiner Müller cemented the postwar German theatre's claim to 'unser Shakespeare' with *Hamletmachine*, in which cultural memories of the play rub up against the contradictions of actually-existing socialism, and in which Ophelia speaks with the voice of the Baader Meinhof; three years later, at the RSC, John Barton was applauded for his ingenuity by contriving *Hamlet* as a play (abstracted from politics and history) about theatre, role-playing and performance.

Since the 1980s, much of the energy of new performance has derived from its increasingly hybrid nature, with theatre making, the fine arts, dance, sculpture, video and media work engaging in exchange and dialogue between practices and across previously separate disciplinary boundaries. In the Shakespearean theatre, such attempts as there have been to reflect these developments have been greeted by critical disapproval (a notorious example being Robert Lepage's mud-caked intercultural *Dream* at the Royal National Theatre in 1992[13]). Despite the recent emergence of an eclectic, self-referential postmodern design aesthetic which, albeit cautiously, favours the division and fragmentation of stage space and temporality, Shakespearean theatre remains deeply loyal to a poetics of spatial and narrative coherence.[14] The general absence from the scene of the mainstream Shakespearean stage of the technologies of mediation which have become indispensable to postmodern performance (the microphone, the video monitor) is symptomatic: if, as Johannes Birringer suggests, performance art's fondness for the screen image represents a 'popular embrace of the multiple, artistically challenging crossovers between the visual media and the new possibilities of technological intervention',[15] the Shakespearean theatre's relation to technology is shaped by its continuing commitment to verbal integrity and unproblematised actorly presence. In this light, the fact that the opening of Shakespeare's Globe on Bankside, which is emphatically constituted in terms of the refusal of technology, could be acclaimed as 'a radical move into uncharted territory'[16] and the building itself widely hailed as an 'experimental' space, is an index of the differential weighting of the 'radical' and the 'experimental' within the field of the Shakespearean; but it also signals that the postmodern preoccupation with the relations between the live and the mediatised is not one that the official Shakespearean theatre currently shares.

This is not necessarily a bad thing, of course; and if Taylor is correct in identifying a loss of dominance, Shakespeare's continuing significance might be in part due to its forcefulness as an example of what Raymond Williams has termed the 'residual' within culture, in that 'certain experiences, meanings, and values which cannot be expressed or substantially verified in terms of the dominant culture, are nevertheless lived and practised on the basis of the residue – cultural as well as social – of some previous social and cultural institution or formation'.[17] If the Bard really is, as Taylor has it, 'shrinking', one of the tasks of theatre scholarship might be to reassess the scale and shape of performance to determine the changing ways in which it is (still) both like and unlike other modes of drama, theatre and performance. In the past, performance criticism has had a fondness for ascribing to Shakespeare attributes which are endemic to the medium at large: multi-dimensionality, polyvocality, the thrill of embodiment, and so on. In the context of a shift from Shakespeare-in-performance studies to cultural and performance studies, these characteristics may be more carefully located and differentiated. A further methodological twist is possible here, which involves making a distinction between performance and the consensual version of Shakespeare which has been constituted to encompass it, and which has assumed (or argued for) the continuity between effective contemporary performance practice and the authentic historical character of the text. Within this model, as proposed, for example, by Thomas Clayton, evaluating 'legitimate production' is a matter of defining 'what a play meant for its playwright and original audiences, what a play in production signifies in contemporary performance, and how far a modern production is consonant with, and an extension of, the play as originally conceived and performed – so far as we know and can reasonably infer'.[18] Performance, in this account, can, and perhaps should, ultimately defer to the text and to history for authorisation. Because performance is required to answer to an intentionality which is distributed between the author, his theatre and originating historical circumstances, theatrical legitimacy is defined in terms of the subordination of the more recalcitrant and contingent aspects of the medium, and, as in any such power relationship, it will inevitably breed its own resistances. In order to argue for the relative autonomy of performance, therefore, it is firstly necessary to disentangle questions of the efficacy of contemporary performance from those of historical authorisation and precedent. More importantly, it may be that there are characteristics of the medium itself that are deeply antithetical to the performance versions of Shakespeare currently dominant. This understanding of performance seems to be partially endorsed by performance criticism, one of whose axioms is that its object of investigation is intrinsically transient and, in the words of Stanley Wells, 'notoriously ephemeral'.[19] An individual production varies from one performance to the next (and from the perception of one spectator to the next, as, Peter Holland suggests, 'the audience fragments into its constituent individualities, dissolving the myth of a unity of reception and creating instead an unassimilable and unmeasurable diversity'[20]), and the documentary traces it leaves behind are partial, fragmentary and unreliable, sad vestiges of an experience written on the wind. Further, performance itself is profoundly contingent, only ever an approximation to its own ideal, and heir to the thousand natural shocks of (as Richard David puts it) 'an attack of indigestion, a badly fitting wig, a touch of spring, a draught on the stage, a row at home', or of 'the precise degree of warmth or indifference with which the "house" responds to it'; it is also 'subject to the second law of thermodynamics', in that there is an inherent tendency to become 'less tightly organised, more random, as time goes on'.[21]

David is, as I read it, quite philosophical about both the entropic tendencies of performance and its vulnerability to the irruptions of the quotidian, but it is now both possible and necessary to view the little failures, approximations and near misses that are intrinsic to the processes of enactment less as incidentals and more as fundamental to the work that performance does as it negotiates with, and eventually dissolves into, the realms of everyday life that give it meaning and value. As Alan Read puts it, the act of putting theatre and the everyday together 'might appear to suggest a binary opposition', but 'examining both more closely reasserts the need to think not of an inside or outside of theatre but the way theatre is in dialectical relation to the quotidian.'[22] Performance writing is occasionally tinged with nostalgia, but performance critics not only mourn but revel in theatre's impermanence, perhaps in part because it is precisely this quality of transience which releases a kind of licence unobtainable elsewhere. Peggy Phelan proposes:

> Performance's only life is in the present. Performance cannot be saved, recorded, documented, or otherwise participate in the circulation of representations *of* representations: once it does so, it becomes something other than performance. To the degree that performance attempts to enter the economy of reproduction it betrays and lessens the promise of its own ontology. Performance's being, like the ontology of subjectivity proposed here, becomes itself through disappearance.[23]

It is, Phelan asserts, this capacity to evaporate into the domain of the unwritten, and to evade the legislation and regulation of textuality, that constitutes performance's truly subversive quality. From this perspective, a full recognition of the implications of performance's dispensation towards vibrant self-destructiveness is, potentially, dangerous and destabilising for both performance and performance criticism, since it threatens to dissolve the hegemonic unity of performed Shakespeare into a lawless and unpredictable space of textual–theatrical freeplay composed of an indeterminate miscellany of significations, experiences, perceptions, and momentary apprehensions. But, of course, performance (and in particular Shakespearean performance) continues to generate writings which purport to document or even explain it: the question that faces us is not whether this should be so, but why, and how. Officially, what ultimately keeps performance in its place and returns Shakespeare firmly to the realms of ordered legibility, is the persistent and reassuring presence of the text. The dynamic, worrying uniqueness of performance is recuperated in relation to an entity which is, as history demonstrates, infinitely repeatable. That this need not be the end of the story is one of the principles of this book.

To this end, I consider a series of meetings between performers, spaces and scripts not in order to map the trajectory of the text into performance (or the immanence of the performance in the text), but as aspects of an activity in which various kinds of 'Shakespeare effect' can be seen to operate – effects which are not released or realised by performances but actively produced by them. My concern is also with the ways in which the components of performance not only interact with each other but, within the shaping rhetoric which 're-produces' theatre as discourse, and as part of this disciplinary work, take on each other's characteristics: in unexpected and sometimes startling ways, Shakespeare's texts, and the performance spaces they inhabit, acquire the attributes of bodies; actors' bodies become readable as texts. The material discussed in this book is drawn from a century of performance, beginning with a number of Poel's 'desperate experiments' (Shaw's phrase[24]) – attempts to revive the spirit of the Elizabethan stage in facsimile – and closing with Forced Entertainment's workshop exploration of *King Lear*. It is a trajectory which takes us from the beginnings of modernist theatrical Shakespeare to the threshold of postmodern Shakespearean performance. Following the discussion of Poel, the second chapter evaluates a theatrical venture that has achieved notoriety as a scandalous convergence of amateurism and the avant-garde, Terence Gray's Shakespeare productions at the Festival Theatre, Cambridge, during the 1920s and 1930s. The following two chapters focus upon the figure who has been acclaimed as the prime mover of the postwar revival of open stage architecture, Tyrone Guthrie, examining first his 1937 production of *Hamlet*, which was taken to Kronborg Castle in Denmark and, second, his role in the foundation of the Stratford Festival in Ontario in 1952–53. Moreover, because Guthrie's legacy to the Shakespearean stage has been tied, in part, to his status as a 'personality', my account also investigates the auto/biographical fashioning of Guthrie by himself and others as both a 'Shakespearean' and a 'theatrical' icon. The penultimate chapter investigates how the Shakespeare effect may operate in performance from a different angle. Whereas the rest of the book deals with Shakespearean plays in production, the subject here is Edward Bond's 1973 drama *Bingo* and its production history in British theatre and television. *Bingo* is a play which trades upon expectations about what the experience of Shakespeare in performance is or should be, in that the spectator is, in a literal sense, 'looking at Shakespeare' for its duration.

This is, self-evidently, not a straightforward history of twentieth-century Shakespearean performance (which would merely duplicate the work of a number of comprehensive and authoritative studies already in print[25]), but a selective re-reading of aspects of that history, and, perhaps more importantly, of the ways in which it has become important, significant and memorable within the disciplines of theatre history and performance criticism and beyond. It is as much a consideration of the texts that are generated by Shakespearean performance as it is about performance itself (if, indeed, such an entity is ever recoverable); for this reason I consider the theatrical memoir, the newspaper profile and the cartoon alongside the journalistic or academic review, the promptbook and the production photograph. My concern is not just with what happened in the places and at the moments in time which these textual traces inconclusively document, but with how the exchanges between texts, spaces and bodies might have conveyed meanings above or beneath those apparently contained within the remit of Shakespeare. The diverse appropriations charted in this study are examined less for their success in realising the Shakespearean dream than as compelling evidence of the theatre's productive capacity for misreading, for accidents, coincidences, mistakes and for failure. The tendency for performance to fall short of (or move beyond) its official function might be considered its fundamental weakness, but for my current purposes it is its greatest virtue. That Shakespeare will continue to occupy a secure position in the theatre is hardly in doubt; by reviewing the implications of some of the modern performance tradition in the light of its alleged failures and outrages as well as its successes, the question of what kinds of Shakespeare, what kinds of theatre, will shape the future may yet become a genuinely open one.

Part 1
Desperate Experiments

1
The Last of the Pre-Raphaelites

I

As the foundational moment of the Shakespeare revolution, William Poel's staging of the First Quarto of *Hamlet* at St George's Hall in 1881 has generated a quantity of discussion that would have surprised its original participants and witnesses, given that in most contemporary accounts it was judged to be a misguided venture bungled by its amateur performers.[1] For a long time, the historical significance of this early venture lay in its epoch-making preliminary engagement with the principles and practice of non-illusionist staging; more recently, the attention that has been paid to Q1 *Hamlet* has prompted a renewed interest in it as a pioneering production of this text, and as the inaugurator of what the play's Cambridge editor describes as a 'surprisingly rich performance history'.[2] I shall discuss the staging and acting below; first, however, I want to examine the implications of Poel's choice of text, which for most contemporary commentators was the event's chief source of significance or, rather, notoriety.

It is well documented that the decision to play Q1 *Hamlet* was almost universally regarded as a perverse, unnecessary exercise, and at worst a monstrous affront. The opinion of Dutton Cook, critic for the *Pall Mall Gazette* and *The World*, is representative: referring to the text's 'poverty and clumsiness, its execrable blank verse, its garbled lines and general slovenliness and debility', describing it as 'unscholarly, awkward, and even uncouth', as 'early and addled', and 'muddled and mangled', and judging the entire venture as 'wearisome and depressing', an experiment of 'an absurd and reprehensible sort, involving ... some degradation of the poet in whose honour it purported to be undertaken', he attacked Q1 in no uncertain terms:

The quarto of *Hamlet* of 1603 ... has been usually accounted a piratical, imperfect, stunted, botched, and corrupt edition of the
tragedy: curious and interesting to antiquaries and Shakespearean
students, but to the general public valueless enough. Certain sages
or wiseacres, however, encouraged by sundry supersubtle German
commentators, have made this wretched abortion of book almost
an object of adoration.[3]

While we may now wonder what it was about Q1 that was capable of
arousing such a visceral reaction (and I shall return to the peculiarly
physical qualities of anti-Q1 polemic below), it is the allegations of
distortion and corruption that provide an initial focus of interest.
Whatever Q1 was purported to be, it is framed in this rhetoric as not-
Shakespeare, not-*Hamlet*; that is, as somehow not only imperfect but
also illicit, dishonest, or fraudulent. In order to make sense of these
charges, and of the strong passions that were (and perhaps still are)
invested in them it is necessary to work back from Poel's 1881 production in order to establish the cultural location of Q1 (and, more
particularly, the 1880 facsimile edition of Q1 from which he was
working) in terms of its nineteenth-century history of transmission,
mediation and duplication.

In 1821 Sir Thomas Charles Bunbury, sixth baronet of Barton Hall,
Member of Parliament for Suffolk and winner of the first Derby, died
without heir, leaving his nephew, Sir Henry Edward Bunbury, to
inherit his estate. A staunch Whig and social reformer, Bunbury's
fortuitous legacy can justly claim to have altered the course of English
political history during the first half of the nineteenth century:
returned in 1830 as MP for Suffolk in a formerly safe Tory seat, he
voted for the second reading of the Reform Bill, ensuring that it was
carried by a majority of one. His significance for literary and theatrical
history was that he was also an antiquarian and bibliophile, and with
the Barton estate acquired the library of his uncle's great uncle, the
eighteenth-century Shakespearean Thomas Hanmer. In Bunbury's
account, in 1823 he found 'the only copy' of the 1603 *Hamlet* 'in a
closet ... it was a small quarto, barbarously cropped, and very ill-
bound. I exchanged the volume with Messrs. Payne and Foss, for books
to the value of £180, and they sold it to for £230 to the Duke of
Devonshire.'[4] Payne and Foss did not altogether surrender their stake
in the work, however, and in 1825 it was issued as a reprint by the
Shakespeare Press. A brief preface announced that the work was an
'accurate reprint of this tragedy as originally written by Shakespeare,

which he afterwards altered and enlarged',[5] thereby identifying the text as the lost original for *Hamlet* which had been the subject of editorial speculation since the end of the previous century. Drawing attention to 'several lines of great beauty', it deals lightly with the features that would subsequently provoke such vitriol: 'the typographical errors and even negligent omissions in the text are common to all the editions published during the lifetime of Shakespeare'. Even the absence of the last leaf and hence of the arrival of Fortinbras was a minor inconvenience (and, coincidentally, in accord with contemporary theatrical convention): 'as the play is perfect to the death of Hamlet, the loss is of comparatively small importance'.

The Shakespeare Press edition thus introduced Q1 into the sphere of public scholarship (a reprint was also published in Leipzig by Ernst Fleischer, thereby making it available to the 'German commentators' that would later rouse the ire of Dutton Cook and others). Around the same time Edmund Malone's revisions to the second edition of his complete works – to incorporate findings from Henslowe's *Diary* – renewed interest in the question of whether there had been a performance of *Hamlet* at the end of the sixteenth century, although whether Q1 represented any kind of record of this remained open to debate.[6] The next important moment in the text's cultural history came in 1858, which saw the publication of the first photolithographic facsimile of the Duke of Devonshire's copy, paid for by himself and conducted under the supervision of the great Shakespearean forger John Payne Collier. Only forty copies were made, and distributed to a select group of scholars and librarians. Two years later, a further reprint was published by Samuel Timmins, *The Devonshire 'Hamlets'*, which presented the Duke's copies of Q1 and Q2 on facing pages. Unlike its predecessors, however, this could be offered as a complete text. In 1856 a second copy of Q1 had emerged, now conveniently supplied with the missing final leaf but lacking the title page. A Dublin bookseller by the name of Rooney reportedly obtained it from an unknown Trinity College student who had brought it with him from Nottingham. Rooney cannily offered the student one shilling for it and then, having copied the final leaf, sold it to the book dealer, Mr Boone, for £70. Boone in turn doubled his money by selling the text to J.O. Halliwell for £140, from whom, in 1858, it went to its final resting place in the British Museum.

The Devonshire 'Hamlets' established the template for all subsequent facsimile editions by offering a discreet conflation of the Devonshire and Halliwell (subsequently the Huntington and British Library) copies; while its placement in conjunction with Q2 so that 'the development of the characters, and the changes of the text, may be readily examined and compared' endorsed the early-draft hypothesis.[7] In 1866 a hand-traced facsimile was issued as part of Halliwell and Edmund Ashbee's series of early Quartos. Only thirty-one copies were printed, and (after the fashion of elite Victorian pornography) offered for private circulation only, each copy being individually numbered and inscribed by hand by Ashbee and Halliwell. These retailed at five guineas (by way of comparison, Collier's nine-volume edition of the complete works was on sale at the same time for £4 16s). Whatever view might be taken of Q1's artistic merit, its status, even in reproduction, was that of a rare and valuable commodity: Ashbee and Halliwell knew their business well enough to franchise their facsimile to the New Cambridge and New Variorum Shakespeares of 1866 and 1877.

When F.J. Furnivall, under the auspices of the New Shakspere Society, published in 1880 the edition that provided the impetus for Poel, the issue of price and availability had become a visible and indeed controversial item on the scholarly agenda. Announcing that 'every genuine student of Shakspere has always desired to own those Quartos of his Master's Plays and Poems which are the necessary foundations of the Text', Furnivall noted that, despite the exorbitant cost of Ashbee's 'hand-traced' facsimiles, they were nonetheless 'in a nonworking form and without any information as to the original Quartos'. Presenting the Quartos 'in a new and workable form, for *six shillings*', Furnivall's New Shakspere Society editions offered access to cultural capital – that had formerly been restricted to a moneyed scholarly elite – to an expanding constituency of petit-bourgeois Shakespeareans who took their responsibilities very seriously indeed. Indeed, the opportunity for ownership of such texts answered to a combination of desire, right and duty: 'every true and faithful worker at Shakspere's text *must* want to have in his own hand, under his own eye, and as his own, trustworthy facsimiles of these truest representations of the poet's own manuscript'.[8] In the case of Q1 *Hamlet*, the first in the series, the thorny issue of attribution was presented objectively, encouraging the scholar-sleuth to draw his (sic) own conclusions: 'is there ... any evidence that the passages special to it only are not by Shakspere, or mistaking reports of what he wrote?' In this edition, Furnivall had 'starrd [*] all the lines that appear in Q1 only: to them let the reader turn, and judge for himself' (p. vi). The text was valued in terms of the scope it offered for investigation and debate; dedicating the volume to the Duke of Devonshire, Furnivall saluted Q1 as 'the gem of his collection' (p. xii).

If facsimile publication was a significant component of the modernisation of the late nineteenth-century Shakespeare industry, it was one made possible through the rapid pace of technological change. Collier's photolithographic edition twenty years earlier demonstrated the application of a technique that had recently emerged from a convergence of photography and a print technology that had only been in existence since the end of the eighteenth century. The first daguerrotype-based lithograph was published in 1839, the year that Louis Daguerre unveiled the invention that bears his name; a decade later, the French lithographer Rose-Joseph Lemercier took advantage of the invention of the photographic negative to advance the process a stage further, making the photographic image itself the object of reproduction and publicising his work at the Great Exhibition. In 1855 the process was patented; and 'within fifty years of its inception the topographical artist had been more or less replaced by the camera', while 'the appearance of photolithographic plates ... foreshadowed the eventual disappearance of the professional lithographic draughtsman'.[9] What had originated as a method of drawing upon, and printing from, stone plates as a means of putting pictorial imagery (of landscapes, architecture and persons) into mass circulation had, by the late 1850s, become fully integrated with a means of mechanical reproduction which, in its official uses, was profoundly implicated within a developing culture of documentation and surveillance (of places, faces, and, now, literary texts). During the Victorian period, John Tagg writes, there emerged 'the instrumental deployment of photography in privileged administrative practices and the professionalised discourses of new social sciences ... all of them domains of expertise in which arguments and evidence were addressed to qualified peers and circulated only in certain limited institutional contexts'. Situated within the context of the gradual formation during the period of systematic disciplines and structures (both amateur and emergent professional) of bourgeois Shakespeare scholarship, the turn to photographic facsimile reproduction revealed how a new attention to the early modern playtext as a material entity construed it as the object of new kinds of knowledge. This scrutiny conformed perfectly to a 'rhetoric of photographic documentation at this period' characterised, in Tagg's account, by 'precision, measurement, calculation and proof, separating out its subjects of knowledge, shunning emotional appeal and dramatisation, and hanging its status on technical rules and protocols whose institutionalisation had to be negotiated.[10]

Announcing their authoritative, authentic status, the Shakspere Quarto Facsimiles that began to appear during the 1880s fully endorse this positivist and empiricist rhetoric, echoing, and perhaps amplifying, what Barthes characterises as the photograph's claim to be 'somehow co-natural with its referent'.[11] The duplication process is also, the editions make clear, judiciously policed: 'executed under the superintendence of F.J. Furnivall', photolithographic reproduction of the Quartos is announced as conducted by Mr W. Griggs and Mr Charles Praetorius, a pair of technicians whose 'long experience at the India Office and the British Museum respectively' guaranteed 'the faithfulness of their reproductions' (p. 26), bringing to bibliography a probity and authority derived from the successful administration of both heritage and empire. The New Shakspere Society series is also a symptom of a more general realignment of scholarly labour, conducted as a human science rather than an art of letters, based upon a new understanding of the status of a primary text, and of the uses that can be made of it. Rather than resting as rare commodities in the libraries of the bibliophile elite, made available only in a limited sense to a more general readership through the fallible (or fraudulent) human intervention of the copyist, they are encouraged to circulate in a replica form which mechanical reproduction alone can guarantee as trustworthy. But as Gary Taylor points out, although the appeal of the facsimiles is that they 'compound the modern technological authority of photography with original historical authenticity of "documents"', both claims 'prove, upon examination, questionable'.[12] The combination was nonetheless a powerful one for the New Shakspere Society's subscribers. A comment by photographic pioneer Lady Elizabeth Eastlake dating from 1857 points towards another way in which photography, with its empiricist aesthetic of relentless exposure, might be particularly attuned to the reproduction of early modern texts: 'the forte of the camera lies in the imitation of one surface only, and that of a rough and broken kind ... the mere texture of stone, whether rough in the quarry or hewn on the wall, its especial delight ... if asked to say what photography has hitherto best succeeded in rendering, we should point to everything near and rough'.[13]

Once the production of facsimile texts is seen as part of the uneven modernisation of a Shakespeare industry it may be seen that the strong reactions to Q1 in performance are connected with a more widespread disquiet about the direction in which Shakespearean cultural production appeared to be heading during the closing decades of the nineteenth century. As the profits generated by trading in the Q1 *Hamlet* in itself and in facsimile demonstrated, the advent of new technologies of reproduction and distribution indicated that there was no necessary correlation between this aspect of the business of scholarly publishing and longer-established kinds of textual value; moreover, the methods of scholarship that were being developed to process early modern texts newly revealed as raw data viewed the material with the detachment of the palaeographer rather than the reverence of the bibliophile or bardolator.

In that the preservation of typographic materiality was a crucial index of historical authenticity, there were clear affinities between the thinking that informed the production and use of photolithographic facsimiles and Poel's production philosophy and methods, defined as a principle of 'reviving the masterpieces of the Elizabethan drama upon the stage for which they were written, so as to represent them as nearly as possible under the conditions existing at their time of their first production – that is to say, with only those stage appliances and accessories which were usually employed during the Elizabethan period'.[14] That Poel himself sensed such an affinity is evident from an account of the Q1 performance which he subsequently incorporated into a flyer advertising his Shakespearean reading class, which recorded that 'in 1880 the first quarto was reproduced by photography, and the great value of this earliest version, as showing Shakespeare's original drift and intention, caused Mr Poel ... to reproduce it at St George's Hall'.[15] If the doubling of the term 'reproduce' suggests that Poel saw his staging methods as akin to photographic/ photolithographic duplication, it may also imply a kind of faith in facsimile that regards these techniques as a means of eradicating the contaminating errors of mediation (the first usage of the term recorded in the *OED* in the sense of 'to repeat in a more or less exact copy' dates from 1850, the period in which photography began to become commercially available). The photographic impulse reflects the reforming and modernist orientation of Poel's alleged antiquarianism, in that he opted to embrace the possibilities of one of capitalism's most advanced technologies in order to strip the text of what he saw as the lies and distortions imposed upon it by three centuries of cultural appropriation. But the connection with photography and the photographic sensibility goes further than this, in that Poel's work is informed by a complex and fraught relationship between scenography, the claims of oral and aural theatrical tradition, and the emergence of a documentary visual culture. The modern technology impinges upon Poel's understanding of the evidentiary status of the Quarto texts, which he defined as performance-based (as he later insisted, 'the early quartos alone represent Shakespeare's form of construction and his method of representation'[16]).

Making the case for Q1 *Hamlet*, Poel argued that the unknown reporter who had transcribed the original First Quarto had 'endeavoured to reproduce the play as *he* saw it represented'.[17] Although Poel allows for an element of subjective indeterminacy by italicising the subject of his conjecture, the appeal to the authority of vision and of the visual record, is strong: as the memory of the scene of performance, it is afforded a privileged legitimacy which is of a different order to that of the literary text. Q1 is thus a record of a *visual* impression of a performance event, distorted and miniaturised like the reversed and inverted negative image on a photographic plate, which the further intervention of performance can return to its proper size and shape by developing the page for the stage. Poel's position can be contrasted with the related assumptions about the relationship between the arts of memory and transcription, reliable and unreliable reporting, and the status of reported texts, that underpinned contemporary debates about textual piracy. In his introduction to the New Shakspere Society facsimile of the First Quarto of *Romeo and Juliet*, Herbert Evans envisages the practice:

> John Danter, or the anonymous bookseller for whom he worked, employed a shorthand writer to attend one or more performances, and take down as much of what he heard as he could. The notes thus obtained were of various degrees of accuracy: in some places they were tolerably exact, in others, either very imperfect or consisting of mere jottings describing the scene as the reporter beheld it, with perhaps a striking phrase caught here and there and hastily noted down.[18]

Although Evans seeks to discredit his putative wily stenographer where Poel guardedly defends his, common to both of their claims about the accuracy of the text is the emphasis upon vision and audition as unreliable mechanisms of transmission: what the scribe attempts to set down, in a verbal form, is what he *sees* as much as what he *hears*. It is an account of nefarious textual practices which strikes a chord with a culture of increasingly sophisticated apparatuses of recording and duplication, while the shadowy agent of the pirate reporter conducts his criminal activities within the sinister underworld of Elizabethan publishing by combining the roles of witness, detective and newspaper journalist. On the one hand the surreptitious playhouse scribbler is capable of prodigious feats of transcription, the accuracy of which, given the circumstances, is as astonishing as its audacity (actually, as Richard Proudfoot notes, 'no shorthand system known at the time could have produced such good results'[19]). On the other, especially as judged by the forensic standards of the culture of the facsimile, he is a cloth-eared, insensitive and unreliable witness. Groundling that he is, he is easily impressed by dumbshows and noise but prone to lapses of memory and concentration: thus in Evans's discussion of the reporting of the fight between Montagues and Capulets in I. i: 'amid the wrangling and scuffling on stage, the reporter gets confused, and on the entrance of Benvolio drops his pen altogether, contenting himself with a descriptive stage-direction in place of the rest of the dialogue' (pp. ix–x). According to this view of the stage, the theatrical medium was one in which the deleterious effects of sharp practice were compounded by the endemic multiplication of inaccuracies, as the actor would 'while preserving the general sense of his author ... express it in his own phraseology ... make terrible havoc of the metre' and 'foist lines from another part of the play into the wrong places' (p. viii).

From this perspective, performance is, by the very nature of its location within the quotidian, and its subjection to the contingencies of vision and audition, a medium lacking any decisive claims to authority; and since what took place on the Elizabethan stage was already a corrupt and distorted version of the ideal original, further mediation of this through performance-based texts only multiplied the errors and corruptions. This perception is rooted in a deeply Victorian mistrust of theatricality itself as inherently duplicitous, and of Shakespearean performance in particular as, fundamentally, an act of betrayal. For many respectable commentators, Nina Auerbach suggests, the theatre was 'that alluring pariah within Victorian culture', standing for 'all the dangerous potential of theatricality to invade the authenticity of the best self'. Within this scheme, 'the nineteenth-century Shakespeare came to stand for human inviolateness'; hence 'the Victorian mission to redeem him from theatricality is part of a cultural passion to preserve all lives from their inherently deceitful potential'.[20] In the theatre, from the middle of the nineteenth century onwards, the work of regulating Shakespearean theatrical meanings took place within the visual regime of pictorialism, in 'stage representations of historical periods and geographical locations central to the Victorians' construction of their cultural heritage';[21] while realism's merging of the theatrical sign and its referent attempted to abolish the troubling gap between actor and role.

This was conducted, however, in the full knowledge that this was, historically speaking, not quite 'authentic' Shakespeare; and, indeed, that it was the task of the modern stage to tame, civilise and improve upon its raw theatricality. Introducing the collected Henry Irving Shakespeare in 1888, the eminent actor-manager balanced the assertion that 'Shakespeare was one of the most practical dramatists which the world has ever seen' with the recognition that 'he lived in an age when the drawbacks which existed to the proper representation of stage plays were very many'. Countering objections to 'the employment of the sister arts of music and painting in the stage representation of Shakespeare, and to the elaborate illustration of the countries in which the various scenes are laid, or of the dress and surroundings of the different characters', he emphatically concluded that 'their value has ceased to be a matter of opinion; they have become necessary. They are dictated by the public taste of the day.'[22] Beerbohm Tree, towards the end of the century, was more belligerent: 'be our method right or wrong, we are enabled to give Shakespeare a wider appeal and a larger franchise ... his words are not only, or primarily, for the literary student, they are for the world at large'.[23] But despite such efforts to confer legitimacy upon performed Shakespeare, and to draw respectable bourgeois audiences to the theatre, high-minded scholarship remained less hostile than indifferent to contemporary theatrical practice. Modelling itself upon the natural sciences, Victorian philological scholarship concerned itself with the material documents of Renaissance culture in order to excavate a deeper truth: the evolutionary development of the life, mind and art of Shakespeare (a set of concerns adumbrated in the subtitle of what has been called 'the official programme of late Victorian bardolatry', Edward Dowden's hugely influential *Shakspere*, first published in 1875).[24] Amidst the formation of the methods and institutions of modernising professionalism, and the consolidation of his position as a semi-secular national religion, Shakespeare's presence in the contemporary theatre is only peripherally relevant to this project. It is not just that Victorian scholarship of the kind instituted by the New Shakspere Society and its followers did not take performance seriously, but that it would hardly have known what to do with it had it wanted to since the (tainted and compromised) material evidence of performance was not of a kind that could be efficiently administered within its existing systems. In this respect, the invention of photography and its subsequent application to the documentation of performance (and Poel played a pioneering role in this development) was instrumental in the birth of Shakespeare performance studies. Here, for the first time, performance became available in a documentary form which could be preserved, scrutinised and reproduced.[25]

I have stressed this point because it is important to recognise the nature of the critical context within which Poel's early experiments were conducted. There was plenty of serious and sustained theatrical commentary in circulation during the period in which Poel began his work, but it was confined almost entirely to the medium of print journalism. This marked a change from the position at the beginning of the century, which had seen literary professionals such as Lamb, Coleridge and Hazlitt ready to engage with performance (even if they were unhappy with it) as something worth documenting, discussing, and critiquing in relation to other reading practices; as Hugh Grady observes 'Romantic criticism shared with that of the previous century a locus in a generalized, public sphere of coffee-house, magazine, and lecture-hall' and chose the objects of its scrutiny accordingly; as criticism became professionalised 'it passed out of the sphere of public discourse properly speaking, becoming instead a power/knowledge of new bureaucratic institutions',[26] and theatre, consequently, moved beyond its remit. Acknowledging the scale of the division that had grown between the theatre and the increasingly specialist scholarship of the later part of the nineteenth century may help us to appreciate the sheer nerve of Poel's approach to Furnivall in October 1880 with an offer to present a paper on acting editions of Shakespeare to the New Shakspere Society. As a glance at the published transactions of the Society from 1874 onwards instantly reveals, this was a significant departure for a forum which had defined its remit (and its work ethic) in terms of meticulously detailed empirical investigation of documentary evidence. When Poel wrote to Furnivall with the proposal that he would demonstrate that Q1 was an acting edition (not an argument advanced by Furnivall in his introduction to the New Shakspere facsimile) by means both of a paper and an amateur performance, he was declaring his credentials as a serious scholar, but he was also presuming upon the authority of performance in a radically new way. The performance took place on 16 April 1881. Poel's paper, 'Acting Editions of Shakespeare', was read to the Society on 10 June and published in the *Era* on 2 July.[27] Effectively announcing the initial agenda for his own stage practice (and appealing to his immediate auditors), he declared that 'cheap facsimiles of the quartos as well as the folio should be made accessible to actors, and from these an attempt should be made to standardize stage-versions of Shakespeare's most popular plays, and these stage-versions should be the joint work of scholars and actors' (p. 160). As discussed earlier, the authenticating presence of the facsimile is envisaged as a means of pre-empting the corrupt and fraudulent practices of the theatrical profession (issues of cost and the circulation of cultural capital are still predominant: it is important that these copies should be 'cheap'); in return, performance is required to submit to the disciplines of scholarship. After all, Poel reasoned, experience had shown that the exisiting commercial theatre was not to be trusted with Shakespeare; and to demonstrate this his paper went on to identify the deficiencies of the extant Globe and French's acting editions of *Hamlet*, including their omission of Fortinbras (who should 'appear like Richmond in *Richard III*, as the hero who will restore peace and order to the distracted kingdom') and their unduly pious treatment of the Prince: 'our stage Hamlets try to tone down the inconsistencies and imperfections of the character; they exploit his sentiments, but do not show his inclinations ... a student, a controversialist, and a moralist, what has he to do with revenge or murder?'(pp. 157, 169). Poel countered this sentimental and individualistic view of Hamlet with his own version of the play 'as an epitome of life ... not the career of one individual', and, importantly, cited the 'much abused' Q1 in support: 'mutilated as that version is, care has been taken to avoid confusing the story of the play' (p. 157).

Clearly, Poel was already heading for trouble on a number of counts. The debate about the relative merits of Q1 might have been a relatively arcane affair, conducted at the more rarified levels of scholarship, but Poel's aggressive interrogation of the received image of Hamlet was tantamount to an attack upon his own era's most cherished, but also problematic, cultural myths. As R.A. Foakes has demonstrated, the nineteenth-century cult of Hamlet originated in the Romantic vision of the Prince as a figure who 'seemed to combine so many strong attributes with so many weak ones', and who therefore 'could serve as a paradigm of and excuse for ordinary people who in the normal way regard themselves as having potential, but fail to live up to their ideal of themselves, or fall short of the achievements they hope for'. In general, 'abstracted from the play, Hamlet became a free-floating signifier, taking on the subjectivity of the critic, and typically reflecting his anxieties'.[28] By the end of the century (as I shall develop in the next section) the broadly sympathetic post-Romantic relationship with Hamlet was coming under pressure, as his vacillating sensitivity began to look unmasculine; even as Irving presented Hamlet as (in Clement Scott's description) 'as much of the gentleman and scholar as possible',[29] Dowden was formulating a complaint against the Prince's 'disease of the will' and celebrating the arrival of Fortinbras as 'the restoration of practical and positive feeling'.[30] On the face of it, the melancholy Dane who stalked the increasingly intricate ramparts of Elsinore on the nineteenth-century stage was a secure icon of individuated interiority and masculinity, to a certain extent immune to the compromising inauthenticity of the theatrical medium precisely because he promised that he had that within which passeth show. From a different angle, Hamlet's reflectiveness was both worrying and dangerous: not only was the hero prone to feats of self-theatricalisation that repeatedly threatened to exceed the fragile boundaries of realist performance, but there was the nagging anxiety that the heart of Hamlet's mystery might, after all, be nothing but emptiness. And in this respect, the hero and the text are prone to the same problem: subject to an identity crisis, they are but imperfect versions of what they might have been. To a certain extent, the cultural force of Hamletism explains the extremity of the reactions to Q1, not only because its criminal spuriousness assaults the integrity of the 'real' play, but because it underlines the divisions within the legitimate version itself. Halliwell himself mournfully recorded that his 'sad and strong belief' was that 'we have not the materials for the formation of a really perfect text; and that now at best we must be contented with a defective copy of what is in many respects the most noble of all of the writings of Shakespeare'.[31] Such talk of the text might well be a character evaluation of Hamlet himself. Nineteenth-century productions liked to end with Horatio's valedictory lines inviting flights of angels singing the sweet prince to his rest; the mysterious, noble heart of Victorian literary and theatrical culture was cracked from the very beginning.

II

Poel's paper publicly aired his theories about Q1 two months after the performance which had been intended to vindicate them in practice. At the outset, Poel took care to establish the circumstances of the performance such that it would be received less as a theatrical entertainment than as a sober scholarly venture. Poel first proposed the

performance to Furnivall as something which 'might be of some interest to students', and the *Academy* anticipated that 'Dr W. Pole [sic], and
some amateur friends have resolved on giving what Shakspere students
and critics have long desired to see, a performance of Shakspere's first
sketch of his *Hamlet* as represented by the first quarto of 1603 ...
opportunity will thus be given to test the opinion of those many critics
who have held the first sketch to be a better acting drama than the real
play.'[32] As a performance conducted in the earnest spirit of positivist
experimental science, this was very much attuned to the New
Shakspere Society way of thinking, in that the 'test' of performance
was intended to provide an empirical demonstration of a theoretical
proposition about the text. The laboratory space designated for the
experiment (and for many subsequent ones by Poel and the
Elizabethan Stage Society) was St George's Hall, a concert hall in
Langham Place which possessed the advantages of being both relatively inexpensive to hire, and, as a venue for generally high-minded
and philanthropic cultural events, respectably middle-class. Since its
opening in 1867, St George's Hall had been dedicated to the mission
of providing live entertainment for family audiences who would have
considered it improper to frequent the theatre (or, even more dangerously, the music hall). Its programme supported the culture of amateur
performance which the middle classes had developed as an alternative
to professional entertainment, and which was rooted in the ethics of
self-help and self-improvement that had given rise to the New
Shakspere Society and similar organisations. A flavour of the hall's
prevailing air of seriousness can be caught in a comment by its new
manager in 1900, which urged audiences 'to consider as obsolete the
old custom which has strongly prevailed in the Building of repressing
laughter, as the manifestation thereof greatly encourages the performers'. As O'Connor reads it, this looks like 'a sneer at the efforts of those
amateur groups – such as ... Poel's own Elizabethan Stage Society'
familiar to the hall;[33] it also indicates that the polite smothering of the
more raucous or spontaneous elements of audience response (whether
to displays of incompetence or to intentionally amusing moments)
was for a long time considered to be appropriate conduct within this
building. An engraving published in the *Illustrated London News*, of 29
June 1867 (reproduced by O'Connor and in Mander and Mitchenson's
Lost Theatres of London[34]) depicting the hall's interior suggests that this
atmosphere of chilly detachment was not inappropriate. The hall was
a high-ceilinged, cavernous space, with a stage positioned at the end
of a galleried room built to seat 1500; the *Era* (28 April 1867) reported

that the '*salon*' was '110 feet in length, 50 in breadth and 45 in height'. Intended for use as a concert hall rather than as a theatre space, the hall was lit by means of a row of skylights running either side of the roof, and by lights set into an elliptical ceiling whose arc recalls the engineering of the capital's new railway stations. When St George's Hall was reopened after extensive refurbishment in 1905, it attracted particular praise for its acquisition of 'no less than 3000 electric bulbs',[35] but Poel's performance of Q1 *Hamlet* was lit by a mixture of gaslight from the ceiling and stage footlights, with the late April afternoon daylight filtering down from outside. The combination was enough to persuade the *Era*'s exasperated critic of the fatuity of the exercise, as he described 'the performance of the Shakespearian enthusiasts who dragged us from the bright sunshine, and occupied nearly three hours of our time at St George's Hall, on the afternoon of Saturday last' (23 April 1881).

If this sense of stubborn perversity set the tone for the criticism that would be directed at him for much of his professional life, Poel was in turn determined to establish the validity of the enterprise in terms of its scholarly rather than conventionally theatrical virtues. As if to underscore the textual authority and visual authenticity of what the audience was to witness, the front cover of the programme reproduced a facsimile of Q1's title page, but this policy of direct and plain dealing did not extend to the listing of performers, since (presumably as a precautionary tactic) some of them, as the *Academy* had revealed in an advance notice, 'assumed *noms de théâtre* for the occasion' (9 April 1881). Furnivall, at least, was willing to lend his name to the venture, and he prefaced the performance with a short speech in which he admitted to some emendation of the text ('correcting only the manifest blunders' according to the *Academy*) and, tactlessly perhaps, craved the audience's indulgence for 'whatever was amiss, for the absence of much that they might reasonably have expected from a regularly trained company' (*Saturday Review*, 23 April). As the *Daily News* (18 April) reported it, he also probably set a few teeth on edge by citing, 'in defence of these strange proceedings', the view 'elsewhere expressed by the late Herr Devrient, the German actor, that the first quarto is "the better acting play"'. From the start, however, not only the results of the experiment but the very grounds upon which it was conducted were open to dispute. Leaving aside the alleged deficiencies of the performance itself, many critics emphatically rejected the idea that any performance would be able to contribute meaningfully to critical debate; as far as the *Saturday Review* was concerned, it was 'self-evident' that 'a performance on the stage can neither help nor hinder the settlement of a literary question as to the source of this edition'.

According to the same newspaper, Furnivall also drew attention to the production's visual economy, declaring it to be presented with the aim of 'showing us exactly how the piece looked when first played, without scenery and in the dress of the time'. Enough has been said already about how this aesthetic principle incorporates and reproduces the materialist emphases of facsimile bibliography; its key practical features (gleaned from the reviews and from the production prompt-book) can be briefly summarised. The *Daily News* recorded that the raising of the curtain disclosed 'nothing in the way of scenery beyond a pair of screens covered in red cloth, and nearly meeting at the back of the stage. There was also a door at each side of the proscenium, which, together with the central aperture between the screens referred to, furnished the only means of exit and entrance.' Q1's Ofelia's grave was 'represented by something that looked like a seaman's chest' (*Era*), and the players' stage by 'something like that provided by a painter for his model' (*The Times*, 21 April). The closet scene featured no bed but there was 'a chair downstage centre right and an easel with the old King's portrait upstage left'.[36] Mention should be made here of the sheer scale of the stage platform: designed primarily for musical events, it measured 50 by 49 feet, about double the size of those of most London theatres of the time.[37] The lighting seems to have been maintained at an even level more or less throughout, with cues recorded in the promptbook for the dimming of the lights 'for the first two battlement scenes ... and for the entrance of the Ghost in the closet scene'.[38] The *mise-en-scène* was generally received with equanimity: although there were grumbles about its 'primitive ideals' and 'self-denying ordinances' (*Daily News*) and the comment that the conditions 'rendered success more than an improbability' (*Morning Post*, 18 April).

The bulk of the critics' abuse was reserved for the text and the acting. A few commentators, entering into the scholarly spirit of the proceedings, were willing to debate the provenance of the text: Joseph Knight, the renowned critic of the *Theatre*, devoted a lengthy section of his review (May 1881) to an account of the circumstances of the discovery of Q1 and of the competing theories about its origins and status, concluding nonetheless that 'speculations to which no answer is possible are amusing occupations for the dilettante, but a man with serious work to do will do well to eschew them'. Knight's characterisation of the scholarly wrangling over Q1 as effete and unmanly is balanced by a relatively dispassionate view of the text itself, which he describes as a 'mutilated and imperfect version' of the play; and in conclusion he actively promotes 'Mr Grigg's [sic] photolithographic reprint of the text of the quartos, which of course reproduces with minute accuracy every feature of the original, and brings at slight cost the rarest of Shakespearean volumes within the reach of all.' Others were more forthright in their condemnation, augmenting the text's criminal record by means of a graphically physicalised rhetoric of vituperation. Dutton Cook's reference to this 'stunted, botched ... wretched abortion' was echoed in references to 'the botcher's text, the barbarously mutilated and imperfect version of the piratical printer' (*Era*), and 'the muddled and mangled text ... the corrupt play' (*Morning Post*). In a way, there was nothing new in this, since the deployment of a rhetoric of physicality in relation to Shakespeare's text can be traced as far back as Heminges and Condell's discrediting of the 'diverse stolne, and surreptitious copies, maimed and deformed', and their promotion of the Folio as the repository of works 'cur'd, and perfect of their limbes'. Even so, there is something uniquely and revealingly Victorian about this discursive combination of the grotesque, monstrous or morally questionable textual body, mutilation and barbarism, especially when we reflect that the final term has in this historical setting a particularly imperialist loading, as the antithesis of an English civilisation whose practices of science, law and rational order are fully articulated in the poetic-philosophical system that is Dowden's 'Shakspere'. Like a returned and unwelcome colonial subject, duplicitous, malformed, coarse and vulgar, Q1 was inferior and also faintly dangerous: the *Daily News* even suspected a threat of revolutionary dispossession that has more than a hint of the barbarians at the gate, describing the aim of the performance as 'nothing less than expelling from the stage the play as we know it'. Since most critics dismissed the idea that Q1 was an early draft of *Hamlet*, this implied a de facto acceptance of the piracy theory of transmission; I suggest that their distaste for the text was fired not only by the criminality of its appropriation but also by a horror of its proximity to the primary scene of violent and degraded embodiment, the Elizabethan theatre, itself imagined as barbaric and primitive.

The preoccupation with the body is not confined to discussion of the text (with heavy-handed levity, the *Era* critic glosses his remark about the 'seaman's chest' with 'we mean a big box, and not the breathing apparatus of a mariner'): it was also evident in the reviewers' uniformly sarcastic remarks about the efforts of the performers, in that the general amateurism of the performance was characterised in terms of the loss or violation of bodily decorum, coordination and control. The *Era* wrote of Mr Macklow's Ghost that his corpulent appearance betrayed a lack of faith 'in a ghost that doesn't weigh about fourteen stone and can't eat a good square meal'; the *Morning Post* isolated Mr Hallward's Horatio for commendation since at least 'his hands and legs seemed not only to belong to him, but even to be under his control'. Elsewhere, however, according to the same review, the physical disarticulation that is the mark of the amateur performer merged with the bodily attributes of the text to discredit what it presumed to be the objective of the experiment: 'it was decidedly injudicious to entrust to amateurs the onerous task of proving a mutilated Hamlet superior to the whole and perfect prince'. The aberrant bodies of the cast also seemed to be unevenly, and unpredictably gendered: the Ghost 'cut a remarkable figure' when he appeared in his nightgown to Hamlet, 'enveloped in a white veil, look[ing] like a stout female going to the altar, to blush as a bride or pretend to' (*Era*). Although Horatio, at least, contributed 'a manly piece of acting' (*Theatre*), Poel, according to the consensus, did not. His 'unmanly' portrayal was 'sure to be ridiculous', as it alternated 'for the most part between tearful peevishness and unmanly fits of sobbing' (*Illustrated Sport and Dramatic News*, 23 April); in a formulation which equates irregularity of gender identity with that of metre, and which evokes a performing body shamefully incapable of regulating its own secretions, this was a Hamlet 'who sheds tears copiously, and who could not or would not mind his stops' (*Era*).

There was more: 'now and then he bursts into loud and violent utterances – generally when the text would expect him to be calm', in a performance characterised by 'curious perversity' (*Daily News*); 'he was lachrymose and ever in a hurry ... for the most part he ran [his lines] into one another in a way which destroyed their meaning, and made many of them very comical' (*Era*); querulous delivery of the lines '"O my prophetlike soule, my uncle! my uncle!" ... ended in an absolute whine' and resulted in 'a general laugh' (*Saturday Review*). Despite the best efforts of Poel and Furnivall to establish an atmosphere of scholarly solemnity, the unruliness of the speaking bodies of Poel and his co-performers (and, perhaps, the perception that Poel was really too 'plebian' for Hamlet[39]) worked upon critical bodies until they could contain themselves no longer. With his uncertain grasp of his lines and 'eccentric notion of spectral elocution', Macklow's Ghost seemed to epitomise a production rooted in the embarrassing, chaotic and all too solid flesh rather than in the spirit; it could not but fail a play and hero which in the hands of Irving had become 'an extreme extension of Romantic subjectivity'[40] and, as such, might hope to escape embodiment altogether. The recalcitrant presence of Macklow's disordered body reveals a further schism between amateur and professional performance, and, in connection with this, between Poel's incipient anti-pictorialism and the technologies of the picture frame stage. The relation of spectre to spectacle was one of the nineteenth-century stage's greatest challenges, with devices such as traps and gauzes carefully contrived to achieve 'the ghost's eery dematerialization'; thus at a production at the Lyceum in 1864 had the ghost 'stood behind a large concealed wheel which, when started, caught up, at each revolution, a fresh piece of some almost transparent stuff, artfully tinted to match the background, until the requisite thickness was obtained. The ghost apparently melted into thin air.'[41] The apotheosis of this painstakingly ingenious application of technology, and the technique which, as illusionism's ultimate neurotic symptom, finally realised the project of enabling the spectator to see through a body made of glass, was the machinery that produced the effect known as Pepper's Ghost. Although it was a mechanism of disembodiment never to my knowledge used in a production of *Hamlet*, it might well be considered this Ghost's, and this *Hamlet's*, antithesis.

Something else of major significance happened to Poel in 1881. He was appointed by Emma Cons as manager of the Royal Victoria Coffee Hall, the philanthropic entertainment venture that would become the Old Vic. In an interview with the *Daily Chronicle* over thirty years later (13 September 1913) Poel described the experience as formative:

Fresh from contact with poverty and want and suffering ... how it came home to me, the frightful contrast, the awful difference, between the lives of the rich and the lives of the poor ... ever since those days I have striven to change the dramatic world, to alter life on the stage as we know it, to make it what it obviously should be, and what plainly it must one day become, an experience of the spirit of man evolving through beauty and knowledge towards the fullness and perfection of existence.

It is here, rather than in a spirit of antiquarian pedantry, that we find a motivating agenda for Poel's revivalism. As Simon Shepherd and Peter Womack emphasise, Poel 'was a Fabian whose hostility to commercial theatre was a matter of political principle as well as immediate circumstances'.[42] Throughout the 1880s and 1890s Poel's project can be readily aligned with those of Ruskin and William Morris, whom he described as 'that apostle of radicalism';[43] his Elizabethanism extended the concerns of the Arts and Crafts movement, and the Gothic Revival. In the spirit of his utopian mentors, Poel revived early modern forms of theatrical production in order to attempt to retrieve an unalienated mode of social existence, wherein everyday life, work and culture could become organically integrated; following the lead of the Pre-Raphaelites, whose commitment to 'truth to nature' Ruskin championed, Poel promoted a medievalised, vibrantly colourful, stylised-realist art as a way of restoring a lost wholeness of life to an increasingly mechanised industrial society. For Poel, to revolutionise the Shakespearean theatre was a step towards changing the world.

III

Poel tackled *Hamlet* again in 1900, under the auspices of the Elizabethan Stage Society, which, after a spell as instructor to the Shakespeare Reading Society and 'dramatic readings' of Shakespearean and non-Shakespearean texts, he had formed in 1894. Poel's modernising historicism was now fully-fledged, and had acquired a material form in the shape of the Society's mock-up of the stage of the original Fortune Theatre. A portable construction of timber and canvas designed to occupy both the stages of such proscenium arch theatres as could be found to accommodate the work, and the halls which were used at other times, the Fortune fit-up was effectively a stage set. Modelled according to the specification of Peter Street's 1600 Fortune contract, it consisted of a 'substantial stained oak stage' of 30 by 24 feet, 18-foot pillars supporting a roof decorated with a 'facsimile ceiling piece of blue ground and gilt stars', a working balcony, painted flats depicting the galleries, and sets of curtains between the pillars, and across the entrances and back wall.[44] In effect, it was a palimpsest, a hybrid of the three- and two-dimensional, combining some solid material features of the early modern stage (in a scaled-down form) with the curtains and canvas of the late Victorian touring theatre. It was also, as has been pointed out more than once, a pictorial representation of a platform stage and as such was embedded within the scenic logic that Poel otherwise so fiercely contested.

This did not prevent as eloquent a champion of the Elizabethan Stage Society's work as George Bernard Shaw from asserting in a review of the 1896 *Doctor Faustus* at St George's Hall that 'the more I am convinced that their method of presenting an Elizabethan play is not only the right method for that particular sort of play, but that any play performed on a platform amidst the audience gets closer to its hearers than when it is presented as a picture framed by a proscenium' (*Saturday Review*, 11 July 1896). Shaw's elision of an early modern variety of immediacy and authenticity with the ideal conditions of articulation for modern drama anticipates the Poel who later claimed that his aim was to present Shakespeare 'as naturally and appealingly ... as in a modern drama';[45] but it also implicitly aligns the free and democratic working of performance with the meeting-hall ambience of popular political rhetoric and debate. For less sympathetic witnesses, though, the Fortune fit-up provided more opportunities for mockery and jokes. Its first use was for the production of *Measure for Measure* at the Royalty Theatre in 1893 (which had also featured an onstage 'audience' in Elizabethan dress); the curtains and pillars led to it being teasingly (but justifiably) described as 'Poel's four-poster'.[46] As the space of both sex and death, the association with the iconic furnishings of the Tudor bedchamber suggests, however inadvertently, a highly appropriate setting for *Measure for Measure* (and, for that matter, for *Hamlet*); but the tactic of placing a pseudo-Elizabethan playhouse within a proscenium stage also suggests an intriguing configuration of (meta)theatrical frames around the performances operating within them. As Cary M. Mazer concludes, Poel 'placed on the stage ... a verisimilar picture of the theatre in which the plays were originally performed', and required audiences to believe 'that they were witnessing an archaeological picture of a past age'.[47] One consequence was that the intended effect of realness, authenticity and immediacy was displaced by an inadvertent, *avant-la-lettre* Pirandellian self-reflexiveness: as *The Times* (11 November 1893) complained of *Measure for Measure*, 'the persons of the play ... were merely so many abstractions, like the characters in a fairy tale'. It is appropriate here to regard Poel's project as a utopian one; and, in this respect, the multiple framings of Poel's productions rehearsed one of the central paradoxes of utopian fiction. The more precise and detailed the imagined world (and the detail is defined strategically or satirically against, or in opposition to, the existing order that is being critiqued or satirised), the more obviously a 'no-place' it becomes; characteristically, the techniques of realist mimesis work to *estrange* the real rather than endorse it. Whether it takes the form of the ancillary documentation and corroborative narratives of More's *Utopia* or the explanatory device of the dream-framework of William Morris's more or less contemporaneous *News from Nowhere*, assertions of facticity and authenticity affirm both the earnestness of the utopian order and its latent preposterousness. The more emphatically Poel insisted upon archaeologically and historically accurate details of playhouse architecture, music, costume and so on in the interests of authenticity, the less seriously could they be taken; the more insistently pedantic the practice, the more hilariously indeterminate its results. In a sense, the amused scepticism which greeted Poel's work was structurally inevitable.

Following the established practice of the Elizabethan Stage Society, *Hamlet* was staged on the Fortune fit-up, at the Carpenters' Hall in Throgmorton Avenue, on 21 February 1900. Although Poel's outlook had hardened considerably in the two decades since his first attempt at *Hamlet*, he took fewer risks with the text this time. Poel had announced at the Elizabethan Stage Society annual meeting the previous year that he planned 'to act the play as it exists in the First Quarto, so that students might see clearly the development which this great drama underwent before it reached the final shape';[48] the programme, which again carried a facsimile of the title page of Q1 on the front cover, declared that the performance was 'acted from the first published quarto of the play in 1603, on an Elizabethan Stage after the manner of the period', that 'in the present revival, the text of the play, where corrupt and imperfect, is revised from the First Folio'. According to Lundstrom, however, the promptbook reveals that 'he used the Folio text, cut and arranged in the First Quarto order, with occasional interpolations from the latter'.[49] The discrepancy may or may not indicate an intent to mislead spectators by passing off an opportunistic patchwork of Quartos and Folio as a tidied-up version of Q1, but it is in keeping with the generally pragmatic character of Poel's fundamentalism. In many respects, the performance was one of the Stage Society's most scrupulously Elizabethanised to date. Period musical accompaniment was supplied by the Dolmetsch ensemble, who in previous Elizabethan Stage Society performances had sat at the side of the stage in Elizabethan costumes; the programme recorded thanks to Captain Hutton, F.S.A., for the loan of Elizabethan rapiers and for orchestrating the duel as 'a correct revival of one of the period'. The costumes were elaborate and intricately detailed: Hamlet wore a pirate's costume for the graveyard scene, Claudius a pilgrim's hat rather than a crown (supporting Poel's view of the play as a domestic tragedy), and Ophelia a Mary Queen of Scots hat. According to the programme, the Clown's costume was 'copied from the picture of Will Scarlet, the Peterborough Sexton, which is still to be seen in

Peterborough Cathedral: he buried Mary Queen of Scots there'.[50]
Poel's attention to detail was ostensibly rooted in a historicised local reading of the play. Suggesting that it might be called 'The Revolt of Youth', he wrote in the programme that it 'seems to give expression to the growing restlessness of young England, now becoming impatient of the tyranny of Court intriguers ... Fortinbras succeeds to the throne, but the aspirations of the younger generation are defeated, for the influence of the King is entirely reactionary.' Unsurprisingly, however, the topicality that Poel detected in the play had contemporary resonances also, in that the performance took place barely a month after the death of Queen Victoria and the subsequent assumption of the throne by the controversial figure of Albert Edward, Prince of Wales (described by Kipling as 'a corpulent voluptuary of no importance'[51]). As a Fabian, Poel shared the anti-royalist sentiments of his mentor William Morris, who had described monarchy in terms of 'monstrous stupidity', and had urged that 'we must not after all forget what the hideous, revolting and vulgar tomfoolery in question really means nowadays',[52] as well as his disappointment at the failure of the republican agenda to make significant headway in the Britain of the late nineteenth century. The thwarted 'revolt of youth' projected by Poel was that of his own time.

The most contentious aspect of this revival, however, was the employment of an all-male cast. For Poel, this was an experiment which was not to be repeated, but it was (and remains) one of the more sharply debated aspects of authenticity. Poel's views on cross-casting appear to have been rather mixed, and was connected to what was (despite the preponderance of women in the Society) an ambivalent attitude towards female performers of Shakespeare. At times, Poel seemed to operate gender-blind casting, using women for male parts according to his sense of the balance and orchestration of voices: in 1895 he had presented a reading of *Romeo and Juliet* with women in both lead roles, prompting Speaight to observe that 'he was indifferent to the sex of the performer ... provided that the actor or the actress spoke in tune'.[53] He later demonstrated feminist sympathies, arranging, for example, a recital of *All's Well that Ends Well* at the Ethical Church in Bayswater in May 1920 and asserting in a programme note that 'the play has a special ethical significance which gives it a place in the history of women's emancipation'. But, for Poel, women were not altogether to be trusted. In particular, he suspected the capacity of the attention-seeking woman performer to usurp the role assigned to her, to attribute what he saw as a false prominence to female character and female presence: 'the introduction of women players', he wrote in 1916, 'led to one of the evils of the star system. So long as boys acted the women's parts there was no danger of any woman's character being made over-prominent to the extent of unbalancing the play. But when Mrs Siddons became famous by her impersonation of Lady Macbeth ... the character ceased to represent Shakespeare's point of view.'[54] As far as the boy player was concerned, Poel claimed that this was one area of Elizabethan stage practice in which illusionism reigned unchallenged: 'in appearance he was a girl. His voice was like the "maiden's organ shrill and sound" and all was "semblative a woman's part"'; incontrovertibly, 'the boys were successful in the delineation of female characters'.[55] Having eradicated sexual ambiguity from the historical Elizabethan stage, Poel answered the charge that 'to make the revivals complete Shakespeare's women should be acted by boys' by asserting that 'a boy dressed up as a girl and a girl dressed up as a girl is, to the eye at least, the same thing', and that 'there is no particular advantage in excluding the fair sex from their modern privileges' (Letter to *The Times*, 2 June 1905). This seems straightforward enough, but it cannot deflect the suspicion that these questions of Shakespearean gender were, particularly in the *fin-de-siècle* context of the 1900 *Hamlet*, less clear-cut than Poel wanted to admit. In 1881, the year of Poel's much derided 'unmanly' Prince, the American scholar Edward Vining had identified Hamlet as 'essentially feminine', employing 'stratagems that a woman might attempt, and that are far more in keeping with a feminine than with a masculine nature'.[56] By 1899 Sarah Bernhardt had added to a tradition of cross-dressed Hamlets that extends back as far as Sarah Siddons at the end of the eighteenth century, by portraying a figure satirically described by the *Saturday Review*'s Max Beerbohm as the 'Princess of Denmark'.[57]

What is at issue here, of course, is not just the interpretation of a Shakespeare character, but the very nature of masculine and feminine identities at a moment of critical social change, at the end of a decade which witnessed both the emergence of the women's movement and concerted counter-efforts to suppress it; both of which are evident in the cultural prominence of the maligned and contested figure of the 'New Woman', that masculinised hybrid of educational and economic independence, sexual decadence and biological irregularity, and social and economic activism verging upon revolutionary politics, that allegedly had emerged to threaten the institutions of church, family and state. As Sally Ledger summarises, 'the recurrent theme of the cultural politics of the *fin de siècle* was instability, and gender was arguably the most destabilizing category'; as a consequence, 'the New Woman materialized alongside the decadent and the dandy'.[58] Together with the transvestite men and women of the popular music hall and pantomime, and the codedly polymorphous sexualities of Wilde's comedies, cross-dressed Hamlets were a sign of the theatre's negotiation of these instabilities. For some, the changing patterns of control and consumption also heralded the prospect of a feminised theatre culture in which the spectators themselves became emasculated, especially in relation to the issue-centred new drama with which Poelite experimentation was temperamentally, and organisationally, connected. As Peter Womack notes, 'the small-scale theaters of the *fin de siècle*, whose directors, actors and audiences championed the provocatively new in drama, were also the places where "Elizabethan" plays were first revived, and Elizabethan principles of staging reapplied'.[59] Kerry Powell writes that 'toward the close of the Victorian period an increasing number of women produced plays written by women or, like Ibsen's dramas, seriously concerned with women, before audiences largely constituted of women'; a typical male response being to characterise the audience as 'consisting of people of dubious gender, out of place in the playhouse and in life ... "masculine women and effeminate men"'.[60] The occasion described is Madge Kendal's 1889 production of Ibsen's *The Pillars of Society*, but the rhetoric might equally tellingly define the climate of reception for the Elizabethan Stage Society's productions.

Regarded in this light, Poel's antiquarian gesture of presenting *Hamlet* with an all-male cast assumes a modernist inflection. As far as the majority of reviewers were concerned, however, the transvestite spectacle of Edgar Playford as Gertrude and Master Bartington as Ophelia was not particularly upsetting: the *Standard* (22 February 1900) reported that 'the cast was entirely a male one, according to the old style', and that 'all gave painstaking impersonations', and *The Times* (22 February) that the Society were 'more Elizabethan than ever' as 'all the female parts were taken by boys and men'. Yet the authenticating rhetoric of historicism could not altogether control the incidental irregularities of the performers' bodies: altering the charges that had been levelled against the tearful Poel in his earlier production, the critic from *The Times* nonetheless felt of Playford's 'fair' Gertrude that 'her sobs were too manlike and tempestuous and her cheeks made one appreciate the old joke about the audience being kept waiting while the heroine was getting herself shaved'. Bartington's Ophelia was, according to the *Stage* (March 1900), 'truly girlish and delightful', but Gertrude provoked the complaint, 'why not have a real boy to play the Queen, not a man with a voice that reasserted his innate masculinity?' The delicate negotiations around the true, the real, and the innate point to the sensitivity of the gender roles that the discourse is working so assiduously to police: even as masculinity is affirmed as a given and immutable quality, an essence of self revealed in the very grain of the voice, it is doubled with the figure of the provisional gender identity of the (pre-) adolescent male.

But this was tame compared to the criticism voiced by the *Era* (3 March 1900):

> We never see one of these rather pedantic productions without thinking of the celebrated dinner 'after the manner of the ancients', which was given by the enthusiastic antiquarian in Smollett's novel; and we feel something of the distaste which led one of the guests to reject the archeologically correct, but actually repulsive, dish of snails ... There is no good served by reverting to the primitive practices of the early Shakespearean stage, and by the spectacle of a stalwart youth appearing as Gertrude, or a clever boy repeating in mild but masculine tones allotted to the fair Ophelia.

The *Era*'s distaste for the Elizabethan Stage Society rested upon the primitive/civilised antithesis that has already been identified as central to late Victorian thinking about Shakespearean staging (when Frank Benson staged a five-hour *Hamlet* in the same year it was alleged that 'he has put the clock back three centuries ... He has reconverted the manufactured article into raw material'[61]), but there is something particularly intense here about the association of transvestism with the violation of the fundamental cultural distinction between the edible and the inedible, or the raw and the cooked. For the *Era*'s writer, snails and boys in dresses (by whom 'no good' is 'served') are absolutely, not relatively, disgusting; indices of a barbarism, at once stomach-turning and fearsome, that has no place at the dining tables or in the theatres of empire. This was evidently a very different culinary experience to that enjoyed by C.E. Montague several years later, who commended the Elizabethan Stage Society's touring productions of *Doctor Faustus* and *The Comedy of Errors* as 'a real banquet of tit-bits of antiquarian research and conjecture' (*Manchester Guardian*, 8 November 1904). But it is not altogether surprising that these questions of theatrical taste took such a literal turn, since they operate within an extended network of interconnected food-related metaphors of consumption and production, nutrition, and bodily cleanliness and health, whose moral and ethical preoccupations are evident in Poel's rhetoric and practice. The Elizabethan drama, Poel wrote, was 'wholesome and virile', but the modern theatre offered 'unwholesome productions' to a public 'whose taste has been systematically trained to appreciate a depraved quality of entertainment'; academics reduced Shakespeare to 'intense stodginess'; arguing for a government-regulated national theatre he drew an analogy between the wiles of the commercial theatre and the dishonest adulteration of food: 'in the poorer districts of London, for many years margarine was sold under the name of "fresh country butter"'.[62] Addressing the Annual General Meeting of the Elizabethan Stage Society in 1899, Sir Sidney Lee drove the point home: 'the Elizabethan Stage Society's programme was not designed merely to while an empty hour of an evening. It was not designed to promote digestion by producing hilarity or to pacify excited nerves by sentimental platitudinising, nor could it be depended upon to stimulate a jaded ethical palate ... '[63]

In a similar vein, it is of a more than merely anecdotal significance that Poel's biographers have drawn attention to his own abstemious eating habits: Speaight recorded that 'during rehearsals he was always surprised when the actors grew hungry at lunchtime. Every day he had to be asked if time might be given for this purpose. When the actors had gone, he sat down enveloped in quietude and withdrew into another world. He took out a small envelope from which he ate some nuts or seeds, and that was all.' This could be read simply as evidence of Poel's asceticism and personal eccentricity, as could his belief that 'actors could not begin to perform until they were prostrate with hunger',[64] but there is an underlying logic: the denial of bodily appetites which are regarded as inherently compromised and corrupt is part of a more general cultural politics of radical dissent. There are direct and significant connections here between the production and reception of Poel's work and the Victorian-Edwardian subculture of vegetarianism (within which Poel's advocate Shaw was, of course, an important figure), itself generally regarded as a freakish, even actively disloyal and subversive movement. To eschew meat-eating was, in effect, to challenge one of nineteenth-century bourgeois society's most powerful moral and cultural codes. According to the mythology, to consume beefsteak was to ingest the essence of Englishness, and to confirm one's own superiority and affluence, indeed, one's very masculinity, but the vegetarian was a wan, ambiguously-gendered figure. The human carnivore was defined along the axes of race, gender and class. 'Nineteenth-century advocates of white superiority endorsed meat as superior food', writes Carol Adams, '"Brain-workers" required lean meat as their main meal, but the "savage" and "lower" orders of society could live exclusively on coarser foods ... cereals and fruit were lower than meat on the scale of evolution, and thus appropriate foods for the other races and white women, who appeared to be lower on the scale of evolution as well.'[65] To opt for a meatless diet was thus to buck the trend of progress, to refuse civilisation, and to embrace degeneration; for their own part, vegetarian apologists hit back with the charge that it was meat-eating itself which was savage and barbaric; in the words of one Edwardian anti-meat polemic, which dealt with the atrocities that had been perpetrated by British soldiers at war in China in 1901: 'is there not some direct relation of cause and effect between the food of these executioners, who call themselves "agents of civilisation", and their ferocious deeds?'[66] One way or another, the impassioned debates around the 'primitivism' of Poel's theatrical methods tapped into more widespread controversies around the current state of civilisation, whose boundaries of good taste had to be continually preserved, and which the experiments of the Elizabethan Stage Society, wittingly or otherwise, repeatedly threatened to erode.

IV

In 1919 Poel visited Stratford-upon-Avon to witness William Bridges-Adams's production of *Romeo and Juliet*, with Basil Rathbone and Joyce Carey in the title roles. As recorded in one of the monthly letters that Poel circulated to the London Shakespeare League, the occasion was not, for him, a happy one, either for its scenic arrangements or for its portrayal of the lovers: 'not only was the continual drawing of curtains at altogether impossible moments a disturbance, but the spectators utterly failed to believe that the lovers were really in love with each other'. He offered a substantial list of criticisms of the staging, mostly in relation to costuming gaffes: the Chorus 'should not have resembled a pantaloon in a pantomime. He is suppose to represent the author, and should have appeared in black, with an academic gown, a plain white collar, bands, and a laurel wreath on his head.' For current purposes, however, the important element of Poel's analysis lies in its implicit equation of traditional pictorial staging with erotic dysfunction, whereby elaborate, intrusive settings and restless curtains thwart both the articulation of desire and the play's journey to climax.

Thespian egotism, coupled with traditional English reserve, compounded the problem even further: 'the protagonists were scarcely conscious of their own frigid deficiencies … "warm, youthful blood" is the inheritance of the young of all nationalities, but among the English the physical indications of its existence are barely noticeable'. As a counter to this, Poel offered a vivid account of an ideal Juliet:

> As a curious coincidence, the present writer found himself, on his return to town, in the same railway compartment with a girl who was not English, and certainly had the temperament of a Juliet. She was travelling with her father and mother and two younger sisters. In appearance she was a miniature copy of the famous Venus of Milo. She had the same supple grace. Love was to her as the very breath of her being. Old and young, rich and poor, would be impressed by her youth, her beauty, and her soft confidings. It is said the most lovable heart is the one which loves the most readily, and which instinctively gives its affections where they are not sought. So that when the gentle Romeo comes into this Juliet's life his image will completely fill the niche shaped by her dreams for one like him – for that lover's image and no other. On the instant she will surrender herself to him; she will become *his* Juliet, and love and be loved for the pure joy of loving. And there were in this counterfeit of a Juliet glimpses of gloom, latent in the inmost depth of her eyes, as we see when peering into a clear bottomless pool – a gloom revealing the soul's steadfastness, an untold excellence, for which the mocking gods exact from its possessors a penalty often paid in terms of precious sorrow, or by even costlier anguish – one which finds relief only in the loving sigh, 'O happy dagger, this is thy sheath, there rust and let me die!' Here, then, was a possible Juliet. Why did not the producer find one like her?[67]

Although Poel diplomatically incorporates the presence in the railway carriage of parents and siblings as chaperones to this unnervingly immediate vision of femininity, thus freeing his account from any danger of impropriety, this brief encounter is nonetheless charged with a revealingly voyeuristic eroticism, as the heat of a railway compartment on the line from Stratford to London gives rise to an uncharacteristically rapturous semi-confessional prose steeped in intense and unrequited desire. Importantly, as the screen upon which male fantasies may be indiscriminately projected, the girl is literally transformed into a visual icon: as a diminished replica of the Venus de

Milo, she becomes abundantly readable as a text, but is also defined (in a revealingly double-edge phrase) as a 'counterfeit of a Juliet'. The terms appear designed to hold in place such distinctions between text, performance and real life as are required by the overall argument, but they inevitably conjure forth the spectre of an inherently duplicitous female sexuality.

Moreover, how is this lost object of male desire to be captured and made the subject of theatrical representation? As if recognising the absurdity of the suggestion that a chance encounter with a stranger on a train might magically yield a 'possible Juliet', Poel urges the producer to seek Juliet's fantasy double: not her, but one *like* her, another copy, another kind of counterfeit. But Poel's difficulties are only symptomatic of the kinds of problems that Juliet posed to Victorian and Edwardian sensibilities, and that were indirectly addressed via the play on stage and in the culture at large. At the heart of this are Juliet's multiple identities as both desiring subject and desired object, and as both child and sexually active woman. One of the key terms, ostensibly an innocent descriptive category but, especially in view of her age as stated in the text (fourteen years), fraught with potentially contradictory associations, is 'girl'. Lynne Vallone and Claudia Nelson write that Victorian commentary on girlhood was characterised by an 'anxiety' which 'seems to have arisen in part from the Girl's refusal to be categorized ... depending not only upon her age but also her class, educational attainments, and marital or biological status, a "girl" might be ... a "home daughter" in her early twenties, a wife and mother aged seventeen, or a self-supporting member of the workforce at twelve.' Moreover, before the passing of the Criminal Law Amendment Act in 1893 raised it to sixteen, the age of consent in Britain was thirteen, creating a situation whereby 'upper-class girls were supposed to be the embodiment of purity' while 'their working-class counterparts were acknowledged to be sexual beings at puberty'.[68] This indicates that to be a fourteen-year-old girl in late Victorian England was, both culturally and experientially, to inhabit a strangely indeterminate, in-between state; as a constructed category, Victorian girlhood was both ideologically loaded and unstable, and traces of this instability can be detected in the critical discourse surrounding Juliet, particularly in relation to the question of her age, and to the relevance of this both to her sexuality, and (although this is rather more covert) to her legitimacy as an object of desire. In his survey of nineteenth-century critical views of Juliet, Philip Davis traces the methods employed by a range of male and female critics to return

Juliet's potentially irregular sexuality to the fold of Victorian mores, citing as an example Anna Jameson's defence of the notorious 'Come night, come Romeo' soliloquy (III ii 1.17) as 'infantine in [its] perfect simplicity', and for its 'charm of sentiment and innocence'; a key tactic is the manipulation of the timescheme of the play (following Hazlitt's point that 'in thought it occupies years') so that Juliet's movement from sexual innocence to experience is achieved through an instantaneous, and quasi-miraculous, passage from girlhood to adulthood: 'the fond, impatient, timid girl puts on the wife and the woman'.[69] A similar logic is discernible in Dowden's Arden edition of 1900, which deals with Juliet's fourteen years by suggesting that 'the miracle of love ... transforms her from a child to a heroic woman'.[70] The iconic image of Juliet on the balcony, familiar from stage tradition, nineteenth-century painting, and the illustrated editions of Shakespeare, encapsulates this understanding in spatial terms, placing the child-woman within an elevated threshold space which is neither inside nor outside (and which is, exotically, not English). Liminally poised between domestic, familial security and the partially tamed sexual wilds of the orchard, in calling for Romeo, Juliet hovers at the edge of the bedchamber within which her leap into maturity is to take place.

In the theatre, the precarious balance between moral, dramatic and theatrical propriety had to be maintained through an intricate refinement of age distinctions through which levels of sexual experience and availability might be defined and legitimised. Fourteen-year-old Juliet simultaneously was and was not supposed to desire, and to be desirable; a double standard that was informed by more general middle-class masculine unease about the sexuality of their own adult partners: as Kimberley Reynolds notes, 'many Victorian and Edwardian men felt more comfortable with working-class women, girl children, or with other men', a phenomenon manifested in 'the widespread use of prostitutes and the frequent seduction of servants' and in 'grown men's passions for young girls'.[71] Viewed in this light, the question of Juliet's age in relation to stage representation is a matter of sexual ideology as well as verisimilitude. 'Of course', wrote Dutton Cook, reviewing Madame Modejska's portrayal in 1881, 'it is not to be expected that the Juliet of the stage can be as youthful as the Juliet of the poet', but in this case 'there is a maturity of manner that is almost as disadvantageous to the interpreter of Juliet as maturity of aspect'. Modejska's misdemeanour (apart from not being English, since 'to the foreign player, the Shakspearian drama is, in almost every instance, a sealed book') was, as 'a clever woman of the world', to indicate a sexual self-awareness beyond that conventionally afforded the character: 'in her hands Juliet's love for Romeo declines into an intrigue; it is attended by so much calmness and calculation, it is so completely made a matter of deliberation and self-consciousness'. The result was that 'she cannot reconcile the apparent inconsistency of Juliet's intensity of passion and innateness of purity'. Since this 'inconsistency' is not just a problem of emphasis but a sign of fourteen-year-old Juliet's contradictory status as a sexual subject, it is even less open to reconciliation than the qualifying term 'apparent' might suggest. One way of attempting to hold Juliet's sexuality in check was to connect her perceived artlessness with her function as an art object. This was the tenor of one of Cook's earlier reviews (of Mrs Scott-Siddons at the Haymarket in 1867), which found much to admire in an innocent and youthful Juliet, whose affect was framed in terms of a becoming modesty: 'it is something to see one who is distinctly a lady in the part ... she never offends by conventional extravagance of manner, although she may fail to satisfy from want of experience and thorough possession of the resources of her art'. Where Scott-Siddons did offer satisfaction was in her appearance. Observing that Juliet 'may be likened to a work of art broadly painted in primary colours', Cook noted that 'the part can very rarely have been so well *looked*'.[72] Thus objectified, the perfect stage Juliet became available within a carefully stage-managed regime of viewing pleasures, wherein the desires of both characters and spectators could simultaneously be acknowledged, disavowed and redistributed. It is worth remembering that the literary, critical and artistic discourses deployed to position Juliet on stage were rooted in a network of sexual power relations that were played out in a more overt form on the streets outside. The Victorian theatre in London, writes Tracy Davis, 'was a viewing place that extended into the neighbourhood and interacted with it'; in a West End 'well provided with public houses, dining establishments, private clubs, gambling houses, brothels and other nocturnal resorts' this interaction took the form of an easy commerce between theatregoing and the sex trade, as 'successive entertainment innovations preserved pleasure-seekers' orientation towards this area'.[73] Given the ease with which a Victorian gentleman could complete an evening's entertainment by making use of the prostitutes whose place of work was the theatre district itself, the status of Juliet as sexual object seems all the more complex.

As a good Victorian, Poel engaged with *Romeo and Juliet* by means of careful negotiations with these problematic issues of gender and sexuality. In 1878 he took a short-lived course of acting lessons; among the parts studied was that of Romeo; as he recorded in his diary, he 'wanted more self-abandonment, more throwing myself into the part, real love, variety of expression. It is a part that does not come easy to me.' In March 1895 he arranged a reading with Lillah McCarthy as Romeo. As noted in the previous section, Speaight comments that 'this was the first sign of Poel's eccentricity of putting women in men's parts', adding that 'no convincing explanation of this disconcerting practice was ever given; but at least he never claimed that it was Elizabethan. Probably he found women's voices easier to modulate; and actresses were generally more willing to give him the time he needed for rehearsal.'[74] The cross-casting may have been expedient; or it may have been that Poel saw in the female performer more potential for self-abandonment in the part of Romeo than (as the attacks upon his 'unmanly' Hamlet had demonstrated) the Victorian code of masculinity would allow; but it was not without precedent on the nineteenth-century stage. Jill Levenson records that Romeo had been considered rather too effeminate by the leading actors of the first half of the nineteenth century, and that it took Charlotte Cushman's portrayal of the role for the 1845–46 London season to restore the play to the stage.[75]

According to Poel, though, the play's major problem had less to do with the dynamics of gender. In a talk given to the New Shakspere Society on 12 April 1889, Poel attacked 'the despotism of the actor, on the English stage, and consequently ... the star system', and the consequent 'mutilation of Shakespeare's plays in their representation'. He traced this process of textual disfigurement in a systematic critique of Irving's acting edition of *Romeo and Juliet*. Instancing the omissions and suppressions made by Irving's version in order to adjust the text to the requirements of both the actor-manager's egotism and the picture frame, Poel argued that its exclusive focus on the love interest not only obliterated the social dimensions of the play but also robbed the romance itself of tragic force. In opposition to the spurious coherence of Irving's redaction, Poel presented *Romeo and Juliet* as 'a veritable hodge-podge' which 'seems to defy the laws of criticism ... Bombast goes side by side with poetry; passion with pantomime ... Shakespeare sought to establish rules in accordance with the national taste, his first aim being the combination of the serious and the ludicrous.'[76] The terminology is not dissimilar to that which had been used eight years earlier to characterise Q1 *Hamlet* as an artefact of abject irregularity; rather than attempting to locate *Romeo and Juliet* within the frosty echelons of 'classical tragedy', Poel lays claim to the (female?) space of a popular theatrical culture that has no difficulty accommodating apparently contradictory materials, moods, tones and styles.

The rhetorical force of Poel's paper stems in part from its implicit equation of two rampantly authoritarian figures, who between them embody the sanctimonious and the bullying aspects of Victorian masculinity: the 'virtuous tragedian' Irving, who by enforcing the clowns to speak less than has been set down for them, reveals himself as 'anxious to rob the low comedians of their cakes and ale' (p. 10); and the monstrous Capulet, depicted throughout as an abusive and insensitive patriarch, distinguished by 'his coarse nature' (p. 18), his 'sensuality, his brutal frankness, his indifference to every one's convenience but his own, his delight in exacting a cringing obedience from all about him'(p. 21), whose 'activity is the outcome of a love for domineering, that springs from his pride of birth, and his consciousness of physical superiority' (p. 11). Of crucial importance, for Poel, is the idea that the play depicts a struggle between youth and age, and his own sympathies are firmly on the side of the former. Throughout his essay, Poel refers to the lovers as children, and at one point summons one of the archetypal images of Victorian sentimentality by describing the Juliet of IV iii as a 'poor child' who 'lies prostrate upon her bed in the likeness of death' (p. 20). Apart from the remark that in III v 'Juliet leaps into womanhood, and realizes her position and responsibilities as a wife' (p. 18), Poel manages the issue of Juliet's sexuality by placing her firmly on the juvenile side of the girl/woman divide, a decision which even enables him to read the 'gallop apace' speech as proof that 'Juliet must have been a girl since no "full-grown woman" could talk like that about her young man.'[77]

Poel's conviction that Romeo and Juliet should be seen as children was to prove decisive in the production of the play which he staged under the auspices of the Elizabethan Stage Society between the 5th and the 11th of May 1905, which was also the Society's last. Staged for the final time on the Fortune fit-up, the production featured seventeen-year-old Esmé Percy as Romeo and fourteen-year-old Dorothy Minto as Juliet. In a verbal tribute to Poel delivered at the dinner given in his honour in December 1912, George Bernard Shaw cited this decision as an index of his integrity. He had

the ridiculous habit of going to see what Shakespeare said. When he found that a child of fourteen was wanted, his critics exclaimed, 'Ah – but she was an Italian child, and an Italian child of fourteen looks exactly the same as an Englishwoman of forty-five.' Mr Poel did not believe it. He said, 'I will get a child of fourteen' and accordingly he performed *Romeo and Juliet* in that way and for the first time it became endurable.[78]

Poel's commitment to verisimilitude, according to this account (and in keeping with his distrust of the female performer, as mentioned in the previous section), exposes the traditional portrayal of Juliet for the vain and risible sham that it really is; by reverting to what is simple, natural and authorially-intended, the casting recuperated the play's innocence and integrity. In effect, Poel attempted to solve the problem of Juliet's sexuality by retreating from the point of transition which the dominant tradition, by rendering Juliet adult, elided. The manoeuvre can be seen in the context of the general intensification of sentimentality within the imagery and cultural meanings of childhood that characterised the *fin de siècle*, the period in which the Victorian idealisation of the child as an icon of naive purity and redemptive grace reached its apotheosis (even as it was most keenly felt to be both threatening and under threat), and in which the state of childhood became a pre-eminently powerful subject for nostalgia.

The intent may have been to curtail ambiguity, but the effect of the casting in performance was, on the evidence of a number of cautious reviews, oddly mixed. Percy as Romeo presented fewer difficulties than Minto's Juliet: he was 'a bright and gallant Romeo', and, in keeping with his age, 'when Romeo starts behaving like a spoilt child Mr Percy plays with considerable strength' (*Pall Mall Gazette*, 6 May 1905). The *Morning Post* (8 May 1905) considered that although he was 'very pleasing to the eye' he 'intones his lines, many of which are not at all suited to such ceremonious treatment'. But Minto's portrayal of Juliet was more readily amenable to analysis within the familiar binary reiterated by the *Morning Post* that 'an actress must be either too young to act Juliet or too old to look her': whereas she acted 'the non-tragic portion of Juliet very delightfully indeed', in that 'she never shapes in the least like the Juliet of stage tradition: she is just a young and "unsifted" English girl, sweet, innocent, and impulsive', she nonetheless 'failed to answer the call of tragedy and reminded one of some milder heroine than Juliet, as, say, a Pamela, when Mr B.'s attentions had thrown her into hysterics'. The *Pall Mall Gazette* concurred: Minto was 'a pretty and winsome Juliet, but while charming in the love passages she is hardly equal to those that are tragic'. Looking past the patronising and dismissive tone, it appears that Juliet's double child-adult identity is not only still visible but, significantly, construed in terms of a further binarisation of the artlessness of the ingenue and the knowing (and potentially duplicitous) art of the mature performer, or of the sexually-experienced woman.

The final word rests with *The Times*, which cogently pointed out that Percy and Minto were 'at least young, ardent, and good-looking, though the very natural and engaging performance of the latter was too natural for the setting' (11 May). It will be more than evident by now that the routine invocation of the 'natural' in relation to Juliet and as a counterpoint to the unnatural artifice of Poel's neo-Elizabethan stage presumes upon a complex set of contending assumptions and speculations about the ethics, gender identity, efficacy and cultural value of the revivalist movement. The production and its reviews simultaneously commemorate the demise of a project rooted in a specifically *visual* (and ruinously costly) economy of the authentic, and anticipate a recognition, not least on the part of Poel himself, that the rhetoric of the image which he had so strenuously attempted to harness to the cause of scholarship would now itself become the target of suspicion, interrogation, and even outright attack. It is symptomatic here that, as O'Connor observes, the Poel who had previously been scrupulous in his photographic documentation of the Elizabethan Stage Society revivals had by the early years of the new century reneged upon his commitment to the preservation of the visual record; after the 1901–1902 production of *Everyman* (which caused Poel to become 'paranoid about publicity' and to forbid 'further photographs showing his stages'[79]) the archive yields very few performance-based photographs and a mere handful of publicity shots of costumed performers 'posed in studios, on steps, in gardens – everywhere except upon the stages whereon they performed'.[80]

From now on, even as he campaigned for the establishment of an Elizabethan-playhouse national theatre, the dream would be a theatre of the mind's eye. As Poel reiterated: 'the atmosphere, so to speak, of Elizabethan drama is created through the voice, that of modern drama through the sight'; 'in Shakespeare's time the presentation of a play on the open stage meant to the Elizabethans an actual event; it was not make-believe but reality, not to the eye but to the ear, and thence to the mind.'[81] Writing in 1912, Poel declared that stage pictures stunted and corrupted the imagination:

It can no longer be said that an interest in pictures lessens with the close of childhood. The taste continues and gathers new strength from habitual indulgence until it threatens the adult with paralysis of the imagination ... more and more do men and women distrust their intuitions. They turn to pictures for the realisation of what they themselves hesitate to visualise ... To what end does the present popularity of the pictured page lead? Is it man's destiny to regard life as if it were a vast kaleidoscope, existing for the sole purpose of being looked at, until his brain, wearied by watching the ever-revolving machine, becomes incapable of concentrated and continuous thought?[82]

Thus Poel, who back in 1893 had launched an attack upon 'the extravagence of realism, so often thought healthy and natural' as 'only perverse sentimentality ... realism is exhausting and enervating in its effect, while idealism frequently avails to stimulate and fertilize',[83] deploys the Victorian rhetoric appropriate to masturbatory self-indulgence by characterising an interest in pictures as itself perverse and enervating, as a sign of a profound alienation and disempowerment. His situation had significantly shifted in relation to the theatrical mainstream, since although a reformed pictorialism remained the norm for Shakespeare, producers had begun, sparingly, to adopt some of his methods and principles, notably in Harley Granville Barker's productions at the Savoy (*The Winter's Tale* and *Twelfth Night*, 1912, and *A Midsummer Night's Dream*, 1914), although less as a result of their recognition of his rightness than because the self-consuming scenic ecology of the Victorian imperialist stage was clearly no longer sustainable. And, for Poel, there was a new and even more deadly enemy, one which would help to perpetuate the scenic project of the theatre he opposed, and which would confirm his worst fears about the cultural dominance of the depthless and duplicitous rhetoric of the visual image: the cinema. Against this, Poel continued to evoke a manly and healthy image of an Elizabethan playhouse which 'sprang from the entertainments of the people, and not from those of the Court', was 'workmanlike and businesslike', with 'nothing amateurish about it', and enabled 'the realism of an actual event, at which the audience assisted, not the realism of a scene to which the audience is transported by the painter's skill'.[84] But it is more than that: Shakespeare's stage is for Poel as for so many of his followers, not just a space of play and embodiment but an object of desire, a liminal, shiftingly-gendered, sexualised entity which serves as a focus for much more than fantasies about Shakespearean staging.[85] It is in this spirit, in conclusion, that we might look again at Poel's intense Pre-Raphaelite vision of the 'counterfeit of a Juliet' recounted at the beginning of this section: the Juliet to whom 'love was ... as the very breath of her being', and for whom Romeo's image 'will completely fill the niche shaped for her dreams for one like him'. Spontaneous, universally appealing, graceful, fresh with the infinite possibilities of youth, perfectly attuned to her partner, an infinitely malleable object of desire but also an icon of unattainable mystery, Poel's ideal Juliet is also his ultimate dream of the Shakespearean stage.

2
Cambridge Irish

I

Early in his autobiography *Around the World in Eighty-One Years*, which surveys a lifetime of incident as a jobbing actor, Robert Morley recalls a conversation with Sir John Martin-Harvey during the 1930s. Attempting to ascertain whether Morley had ever been 'up at' Cambridge, Martin-Harvey enquires whether he had ever frequented 'that preposterous Festival Theatre'. Morley diplomatically replies in the negative, but for our benefit goes on to briefly document his experiences as an actor during the 1931 season, which included the premiere of *1066 and All That*, a traumatic *Salome* and 'a Latin comedy in which the cast was faced with masks constructed of absorbent rubber' (this was Terence's *The Eunuch*). He also provides a rare character sketch of the founder, patron and (from 1926 to 1933) director of the Festival Theatre, Terence Gray:

> Grey [sic] was a bearded giant with a most appalling stammer. His notes to the actors were never spoken, but always delivered type-written by a secretary who was also his mistress. Legend had it that, once confronted with the infidelity of a former wife, he had broken down the bedroom door with an axe. He stood poised on the threshold, the guilty couple cowering on the marital couch. Then he discarded his weapon and stuck out his tongue.[1]

Although Morley offers this anecdote merely as an illustration of Gray's personal eccentricity, there are suggestive parallels here with the way in which Gray, and his work at the Festival Theatre, have been characterised in the extant histories of twentieth-century

55

Shakespearean stage production. Irascible, impetuous, tongue-tied yet fiercely eloquent on paper, the sexual adventurer is himself involved in a scenario which casts him as a Shakespearean cuckold fallen into the world of French farce: initially adopting an Artaudian posture of extreme violence, he abandons the pretended threat of assault in favour of mere childish posturing.

Theatre history has had its own mood swings in relation to Gray: he has been hailed as a visionary, an idealist whose practice was far in advance of its time, and dismissed as an iconoclast whose experiments revealed little more than rampant egotism. In the 1920s and 1930s, the Festival Theatre had a controversial reputation as an experimental repertory theatre, attracting national and international attention from well beyond the local constituency to which its work was primarily addressed. For example, in Léon Moussinac's *The New Movement in the Theatre*, which assembled pictorial evidence of experimental work in European and American art theatres of the 1930s, the Festival Theatre (represented by Gray's 1931 *Henry VIII*) is one of only four theatres in the British Isles to be included.[2] By the 1940s, Gray's work had been relegated to the margins of theatre history: in 1947, his former colleague Norman Marshall offered his 'reluctant' conclusion that his 'ceaseless experiment' had 'in the end practically no effect upon the English theatre'.[3] Gray occasionally pops up in surveys of the Shakespearean stage between the wars, usually as a cheeky and irresponsible maverick whose self-indulgences played havoc with the text. Writing in 1964, Arthur Colby Sprague consigned Gray to a footnote in his avowedly performance-centred account of the Histories, citing his *Henry VIII* as a 'perfect instance' of 'silliness and even travesty in their production'; in 1973, Robert Speaight sniffed that Gray 'did what he chose with Shakespeare when he troubled to produce him at all'.[4] Since then, a general reassessment of Gray in the light of his overall contribution to experimental performance has led to his being reclaimed as an unjustly neglected innovator, for example, by Richard Allen Cave, who fulsomely concludes that we are 'deeply in Gray's debt today for what we have harvested from his experiments', and that 'we owe it to him never to forget the Festival Theatre'.[5] Andrew Davies rewrites the record even more firmly, suggesting that the Festival Theatre was 'perhaps the most important of all the experimental theatre projects between the wars'.[6] Dennis Kennedy treats Gray sympathetically in his history of twentieth-century Shakespearean performance (like Styan, he situates Gray's work alongside the 1920s vogue for modern dress), concluding that although he was 'an index rather than an epitome', his example 'has a permanent place in the history of English Shakespearean performance'.[7] This chapter aims to reposition Gray's Shakespearean interventions by exploring some of the broader ideological and cultural contexts within which his work operated, focusing in particular upon his most adventurous, and notorious, Shakespeare production: *Henry VIII*. Even Gray's admirers have regarded *Henry VIII* as a production where Gray went too far, his quirkiness triumphed over his judgement: as Cave puts it, 'mere method won the day and meaning degenerated into nonsense'.[8] This view has been recently challenged by the editor of the third series Arden edition of the play, Gordon McMullan, who describes Gray's production as 'by far the most remarkable production of *Henry VIII* in the twentieth century', and sees in it an attempt to engineer 'a radical break with previous productions'.[9] I shall argue that its Lewis Carroll-style 'nonsense' can be read as an inversion of the 'truth' of official Shakespearean and 'real' histories, and as deliberate assault upon the play and its associated cultural mythologies.

The key elements of Gray's general theatrical policy and practice can be briefly summarised. His first substantial innovation was an architectural one. In 1926 Gray bought the Theatre Royal in Barnwell (an area then on the outskirts of Cambridge), one of the few surviving Regency theatres in England. As the location of Stourbridge Fair, held annually from September to October, Barnwell was an established site for popular entertainment and festivity: from the eighteenth century onwards it had attracted touring players' companies, itinerant acrobats and jugglers, puppet shows, dancers, and the like, often on jerry-built booth stages. As an event which traced its origins back to 1211, the prerogatives of the Fair nonetheless had to be balanced against those of Cambridge's other great medieval institution, the university itself: until the passing of the 1894 Cambridge University and Corporation Act, the licensing of theatrical entertainment in the town fell to the Vice-Chancellor. In 1782 a wood and canvas booth was built for use by the Norwich Players, which was pulled down in 1807; a year later the Barnwell Theatre opened, which lasted until 1813, when it was superceded by the New Theatre of Barnwell, which became the Theatre Royal Cambridge in 1849. In 1878, it went bankrupt, and for the next forty years it enjoyed an intermittent life as a mission hall, before being bought by the Kings College Club for Boys. By the time Gray purchased it, it had fallen into disuse.

Working with the lighting designer Harold Ridge, Gray ripped out the proscenium and rebuilt the stage and auditorium. Backed by a forty-foot high cyclorama, the platform, Ridge wrote in 1930, 'comes out into the auditorium and merges into it down a flight of broad steps, which stretch the full width of the building'.[10] As a spatial configuration, and a modus operandi, for Shakespeare, this was partly in keeping with the generalised sense of the 'open stage' promoted by Poel and his followers, in that it acknowledged the fluidity of the boundaries between performance and audience spaces, extruded action beyond the supposedly repressive and imprisoning confines of the picture frame, and, as Marshall points out, was deliberately contrived so that 'conventional realistic production was almost impossible'.[11] In addition, the steps took a design element which had been introduced by Leopold Jessner in his Berlin Shakespeare productions of the early 1920s (the *Jessnertreppen*) and deployed it to differentiate levels and clarify hierarchies, and to allow varied patterns of movement, and institutionalised it as an architectural fixture. The Festival Theatre, however, was not a neo-Elizabethan reconstruction, and was more obviously influenced by the Athenian configuration of arena and orchestra than by the Poelite model of the platform. Gray did not attempt a Shakespeare play in this space until 1928 (his fifth season), and it was only then that he began to imagine his ideal theatre in terms of a hybrid of the essential principles of Greek and Renaissance entertainment spaces. Gray had trained as an archaeologist, and latterly specialised as an Egyptologist, but his interest in the ancient cultures of the near and middle East happened to be a fashionable one in 1920s Cambridge, and was shaped by theatrical modernism's own attempts to appropriate and rework the form and archetypal subject matter of classical drama to its own ends (the Festival's opening production was *The Oresteia*). Gray's aesthetic was not, however, archaeological: he equipped his theatre with the most advanced technology currently available, including Schwabe lamps and a fifteen-foot revolve at the centre of the acting area, which was 'turned from below by hand gearing'.[12]

Gray was fortunate enough to command the personal means to carry out his architectural modifications to his own satisfaction and without compromise, which afforded him a degree of rather aristocratic, high-minded aloofness towards a commercial theatre which he termed 'trade'. His contempt for the timidity of its repertoire, and for the illusionist practices that it perpetuated, was fuelled by a lordly disdain for the small-minded, little England mentality to which they pandered. As Gray saw it, the proscenium arch's separation of actors from audience was symptomatic of the passive, insipid, petit-bourgeois nature of conventional theatregoing. Writing in *Theatre Arts Monthly* in 1931, he complained that 'in a London theatre the audience creeps in, listens to the play, claps ritually and departs. It has remained utterly apart. It has been an observer merely.'[13] Dismissing 'the old game of illusion, glamour and all the rest of the nineteenth century hocus pocus and bamboozle',[14] Gray claimed that once liberated from the passive role of silent voyeurism, the spectator could assume the role of an active and intelligent participant in the theatre event: 'the basic requirement of the new theatre as regards its audience is that its audience should act'.[15] But Gray's wake-up call to intelligent and critical spectators was offered as much in a spirit of provocation as of participation, and he actively courted controversy, shock and outrage. 'It is not in me', he wrote, 'to fulfil academic expectations and maintain standards of tradition'; his was a theatre which aimed to be confrontational as well as participatory, seeking what he called 'the unexpected reaction, the unanticipated pleasure, the irrepressible wrath and the readjustment of values'.[16] Gray's design aesthetic and staging practice may have been visibly indebted to Appia and Craig, to German Expressionism, and to Russian Constructivism, but this was the accent of an avant-garde with an agenda more scandalous than the 'theatre theatrical': it is the voice of Jarry, or of Artaud, of Dada and the Futurist Manifestos.

At the same time, Gray soothed and cajoled his audiences by indulging and, literally, catering for bodily appetites. In defiance of the anti-incendiary protocols that had governed English theatres from Gray's derided nineteenth century onwards, the programme declared: 'You are welcome to smoke'. It is an invitation which obviously echoes the Brecht of the early 1930s who called for the spectator to adopt 'an attitude of smoking-and-watching' since 'it is hopeless to try to "carry away" a man who is smoking and accordingly pretty well occupied with himself'; the result: 'a theatre full of experts'.[17] Gray evidently concurred, writing in the *Festival Theatre Review* that 'tobacco smoking is a sedative supplemented by the arousal of the aesthetic emotions. It has a soothing influence on the nerves, and contributes to calm thought and continuous mental exertion.' More dangerously, the return of tobacco and matches to the auditorium also reintroduces the possibility of accidental combustion, and of the altogether more volatile relationship between spectators and stage that pertained before the advent of the safety curtain and the smoke-free auditorium (it was hardly coincidental that Gray's plans for an open stage in London eventually foundered over wrangles with the London County Council about fire regulations).[18] The atmosphere of risky conviviality was reinforced by the fact that the opportunity to combine smoking with spectating was, ideally, intended to be post-prandial. Famously, the Festival Theatre incorporated a restaurant which was regarded as among the best in Cambridge, and which offered 'a speciality dish for each night of the week so the audience could select the evening they went to the theatre with their favourite dinner in mind',[19] and which drew upon Gray's expertise as a wine connoisseur to build up one of the best cellars in England.

Although Gray's production methods were often autocratic (it was said that one of the fundamental weaknesses of the Festival project was that he demanded 'disciples rather than collaborators'[20]), there was a strongly anti-authoritarian rhetoric that flavoured his public pronouncements about the Festival Theatre's artistic policy and practice. There were, he optimistically declared in the weekly *Festival Theatre Review*, 'no rules and regulations' in the Festival Theatre. The pages of the *Festival Theatre Review*, which published poetry and sketches alongside theatrical criticism and theory and, occasionally, social and political commentary, provided an outlet for Gray's diatribes against anything he construed as superfluous regulation and bureaucratic meddling. Targets as apparently diverse as the arbitrary censorship powers of the Lord Chamberlain, the absurdities of the licensing laws, and local planning and fire regulations, he all regarded as fair game, all part of a continuum shaped by the passivity of the English people, with what Gray called their 'infinite capacity for submission'.[21]

Gray's boast was that the Festival Theatre would become 'a focal point in the social life of Cambridge'; what he meant by this was the university community, which formed the bulk of his audience. Never one to miss an opportunity to goad his readership, Gray dismissed the Cambridge townspeople as a 'tribal audience' with 'its own jokes and its own circumscribed spheres of interest' and 'fit only for theatrical missionaries'. The university students, however, he considered more promising. As Gray saw it, although the Cambridge undergraduates were 'utterly ignorant of the word art, and still fairly warmly wrapped in the rags of public school prejudice' they were, nonetheless, 'mentally alert', having 'only the general limitations of the scholastic mentality'. Thus they were amenable to schooling in Gray's arts of the theatre, in that 'a theatre can work with a university audience just as its tutors can'.[22] The hope was to foster a closely-knit, alert and appreciative interpretative community, and, of course, Cambridge already had an established network of amateur theatrical activities in place, including the Footlights and the Marlowe Society. Gray's project was also timely and opportune in terms of the political culture of the town and university. The life of the Festival Theatre coincided with the moment at which, as Francis Mulhern has documented, the university became subject to 'the free interpenetration of certain social and cultural contradictions'.[23] These included the incremental but significant changes in the composition of the student body, reflecting increasing numbers of lower-middle and working-class pupils drawn from the state grammar school sector and, in particular, women, many of whom took up the new literary studies which were rapidly eclipsing subjects like classics. In the midst of shifting political and class loyalties, the left found a new, if short-lived, sense of optimism and solidarity. One of the effects of this was that student politics moved from the unfocused and generalized disaffection and 'aesthetic' rebelliousness of the late 1920s to the middle and upper-class communist activism of the 1930s, and to the emergence of the student movement. In such a context the Festival Theatre was prone to its own interpenetration of contradictions; theatrical and cultural questions raised in the work of the theatre were, for many, also political ones, although Gray's anti-authoritarianism appears to have been motivated more by radical anarchism than by a socialist perspective. This was most evident in the Festival's production of German Expressionist drama, in which the theatre theatrical was clearly also the theatre political (and also, perhaps, the political theatrical and the theatrical political). The Festival staged the Capeks' *The Insect Play* in 1927, Kaiser's *From Morn to Midnight* (1928), Toller's *Hoppla!* and *Masses and Man* (1929), and *The Machine Wreckers* (1930); Raphael Samuel notes that the works of Kaiser and Toller were also championed during this period by other experimental theatres such as the Everyman and the Gate in London, as well as by the Birmingham Rep, and were 'immediately adopted by the cultural Left in the Labour movement'.[24] The Festival Theatre energetically promoted American Expressionism as well, with productions of Rice's *The Adding Machine* and *The Subway* (1927, 1928), Glaspell's *The Inheritors* (1927) and O'Neill's *The Emperor Jones* (1928 and 1933) and *The Hairy Ape* (1928). As Steve Nicholson has documented, work like this led to Gray falling foul of the Lord Chamberlain's office more than once.[25]

With all this in mind, it is worth reflecting again upon the nature of the cultural significance that the Festival Theatre may or may not have enjoyed, regardless of whether or not Gray's specific theatrical innovations travelled beyond Cambridge or outlived his involvement in the theatre. The Festival was emphatically an elitist rather than a popular enterprise: with a seating capacity of four hundred and productions that ran for no longer than a week, it was dedicated to the cultivation of a coterie audience; the practice of encouraging spectators to return to subsequent performances for free after paying for the first suggests that the demand for seats was rarely at a premium. It is not irrelevant to its broader cultural role as a shaper of both opinion and fantasy that the Festival Theatre drew its audiences (and its most articulate critics) from a student body which in significant numbers was destined to occupy the key positions in all of the major political, religious, judicial, military, educational and media state institutions, but whose actual or potential political loyalties and philosophical outlook could not necessarily be predicted from such trajectories. In the absence of any systematic data on audience demographics at the Festival during its period of operation, any suppositions that can be made about this must remain highly tentative, but it is amusing nonetheless to speculate about the constituencies from which Gray's audience might have been drawn. Whether they went to see Gray's Shakespeare's or not (in most cases, the likelihood is the latter), there were plenty of Shakespeare scholars in the neighbourhood at the time. At King's there was George Rylands (later acknowledged as a mentor by RSC founders Peter Hall and John Barton), who contributed to the *Festival Theatre Review* and who, seventy years on, remembered Gray as 'a genius and a great spender of money' and the Festival as 'the place for fashionable, avant-garde productions, where London critics would come, and where, even if the play disturbed, the restaurant did not disappoint'.[26] Graduates in the new and thriving English degree programme in the late 1920s included William Empson, Alistair Cooke (who frequented the Festival, and wrote about it in *Theatre Arts Monthly*), Muriel Bradbrook, L.C. Knights and Q.D. Roth (later Q.D. Leavis). F.R. Leavis himself took up his Probationary Lectureship in English just as Gray set up his theatre. Leavis abhorred performance and would no doubt have avoided the Festival as a prime example of the dilettantism that he subsequently worked so hard to root out of literary-cultural life, but it was Leavis, and his brand of Cambridge English with its 'methodology of close textual scrutiny to search out the metaphors upon which performances might be built', that would subsequently shape the formative agendas of postwar Shakespearean production in Britain.[27] Busy editing the new Cambridge Shakespeares were Sir Arthur Quiller-Couch ('Q') and John Dover Wilson; again, 1926 proves an *annus mirabilis* with the publication of *As You Like It*, which unleashed Q's sentimental (and, for English and Shakespeare studies, profoundly influential) envisioning of the Forest of Arden as the idyllic green world of a lost England, aptly described by Terence Hawkes as an 'immemorial, sunlit Liberal Valhalla, a pre-1914 tennis-strewn, cricket-flecked and picnic-studded paradise'.[28] Finally, fresh from his success (in 1926) in establishing the new, modernised English Tripos was E.M.W. Tillyard, who would go on to develop the conservative historicist scholarship (*The Elizabethan World Picture*, 1943, and *Shakespeare's History Plays*, 1944) that would dominate thinking about Shakespeare for decades.[29] Tillyard would later dwell upon order, hierarchy and degree, but at this stage, by his own account, he and the other initiators of change were 'progressives by temperament', and committed to the 'liberalism' of the subject discipline they were shaping; meanwhile the 'tolerant and eagerly receptive' undergraduates of that moment engaged voraciously with a criticism, literature and culture in an excited, high modernist state of flux.[30] In theory, at least, Gray could not have looked for a more amenable or appropriate potential audience for his work.

II

If Gray's Shakespeare operated within the cultural environment which gave birth to a programme of English literary studies whose effects would be felt well beyond Cambridge university, particularly in terms of its contribution to a national culture as well as to a subject discipline, Gray's own attitude to England, the English and Englishness was a sharply critical and often satirical one. As only someone who was born in Felixstowe, raised in England, and educated at Eton and Magdalene College, can, Gray embraced the Irishness which he claimed from his parents, writing mythical dance-dramas (such as *Cuchulainn: An Epic-Drama of the Gael*, 1925[31]) which demonstrated his inclinations towards the mystical Irish nationalism and republicanism, and the idealisation of the Gael and of Celtic culture, expounded by W.B. Yeats. For Yeats, Celtic legend was nationalistic and escapist, offering 'an alternative way of seeing and representing the world, a non-classical, anti-urban, anti-mechanical mixture of the physical and the metaphysical and of the sensual and the spiritual'.[32] Something very similar is at work in Gray's celebration of Celtic and Gaelic folk culture, but here the classical is craftily recuperated. In his 1926 book, *Dance-Drama*, Gray set out his position:

Among these modern peoples Ireland, having an incomparably

more ancient cultural tradition, an isolated history and a separate racial origin, provides an opportunity that approaches most nearly to the classical conditions if these may be regarded as ideal ... Save in Gaelic Ireland, in Gaelic Scotland, and in British Wales, no figures of popular tradition, no gods and heroes survive in the public imagination, there no longer exists in the thoughts or the memory of the people any trace of a folk-history or mythology as a basis for imaginative thought.[33]

According to this roughly-sketched account, the Athenian, the Gael and the Celt share a richly anthropomorphic mode of imaginative consciousness quite alien to the docile, bureaucratic sensibilities of the English. 'Like the surrealists', writes Declan Kiberd, 'who would later explore those rejected images and ideas which had been banished to the sub-conscious, Irish writers seized upon all that was denied in official culture – holy wells, pagan festivals, folk anecdotes, popular lore – and wrought these things into a high art.'[34] Gray's generally idealised view of peasant culture reproduces a persistent strain in Anglo-Irish writing of the 1920s, wherein the appeal of the 'image of the peasant' resided in a 'physical vitalism which could be attributed to the avoidance of the debilitating vices of modernity'.[35] For Gray, 'physical vitalism' was of crucial importance for a theatre art in which it could assume an embodied form. Gray was of course vociferously opposed to the literary bias of the English theatre, and to what he termed 'the tyranny of words',[36] by which he meant both the elevation of the spoken word over other elements of the performance, and the tendency to treat the author's text as sacrosanct. This was a restatement of the Craigian belief in the total theatre experience and the fully integrated work of art, but Gray went further. For Craig, the verbal text remained, ultimately, 'the body of the play'.[37] Gray, conversely, set the body against the word, predicting that 'words will become of less importance in the theatre, their reign of supremacy, their positive monopoly as a medium of expression will come to an end'.[38] He further contended that 'there are moments in great drama for which words prove an inadequate medium for the expression of emotion ... at such moments, in fact, the character should dance'.[39] At the point of crisis or rupture, the verbal surrenders to a corporeal articulacy which it otherwise struggles to contain and repress. There is an air of the coloniser and colonised in this view of the relationship between the word and the dance, and in this sense the Festival's dance aesthetic was an important aspect of its quixotic, metaphorical logic of

Irishness. Working alongside Gray was his cousin, the dancer and choreographer Ninette de Valois, who had trained under Diaghilev, and who also believed that dance was for the Englishman or woman a largely alien, and only painfully acquired, physical vocabulary (she would abuse incompetent dancers as 'stupid little Anglo-Saxon[s]'[40]). As Gray saw it, from his adopted position of exile in the country of his birth, the freedom of dance was another avenue of opposition to the regulated, alienated and puritanical condition of English modernity.

All this had a bearing upon the place of Shakespeare at the Festival, and not only because Gray had reason to be wary of a canon of work whose wordiness was little short of a national religion. For many Anglo-Irish and Irish writers in the first decades of the twentieth century, Shakespeare was a cultural force to be both contested and appropriated. On the one hand, the Shakespeare of British colonialism, the central pillar of its literary and dramatic tradition, was, as the agent of English cultural imperialism, something to be resisted, as was the Shakespeare who represents Ireland and the Irish as barbaric, marginal and linguistically impoverished, and as a source of mischief and rebellion. On the other hand, writers such as Wilde, Yeats, Synge and Joyce attempted to turn Shakespeare against the English by re-reading the works in nationalist and legendary terms. As Kiberd points out, the project was one of restoring to Shakespeare's texts 'an openness which they had once had before being simplified by the administrative mind' and 'reaching back beyond the imperial mission to a pre-modern, carnivalesque vitality, to those elements which survived in Shakespeare's plays, and which seemed to intersect, in suggestive ways, with the folk life of rural Ireland'.[41] Reading against the official imperialist version of Shakespeare (and specifically against Dowden), Yeats celebrated the force of the poetic imagination over history, so that his Richard II became 'no peripheral victim, but the centre of meaning, moral and poetic, in Shakespeare's play'; in *Ulysses*, Joyce mused upon a Hamlet who was 'a variant of the type, "the beautiful ineffectual dreamer who comes to grief against hard facts"'.[42] For others there were direct connections to be made between the manners of the Irish Literary Revival and Elizabethanism; back in 1911, for example the Abbey Theatre manager Lennox Robinson had engaged Nugent Monck for 'teaching in Shakespearian and modern work': Monck was selected 'because of his training under Mr Poel, whose ideals resemble so closely those of the Abbey Theatre itself'.[43] What has been described as the 'absorption of influential Revolutionary Irish Republicans in Shakespeare and Shakespeare criticism' further complicates the picture; as does the determined appropriation of Shakespeare as Celtic by Irish scholars during the period of the struggle for independence.[44] In the post-independence republican Ireland whose theatre was dominated by the Abbey aesthetic of indigenous peasant drama, Shakespeare remained: during the mid 1920s, the Irish actor Anew McMaster surprised many when he decided to tour rural Ireland with a repertoire of Shakespeare plays, a move which proved unexpectedly popular. In his company was Micheál MacLiammóir, who joined forced with Hilton Edwards to establish Dublin's Gate Theatre, with which the Cambridge Festival had much in common, and where Shakespeare formed part of a flamboyantly avant-garde repertoire of Irish and non-Irish drama and visual extravagance (Ninette de Valois was the founder of the Abbey School of Ballet, which was housed at the Gate from 1927 to 1933).[45]

As a visitor to the ancestral homeland in which, as a breeder of racehorses, he eventually settled, Gray may have been aware that the Irishing of Shakespeare was a matter of ongoing and lively negotiation; at the Festival Theatre, the Englishness of stage Shakespeare was disintegrated into a restless and eclectic internationalism. In actuality (although it obviously looms large in a study of this kind), Shakespeare was a relatively minor element within the Festival's overall programme. Of nearly two hundred plays staged at the Festival between 1926 and 1933, Shakespeare accounted for eleven; beginning in the fifth season with *Richard III* in February 1928, these were: *As You Like It* (1928), *Romeo and Juliet* (1929), *Measure for Measure* and *The Merry Wives of Windsor* (1930), *Henry VIII* and *Julius Caesar* (1931), *Troilus and Cressida* and *The Merchant of Venice* (1932), *Pericles* and *Twelfth Night* (1933). Not all of these were Gray's productions: *The Merry Wives of Windsor* and *Measure for Measure*, for example, were produced by Tyrone Guthrie and Evan John respectively during one of Gray's periodic leaves of absence from the Festival. The apparent disregard for Shakespeare served for some as confirmation of Gray's general fecklessness; in practice it meant that Shakespeare at the Festival was in essence a continuation of the work upon the contemporary avant-garde. In some ways, Gray's scenic embellishments and burlesque visual style echoed the work of Komisarjevsky, then at Stratford-upon-Avon, although Gray courted controversy with his propensity not just for strong design concepts but for wheezes, meretricious gimmicks and frankly cheap jokes. Repudiating Q's bucolic fantasy, he conceptualised *As You Like It* by putting the entire cast in silver wigs and Arden in black and white, but sent a Rosalind with woggle and shorts and a girl-guide Celia scouting for boys, costumed as Baden-Powell's finest. For no obvious reason, Sir Andrew and Sir Toby were equipped with roller skates in the 1933 *Twelfth Night*. Happily anticipating *West Side Story* by nearly three decades, Gray and de Valois had the Montagues and Capulets dancing through a flamenco *Romeo and Juliet*, the setting of which 'looked like an illuminated medieval manuscript', evoking Elizabethan mansion staging with 'the houses of Capulet and Montague facing each other downstage, the one with a spitting cat, the other with a snarling dog painted on the front door'.[46] The 1932 *Merchant of Venice*, similarly, placed the houses of Shylock, Antonio and Portia around the stage; Cambridge pleasures mingled with Venetian ones as performers punted between them in miniature gondolas. In this production, notoriously, Shylock (last seen grinding a barrel organ) fished for lobsters in the canal, and, signalling Gray's boredom with the play, Portia's plea for mercy was 'delivered in a listless tone of voice as if the actress was repeating it for the thousandth time' and 'the entire court relapsed into attitudes of abject boredom'; meanwhile (reflecting Gray's fondness for toys) 'the judge whiled away the time by playing with a yo-yo'.[47] In a way, this was a deeply honest response to the play and its set pieces, but such gleeful, gimcrack iconoclasm was bound to make Gray unpopular with more serious-minded critics, even as it would enhance his appeal to undergraduates. His most stylistically cohesive Shakespeare production, and the only one in which he maintained a consistently serious tone, was his first, the 1928 *Richard III*, which was heavily indebted to Jessner's 1920 Berlin production. Gray banished all props apart from the four spears employed to dispatch Richard at the end of the play, preferring mime and the extravagant gesture to naturalistic detail, declaring, with his characteristically lordly disdain for the trappings of the bourgeois theatre, that 'to crown a king with a crown of lead can never be effective as theatre art: to crown him with a magnificent gesture might be exceedingly moving'.[48] A textbook example of German Expressionist *mise-en-scène*, the play was reduced to a series of tableaux played on the Festival stage's 'hollow-box system'[49] of movable cubes, cylinders and steps, lit entirely by spots, and costumed in black, white, red and gold.

  This was an avant-garde Shakespeare conducted both on the plane of high art and in the realms of burlesque, and one which did not necessarily conflict either with frontality or with the picture frame; indeed, the austere visual autocracy of *Richard III* quietly demanded it. Nonetheless, Gray aligned himself with those who called for the abolition of the proscenium arch and, although he vociferously refused to defer to the plays as literature, his modernist theatrical Shakespeare was conducted in a spirit of neo-Elizabethanism which understood itself as a kind of authenticity. The flexible structure of his stage, he wrote, was essentially a dynamic elaboration of Elizabethan stage practice, with technology facilitating the exploration of unfulfilled textual potentialities: 'in Shakespeare's day this structure was simpler, perhaps, often a mere placard, whereas here the structure serves greater purposes in the play; it raises the actors to varying levels, thereby emphasising their relationships and intensifying the drama of the situation, by its form it symbolises the spirit of the place or of the emotion of the scene, or in some way helps to reveal subtleties in the action'. From the revivalist point of view, the proscenium arch theatre, which he characterised as 'essentially two-dimensional' was fundamentally at odds with Shakespearean drama, which was 'essentially three-dimensional'.[50] Deriding the lower-middle-class introversion of the picture-frame stage as the home of 'drawing room comedy and kindred forms of entertainment',[51] he called for a populist Shakespeare, declaring that he 'would rather produce Shakespeare in a barn, a cellar, a church, a concert hall, a boxing ring, a public square, or any other architectural structure than in a traditional Theatre'. The Festival Theatre was, he felt, partly suited to this, as a compromise between a proscenium arch and the arena stage that was the ideal, being 'a stepping-stone towards the real modern playhouse which shall combine the essential characteristics of the Elizabethan inn-yard, the Gothic cathedral and the essential auditorium principles underlying the Hellenic theatre'.[52] Whether such an architectural and cultural hybrid of the holy and the everyday, the permanent and institutional and the improvised, is even imaginable, let alone achievable, is open to debate, but it is evident that Gray's thinking is very close to the modern/early modern/classical model sought by T.S. Eliot, whose verse dramas of the 1930s onwards attempted to afford this modernist synthesis a dramaturgical shape. Gray's vision of the Elizabethan playhouse, complicated though it was, was coupled to a straightforwardly Arcadian view of Shakespeare's world. In an interview presaging his production of *Henry VIII*, Gray attacked the current theatre industry for contributing to the audience's general anomie, in that 'the moribund entertainment-trade has atrophied their senses and rendered them irresponsive to the old original technique of the Greeks and Shakespeare' (*Sunday Times*, 1 February 1931). This 'old original technique' was vital, dynamic, sensual and immediate: 'we want the audience to experience the pleasures which people enjoyed in the reign of Queen Elizabeth, when England was Merrie, and life still held some freedom and joy'. Gray's temporary hankering for a lost England of innocent pleasures and freedoms, a pre-industrial 'organic community' united under the benign gaze of Good Queen Bess was hardly an isolated one in Cambridge at the turn of the 1930s (it most obviously echoes the rhetoric of Leavis and of the newly-emerging *Scrutiny*). However, it sits rather oddly with what was to follow in *Henry VIII*.

III

Gray's production of *Henry VIII* ran from the 9th to the 14th of February 1931. The play was a strategic choice, since its stage history offered Gray plenty of ammunition in terms of its heritage of nineteenth-century illusion, glamour, hocus pocus and bamboozle. From Colley Cibber's production in 1727 through to Beerbohm Tree's in 1910, it had been treated by producers as a densely-textured popular pageant, with narrative subordinated to crowd-scenes, processions and elaborate ceremonial. More recent productions of the play, such as Robert Atkins's at the Old Vic in 1924 and Lewis Casson's at the Empire in 1925, had perpetuated the tradition of pictorial elaboration. The style had an ideological component; as John Collick has noted, the Victorian style of staging Shakespeare's Histories as 'historically accurate and composed like a series of painted pictures' was 'an integral part of the construction of a new nationally symbolic and historical mythology ... to display the legendary sources of a new British consciousness'.[53] Within the pictorial tradition, the totalising density of the visual representation, its ostentatious period verisimilitude and – in the case of this play – frequent quotation from the Holbein portraiture, invests stage representation with cultural and political authority. Moreover, particularly since the nineteenth century, revivals of the play have tended to coincide with royal christenings, coronations and anniversaries; indeed, the persistence of a surfeit of pageantry and spectacle on the stage during the twentieth century has contributed to English royalist culture's project of re-inventing itself – often in terms of the revival of generally bogus 'ancient ceremony'. At the time of Gray's production in 1931, the monarchy was embarking upon a new period of turbulence that would culminate in the abdication crisis five years later.

As a text deeply embedded within national mythology, *Henry VIII* was not an obvious choice for the producer intent on making a

Craigian 'independent work of theatre art', and yet from some angles this seemed to be how Gray, perversely enough, wished to approach it. A week before the production opened, the *Cambridge Daily News* (3 February) learned that 'Mr I. Quetzacoath' (Gray under one of his various pseudonyms) would treat the play 'rather as a rhythmical theatre-poem than a historical drama'; Gray himself accompanied the illustrations of the production in Moussinac's *New Movement in the Theatre* with the assertion that 'if the theatre is to be regarded as an art-form, the representation of life and the expression of emotion and idea must be held subservient to the creation of formal perfection. The beholder must experience a purely aesthetic reaction unvitiated by sentiment, by ratiocination, or by the intrusion of actuality.'[54] Whether a 'purely aesthetic reaction' is appropriate to a play which centres upon one of the most familiar icons of popular history is open to doubt, and elsewhere Gray adopted a rather more light-hearted (and even referential) attitude to historical drama. Writing in the *Festival Theatre Review* in 1928, Gray indicated the direction that he would subsequently take with *Henry VIII*: 'in the modern drama history may be taken seriously, that is to say a dramatist may set out to create a pageant that brings before the eyes of a modern audience a near representation of the outward semblance of a past epoch of the human race; or he may take it satirically, that is to say as a means of poking fun at, or otherwise bringing into light relief aspects of the modern world by contrast with a caricature of an age that is past.'[55] Nonetheless, this satirical approach could be brought into line with revivalism; thus the *Liverpool Post* (4 February) reported that Gray's intention was to recover the authentic theatrical identity of the play through experimental means: 'Gray expresses his hope that his "modernist" production of *Henry VIII* ... will, by its lack of elaborate "effects", enable audiences to catch something of the same thrill as those who saw it in Shakespeare's day.' As oddly retrograde as his earlier invocation of Merrie England, Gray's attempt to constitute his avant garde Shakespeare as, paradoxically, more profoundly traditionalist is uncharacteristically defensive, and for this very reason is as suggestive of the continuity between his outlook and that of the wider revivalist movement as it is indicative of the difference between them.

In the event, the production generally confirmed Gray's reputation for an irreverence that bordered upon flagrant irresponsibility. The provisional and malleable status of the text was emphasised: the production was announced as *The Famous History of King Henry the Eighth, a masque in the modern manner, using the text attributed to*

William Shakespeare and others, a 'precaution', as one of Gray's more sympathetic reviewers interpreted it, 'to anticipate criticism from the Old Guard'.[56] If this billing introduced an element of textual and authorial indeterminacy into the proceedings, it was in keeping with the critical tone of the production. As reported by the *Birmingham Post* (11 February), Gray's attitude towards the play was that 'its history is villainous'; and this scepticism was reflected in an unforgivingly modernist design aesthetic. Gone were the Tudor timbers which had traditionally framed the Henrican world in English oak: the constructivist set consisted of aluminium sheeting which 'under the changing lights took on a range of metallic tones from dull bronze to gold according to the mood of each scene', and which formed a metal ramp curving from downstage right to upstage left, vanishing through the centre of the dark blue curtains at the back.[57] There was a step stage left, and a low set of steps at the centre of the revolve. The action also occupied the auditorium, which allowed for the restitution of an element of convivial authenticity, with 'the King and his masquers enter[ing] just as they would have done in an Elizabethan banqueting hall, through the aisles of spectators' (*Birmingham Post*), messengers tearing 'up and down the gangways' (*The Times*, 13 February), and scenes of festivity surrounding the christening. In keeping with Gray's wish to arouse and involve the spectators, the audience was inducted into the performance, 'in turn addressed as the lords who are attending the Court at Blackfriars: and as the rabble who have forced their way into Whitehall for the Coronation feast' (*Birmingham Post*). There was also an in-joke for Gray's audience in the form of an interpolated scene (*à la Henry V*) entirely in French, which featured gentlemen enquiring '*Ou le diable sont les dons?*', an 'outstanding innovation', according to the *Evening News* (10 February), which, appropriately enough, was 'played in the auditorium'. Inadvertently, perhaps, this was a historicist gesture; the mobile staging made use of what Robert Weimann was subsequently to identify as the Elizabethan theatre's dialectic of *platea* and *locus*, the 'complementary perspectives' of court and populace, high tragedy and low comedy, realistic and emblematic representation.[58] The *Manchester Guardian* (12 February) noted this hierarchical differentiation: 'certain aspects of Katherine's tragedy were isolated on the stage and the groundling humours kept in the auditorium'.

More disconcertingly, the costuming also flouted conventional forms of period authenticity. Gray declared in advance that Henry VIII 'will be dressed, not as Henry VIII was dressed, but in a costume which will be symbolic of Henry VIII's relation to the other characters, whose dress will symbolise their relation to him' (*Sunday Times*, 1 February), a rather Derridean position which pointed towards a language of costume defined not in terms of its referential capacities but as a system of differences. His visual cue, accordingly, was taken not from Holbein but from 'the garden party in *Alice in Wonderland*, as conceived by Lewis Carroll and illustrated by John Tenniel' (*Birmingham Post*). All of the characters in the play were dressed as playing cards, which for one reviewer seemed 'vaguely Tudor' (ibid.), but to another looked rather sinister, and unpatriotically Teutonic, with 'the traditional stiff curled wigs and grotesque make-ups suggestive of the German rather than the English card' (*Evening News*). The scheme allowed Gray and his costume designer Doria Paston opportunities for visual punning: 'Henry's royal attire was (more or less appropriately) decorated with "hearts", and the Duke of Buckingham was a "Knave of Spades"' (*Daily Telegraph*, 10 February); Gardiner was 'the ace of spades and Cardinal Wolsey a diamond', and 'the courtiers were dressed as plain cards, the suit depending on their loyalties in the court'.[59] As a cartoon inversion of the nineteenth-century world picture, the appeal of the Carrollian conceit to Gray's anti-Victorianism can be readily discerned, and the references worked on a number of levels. Gray's appropriation of Carroll for satirical ends was not without precedent: until the end of the 1920s *Alice* was a pantomime staple, a familiarity which was exploited, to take just one example, in an agitprop piece produced by the Hackney-based People's Players in 1929, *Malice in Plunderland*. Andrew Davies records that the skit reworked the trial scene wherein 'the characters were dressed as playing cards, each of them being a prominent political figure of the time, such as Stanley Baldwin and Winston Churchill. The Press formed the jury and the Knave of Hearts, the defendant, charged with organising a secret society named the Labour Party.'[60]

In Gray's *Henry VIII* the scheme afforded the proceedings an *Alice*-like dream logic analogous to the Joycean nightmare of history, and suggested a framework of nonsense and absurdity: this was a caricature of both historical representation and history itself. The scheme also reduced the characters to flat, manufactured and depersonalised playthings, and characterised court politics as a ruthless and arbitrary game. The device paid its strongest dividends in the trial scene, which naturally evoked the climax of *Alice in Wonderland*, in which 'what is on trial is the "law" itself, whether it be the law of Wonderland or, by extension, the law wherever it is encountered ... since the world in which the trial takes place is without order or meaning, the trial is itself a pointless formality, another nonsensical game without rules and without a winner'.[61] Gray's production voiced just such scepticism (even nihilism) about the mechanisms of justice, sense and order. Its evocation of the terrorised court and decapitating monarch of Carroll's text also, perhaps, alluded to the realities suppressed in Shakespeare and Fletcher's 'villainous' version of history, hinting at the despotism and the serial executions of Henry's reign. Despite Gray's apparent disavowal of historical referentiality, this was a design concept which in places allowed the historical unconscious of the play to become visible.

The production's style was established in the opening moments. According to the *Eastern Daily Press* (11 February):

> two members of the cast enter carrying a life-size cardboard figure each. These figures, being placed one on either side of the stage, representing Norfolk and Abergavenny, and lest you should be in any doubt as to their identity a card is hung in front, one with 'Norfolk' written on it and the other 'Abery'. Later these same figures become '1st gent' and '2nd gent', the cards being turned around to inform you of the fact. The two members of the cast, as the chorus, meanwhile take up positions on the steps at either side of the stage, and with megaphones, speak their parts. You thus have the cue to the method. It is 'Why clutter up the stage with minor characters? Cardboard figures will do equally well.'

This opening sequence used a strategy employed in other Festival Theatre productions of large-cast plays; perhaps it was also another in-joke, in the form of a veiled reference to the Festival Theatre's 1929 production of Toller's *Hoppla!* Infuriated at the cuts that the Lord Chamberlain's office had stipulated for the production, Gray had satirised the interventions of the censor by having the stage manager comment from offstage through a megaphone, thus: 'The scene in Room 29 is deleted. Eva is now getting out of bed, but the Lord Chamberlain will not allow you to see it!'[62] The irony was further compounded by the fact that uncensored text of the play was freely available for reading: it was put on sale in the foyer with Gray's comment that 'the audience were allowed to read the play but not look at it'.[63] This opening sequence, which some reviewers thought childish and irritating, established the production's detachment from royalist rhetoric, as well as representing the *reductio ad absurdam* of

Gray's antipathy to realism and, in particular, to the depiction of character. Insisting upon a quasi-Brechtian detachment of the actor from the role, Gray declared that 'the actor will not try and give an impersonation of Henry VIII. He will be Arthur Young ... [He] will act in a completely stylised manner, for his object is not to persuade people that he is Henry VIII, but to express, in a stylised manner, the emotions and ideas which Shakespeare intended to convey' (*Sunday Times*, 1 February). Like Meyerhold (a major influence upon his work), Gray saw the ideal actor as a combination of dancer and marionette rather than an impersonator. Accordingly, mime substituted for props, and each performer was given a repertoire of steps to delineate the essence of his or her role and define its place within the play as a whole; and grouping and movement were choreographed by de Valois to foreground what Gray saw as the dance-drama form of the play. Gray also made use of angles and levels in order to illuminate the court hierarchy and the narrative pattern of rise and fall: actors entered at the top of the ramp, and Cardinal Wolsey was consistently placed at a higher level until his downfall, when 'he literally seemed to wither in stature'.[64] Wolsey executed a 'kind of foxtrot to appropriate music offstage, a rhythmic measure he treads throughout the show', Henry moved by 'thrusting one foot out one way and the other another, his body following in a swaying motion' (*Eastern Daily Press*), and the courtiers, with 'a single communal gesture' attained a 'mocking impersonality'.[65] Anne Bullen was particularly striking, as she postured 'incessantly before an imaginary hand-glass, with curious contortions from the waist'; the *Birmingham Post* suspected that this was another Carrollian reference: 'she must be striking "Anglo-Saxon attitudes"'. For Gray, and de Valois, of course, 'Anglo-Saxon attitudes' were what were most despised, and precisely that which dance-drama sought to challenge.

The most striking moment of directorial inventiveness, and Gray's most macabre joke, came in the final scene, the handling of which was for one reviewer the 'great laugh of the evening' and for another 'the ultimate liberty' (*The Times, Eastern Daily Press*). As Cranmer launched into his eulogy to Elizabeth, the baby was revealed to the audience as a property doll, a cardboard effigy with the face 'of Elizabeth at the age of 60, and an extraordinary caricature at that', complete with 'her hooked nose, and her red hair, and brocade and ruffles' (*Eastern Daily Press, Birmingham Post*). Whether or not there was an intended topical reference here to the second (and future Queen) Elizabeth, it was an unsettling as well as comic image, with the aged and wizened infant offering an apt metaphor for the grotesque anachronism of the modern monarchy. As Cranmer spoke, according to Norman Marshall, the revolve began to rotate, until 'finally with a shout the company tossed the baby into the audience';[66] immediately, 'the entire company dashed through the audience and made their "exeunt omnes"' (*Birmingham Post*). This spectacular stunt might have been interpreted as an alarmingly literal depiction of a revolutionary view of history, signifying the ultimate fate of the ruling class satirised in the production, or as a vaudeville routine inspired by the antics of the Crazy Gang at the London Palladium, but there was no doubting its incendiary effect upon the audience: on the first night, Marshall recalls, it provoked 'a pandemonium equally compounded of cries of rage and shouts of delight' (p. 67).[67]

Joking apart, a number of reviewers clearly sensed that there might be more to Gray's subversive lampoonery than varsity prankishness – 'ragging the Bard', as many put it. For the *Manchester Guardian* (12 February), *Henry VIII* was a politically as well as theatrically radical production, which showed Gray 'continu[ing] to lead the Left Wing with energy and humour'. The *Evening News* notice neatly situated the radicalism of Gray's methods in terms of a geographical disposition of English culture and Shakespearean theatre, commenting that the production 'would have shocked a Stratford audience, but it amused Cambridge'. Cambridge's reputation as the cradle of advanced thinking and political as well as cultural dissent was also alluded to by the *Birmingham Post*, which concluded that as a 'first attempt to adapt Russian methods to Shakespeare in this country', the production was a 'novelty', but 'it would take a whole Bolshevik Revolution to take it much beyond Cambridge'. This comment is worth pausing over since, probably inadvertently, it identifies the real challenge of Gray's work. The immediate sense is clear enough: Gray's 'amusing' experiments are Bolshevik in the general, rather casual, and possibly abusive, sense of innovation, iconoclasm and anti-establishment sentiment, as well as being obviously derived from Soviet stage practice. But Gray's revolt against the picture-frame, scenic realism and naturalistic characterisation attacked not only the dominant theatrical discourse of illusionism but also, implicitly, the humanist consensus that both informs and is sustained by it. By displacing psychological 'naturalness' from its central position, Gray followed the lead of Meyerhold ('there is a whole range of questions to which psychology is incapable of supplying the answers') and Brecht ('the continuity of the ego is a myth').[68] There is more at stake here than mere advances in style and technique.

Meyerhold's concern was with the contradictions beneath the supposedly unified surface of the naturalistic bourgeois character, and with the construction of a post-revolutionary subject, which could be manifested on stage in a physical athleticism that emulated the rhythms of labour. The application of this method in *Henry VIII* resulted in a dance-drama of playing cards which was on the one hand a Dionysian celebration of communal and social identity over bourgeois individualism, and on the other a spectacle of the human subject in history as an arbitrarily-inscribed flat surface, the depthless, hollow and alienated subject of advanced industrial society, the Marcusian figure of one-dimensional man. In the light of the history of the decade that followed, as the transformation of the Soviet dream into the nightmare of Stalinism was shadowed by the growth of fascism, it was a prescient vision. Hints of this can be caught in subsequent comments on the production and upon Gray's methods; for example, Speaight's conclusion that the stylisation of Henry VIII ensured that 'the dramatis personae naturally disappeared with their personalities'[69] confronts Shakespearean character with deeper (and perhaps unconscious) fears of the annihilating anti-individualism of Soviet Communism. Here, perhaps, is one reason why Gray's work has been a source of contention, and why it remains politically ambiguous.

If all this seems a little removed from the Merrie England invoked by Gray, then it is in keeping with the contradictory quality of his Shakespeare. In a production which was seen as both amusing and scandalous, the farcical violence as Elizabeth was tossed into the audience provided the most joyful moment, at which, according to the *Eastern Daily Press*, 'the audience laughed without restraint'. It was a Punch-and-Judy image which carried a subversive hint of regicide, but, more chillingly and prophetically, perhaps also of genocide. Then again, like the production as a whole, it might simply have been a joke. If this is so, then it is a joke which deserves to be taken seriously; for, as Freud reminds us, nonsense or absurdity 'never arises by chance through the ideational elements being jumbled together', but rather is unconsciously 'designed to represent embittered criticism and contemptuous contradiction'.[70] This seems an apt summation of the Festival Theatre Shakespeare. Beneath the clowning and the choreography, there loomed a more disturbing sense of unease, provoked by the rapidly-accelerating social and political crises of the 1930s. Such was the sense of Gray's nonsense: seen in history, *Henry VIII* emerges as a very grim joke indeed.

Part II

The Double Life of Tyrone Guthrie

3
Hamlet and Oedipus Biggs

I

We should be giants, living in a land like this!

(Anton Chekhov, *The Cherry Orchard*, 1904)

On the morning of 15 May 1971, seated at his desk at his family home near Newbliss, County Monaghan, Ireland, Sir Tyrone Guthrie died of a heart attack. Although Guthrie was in his seventieth year, had survived a similar attack eleven years earlier, and had for some time been in a precarious state of health (concealed by an apparently relentless energy and robustness), the announcement of his death was greeted with a widespread sense of shock and genuine loss. If Guthrie's demise was, like many of the achievements of his life, a newsworthy event, it was also the occasion for the reiteration of the superlative and hyperbolic rhetoric within which his work had been couched for decades. A full page obituary in *The Times* (17 May 1971) noted that the director's influence 'came to be felt in practically every country in which the theatre exists'; but Sir Ralph Richardson authentically voiced the mood of Guthrie's professional collaborators when he wrote in the *Sunday Times* (23 May) of 'the astounding range of his achievements, all over the world, suddenly cleaving the skies ... bursting with ideas and filling all he encountered with faith and fire'. For Richardson, Guthrie was an 'eagle' who (to employ one of Guthrie's favourite phrases) 'rose above'. At the memorial service at St Paul's, Covent Garden, Alec Guinness opened his address by announcing that 'A great tree has fallen'; a tribute event at St George's Theatre featured Daniel Massey giving Cleopatra's 'His legs bestrid the ocean ...' (*Antony and Cleopatra*, V. ii. 82); throughout his life Guthrie was described as a founding father, as a pioneer, and, over and over again, as a 'giant' of the theatre.

If there is one thing that everyone who knew Tyrone Guthrie (and quite a few who didn't) agreed upon, it was that he was *big*. The cue for this was, of course, the fact that from the age of seventeen Guthrie was six foot five inches tall, a characteristic which he himself regarded with considerable sensitivity; but the pervasive tendency to characterise 'Tony' Guthrie as a cross between Monty, Johnny Appleseed and Finn MacCool also suggests that there was a quality to Guthrie's work, as well as his personality, that seemingly inevitably transformed his physique into metaphor, summed up in the phrase 'larger than life'. Thus when the man who was born in Tunbridge Wells in 1900, educated at Wellington and St John's College, Oxford, moved between Oxford, Cambridge, Belfast, Glasgow and Montreal before becoming artistic director of the Old Vic at the age of thirty-two, founded the Stratford Festival in 1953 and the Guthrie Theatre in Minneapolis ten years later; was knighted in 1961 and became Chancellor of Queen's University, Belfast in 1963, and who, Falstaff-like, was the source of wit in others in the form of seemingly endless anecdotes, is described in two recent contributions as 'a big man in every sense' and, more ominously, as 'that looming patriarch of British theatre',[1] we might well ask whether the slippage between physique, reputation and philosophy and practice of theatre indicates that there is rather more at stake than the force of Guthrie's own personality.

On the evidence of the testimony of those who knew him, Guthrie was without doubt a remarkably energetic and charismatic figure, and a superbly inventive director; his witty and fluent critical and auto-biographical writings also reveal an adventurous thinker with a keen sense of the social responsibilities of theatre rare within the theatrical mainstream of his time. But the recurrent references to Guthrie's magnitude suggest that his distinctive role as public figure was to embody the hopes, dreams and aspirations not only of what theatre was but also of what it might be. More particularly, he was to assume the mantle of the Shakespearean theatre: as a man who was earthy and profane in his eccentric personal habits and mode of speech, but had a classical and spiritual vision of theatre as ritual and ceremonial ('the purpose of the theatre is to show mankind to himself, and thereby to show to man God's image'[2]), who displayed the dress sense of the aristocratic tramp, and who was always a compellingly *physical* presence, Guthrie seemed a fleshly incarnation of the postwar modernist rough/holy Shakespeare (as described by Peter Brook[3]) that his own theatre practice sought to recreate. In order to make sense of Guthrie's Shakespearean interventions, and of the theatre spaces which shaped and were shaped by them, it is as well to begin by acknowledging that the forms in which the life has been profiled and evaluated cannot easily be separated from the work itself. The Festival Theatre at Stratford, Ontario and the eponymous Guthrie Theatre in Minneapolis are Guthrie's immediate progeny, but his paternity can be traced throughout the postwar open stage movement. As hybrid constructs of Greek-style arced auditorium and semi-Elizabethan platform, both spaces not only gesture towards two of Guthrie's textual touchstones, *Hamlet* and *Oedipus Rex*, but also, by enabling over a thousand spectators to be seated no more than sixty-five feet from the stage (about the length of ten Tyrone Guthries), figure relationships between scale and intimacy, distance and spontaneity, that reverberate through the Guthrie story.

For reasons which will become evident, this chapter adopts a chronological framework which necessarily makes use of auto/biographical materials. My initial points of reference, then, are the two texts which, each in their own way, negotiate between theatrical and personal history: Guthrie's autobiography, *A Life in the Theatre* (1959), and James Forsyth's *Tyrone Guthrie: a Biography* (1975).[4] Rather than treating these as unproblematic source material, I will aim to demonstrate how in these texts Guthrie's theatrical practice has become intertwined almost inextricably with the life story that both he and his biographer have attempted to shape as narrative.

II

How can we justify a need ... to obtain knowledge of the circumstances of a man's life when his works have become so full of importance to us? People generally say that it is our desire to bring ourselves nearer to a man in a human way as well. Let us grant this; it is, then, the need to acquire affective relations with such men, to add them to the fathers, teachers, exemplars whom we have known or whose influence we have already experienced, in the expectation that their personalities will be just as fine and admirable as those works of theirs which we possess.[5]

Reflecting upon the relationship between biographer and subject, Freud suggests that our curiosity about the private lives of creative

individuals is prompted in part by a desire to trace the artwork's characteristics of formal perfection and moral integrity in the person of the
artist. But the relationship is also characterised by the general Oedipal
ambivalence that we feel towards 'fathers and teachers', in that 'our
reverence towards them regularly conceals a component of hostile
rebellion'; thus 'by reducing the distance that separates him from us'
the biography also 'tends in effect towards degradation'.[6] Like most
conventional modern biographies, Forsyth's *Tyrone Guthrie* negotiates
between the conflicting imperatives of commemoration, veneration
and exposure, presenting what is for the most part a positive and
sympathetic account of the 'most important, British-born director of
his time'.[7] Cast, he tells us, as 'The Biographer' only days before
Guthrie's death, James Forsyth writes from the simultaneously privileged and compromised position of a colleague and friend; and hence
his treatment is characterised by respect and circumspection,
enlivened and substantiated by moments of autobiographical reminis-
cence in which he appears as a walk-on part in Guthrie's larger drama
(in general, this means that Forsyth passes over aspects of the life
which might incite controversy or prurient interest; Guthrie's sexuality and marital relations, for example, which are elsewhere a source of
bafflement and amused speculation, are here treated with rather
convoluted tact).

The principle of selection and manipulation of the events that are
held meaningfully to constitute the life story has further implications:
like any good biographer, Forsyth organises Guthrie's history as a
narrative with a clear developmental logic. Theorising the practice of
life writing, Liz Stanley has argued that the strategic deployment of
biographical detail to 'constitute and confirm a more general and
apparently trans-situational biographical self' generally serves as 'an
explanatory framework for understanding and drawing together otherwise unrelated *ad hoc* eries'; at the heart of the practice is the
asumption of a 'a coherent, essentially unchanging and unitary self
which can be referentially captured by its methods'.[8] In the case of
Forsyth's life of Guthrie, this is nowhere more evident than in the
account of childhood and youth, which, viewed from the vantage
point of hindsight, becomes not just a prelude to the professional
career, but an explanation of it. Combining the classic format of the
Bildungsroman, Wordsworthian logic and pop Freudianism, Forsyth
states this explicitly in his first paragraph: 'one of the discoveries of
the century with which he grew is how much of the Man is already
determined in the Boy' (p. 1). As far as domestic life is concerned,

Forsyth paints an idyllic picture of a secure and privileged childhood split between the bourgeois gentility of Edwardian Tunbridge Wells and the rougher rural pleasures of the ancestral home, Annagh-ma-kerrig. The place of Guthrie's birth is initially depicted as a royal spa town deep in the timeless summer of the Garden of England, but is soon demoted to the family's 'winter quarters', as his true home is identified as another 'Summer Place': 'a biggish greystone house amid forests, above a lake and beyond a bog'; a place of belonging and natural abundance, with 'wood cut from our forests, or "turf" from our bog, to feed our fires, fish from our lake, milk from our cows'; a space accessible by means of an epic boat and train journey ('the journey to freedom that gave young Guthrie a lifelong love of trains') that finally led to 'the forests of the General's land and the long lake with the wild swans, and the white-painted cast-iron gates which gave into the long, long gravel drive by the lake; and on through rhododendron bushes up above the lake – "home"' (pp. 9–11). Here was where the real people were to be found, where authentic life was to be lived, where Guthrie acquired a taste for the simple things and a 'life-long respect for original and native intelligence' (p. 9). Even at this early stage, shunting between Tunbridge Wells and Newbliss, Guthrie had to be preternaturally engaged with theatre. Asserting that 'there were assuring signs for his adoring mother that Willie Tyrone ... would probably grow to be among the successes of the new century', Forsyth records that by the age of four 'the Theatre began, mildly, to have an influence on him', an influence which, naturally 'came from his mother's side' (p. 1). Across the street from the Tunbridge Wells house lay Trinity Church, which enabled Guthrie to witness the 'Ritual Street Theatre' of weddings and funerals; within the domestic arena, the boy could engage in 'private theatricals on the drawing room carpet' in the emphatically maternal space of 'the area adjacent to his mother's piano'; thus both house and street afforded 'open stages' for exploration by the theatrical neophyte (pp. 2–3).

In this way Forsyth establishes the polarities with which the reader is implicitly invited to frame the man and his art: reserved, conservative Victorian England versus open, emotionally authentic, peasant Ireland; masters versus servants; the masculine world of work, duty and privilege versus the female and maternal space of play, nurturing – and theatre. Importantly, Guthrie is positioned not as a creative radical opposed to the forces of order and the law of the father, but as a diplomat and a conciliator. The oppositions are sharpened further in Forsyth's second chapter, which commences with Guthrie's entry to

Wellington public school in the September of 1914. As the Edwardian summer sinks into the mud of trench warfare, Guthrie is found adjusting to the spartan drabness of a militarised regime which has 'the same planned isolation from Life as a mental asylum' (p. 20). Physically and temperamentally at odds with this quasi-custodial setting (described as an 'academic cell' with 'the indefinable smell of many young human animals corralled together under one roof and living within walls rubbed smooth by past generations'), Guthrie sets to work on his window box in order to resist Wellington's masculinist ethos with a 'defiant horticultural display of all sorts of flowers', while writing home that 'on a calm clear day, he could hear the sound of the guns on the Somme' (pp. 21–2). Working through this four-year rehearsal for an action that he eventually just managed to escape, Guthrie nonetheless fitted in well enough to end up as a 'proud Corporal in the Corps, captain of his house rugger fifteen and head boy of the Hardinge' (p. 24). Guthrie also encounters *Hamlet* for the first time, at the hands of the inspirational schoolmaster whom Forsyth is quick to identify as 'a father-figure that could not have been a better substitute or more in accord with his eager young soul' (p. 23). Here, too, were opportunities for the further contemplation of the 'open stage' in a College Chapel wherein 'processional ceremonials took place in a sacred playing area or pitch not too different in architecture from that area on which he finally made his revolutionary stage, in Edinburgh, in the Kirk's Assembly Hall' (p. 24).

By the end of the chapter both the war and Guthrie's schooldays are over, and, thanks to a History Scholarship at St John's, he is set for Oxford. But he is also, according to the cumulative narrative logic of familial and institutional circumstances, physique, personality and temperament, indelibly marked with the sign of theatricality. Commuting to London University to study medicine for a year before going up to Oxford (where he would occasionally assume the nom de plume of Oedipus Biggs), Guthrie and his cousin Martin Bretherton 'loudly talked their heads off, giggled at private jokes and carried on conversations in assumed characters'. More importantly, Guthrie takes singing lessons from Gustave Garcia, 'a little old maestro in black velvet jacket and flaming *Bohème* bow', only to learn from his teacher that 'You will not be much of a singer. But you will make a good listener, a good audience. Stick to that' (p. 32). The source is Guthrie's own account in his autobiography (discussed further below); importantly, Forsyth's use of the incident contains a small but rhetorically significant misquotation (in Guthrie's version, Garcia observes that 'you *make* a good listener'[9]). By shifting the remark from the present into the future tense, Forsyth imbues the flamboyant mentor with a gift of prophecy that leaves Guthrie at the end of the chapter as 'a leader of men' (p. 32), poised on the edge of destiny. From then on, the account indicates, Guthrie's career in theatre was not only natural and right: it was inevitable.

Turning to Guthrie's own narrative of his early years, we detect a similar attempt to shape the events of the early days into a pattern which might offer a means of making autobiographical sense of the relationship between the life and the work. Unlike the fact-bound Forsyth, however, Guthrie exploits the autobiographer's privilege to begin in a spirit of musing speculation: 'I suppose few people know precisely why they are occupied as they are' (*Life*, p. 1). If the first sentence is an admission of the inaccessibility of Guthrie's own deepest motives, even to himself (as well as a characteristic tactic of deflection and evasion), it also defines the autobiographical project in terms of an Oedipal enigma of lost or unknown origins: 'I do not know just how or why I came to the theatre' (p. 2). Having struck a keynote of indeterminacy, Guthrie proceeds to detail three aspects of his early life which might help to resolve the mystery. The first of these, prompted by the conjecture that 'perhaps heredity had a bit to do with it' (p. 2) is his account of his ancestry, with particular attention to his maternal grandfather, the Irish actor, Tyrone Power. This presents the opportunity to recount a good story about Power's purchase of real estate in what became Madison Square Gardens, his drowning in the mid-Atlantic, and his subsequent ghostly reappearance; like *Hamlet*, Guthrie's narrative begins with a ghost and a lost inheritance. The second proposition is that 'probably environment weighed heavier than heredity', the key environmental factor being visits to the theatre with his mother. Guthrie identifies the experience of seeing *Peter Pan* ('a dramatic masterpiece ... a work of extraordinary theatrical power') at the age of seven as formative: 'for a year I spoke like Pauline Chase, drew Underground Houses with toadstool chimneys, pretended to fly and dreaded, of all things, that I might lose an arm to a crocodile' (p. 5). As well-versed in psychoanalytic theory as he was by the time he came to write this, Guthrie would have been alert to the castration anxiety encoded in this recollection; a point confirmed by his reading of *Peter Pan* as 'a version of the Oedipus legend the more horrifying because it is coated in rose-pink, poisoned icing-sugar' (p. 6). Usually regarded as a children's play, *Peter Pan* emerges in this account as a thing of menace and dark beauty: 'when the nursery night lights, symbols of Mother's loving protection ... Mother, you remember is at this moment out gadding with that miscreant, Mr Darling ... when the night lights flicker and fade; and, as they finally die away, the music swells up, the nursery windows swing open and in flies Peter – *flies*, mind you, sails through the night air like a bomber, like a moth' (p. 5).

Again, there is the sense of the imminence of death; as in *Hamlet*, there is also the preoccupation with abandonment and maternal betrayal. But *Peter Pan* is also a work which offers an extraordinary, intoxicating magic, as when Peter 'pleads ... for the life of Tinkerbell':

'If you believe in fairies clap your hands' – then hard-bitten hunting-women from the shires, usurers from the city, field-marshals in a bath of tears, rise in their seats and clap and cheer, and clap again, until the twinkling of her light proclaims that Tinker Bell's well again. (Ibid.)

As a vision of theatre in which divisions of rank and geography dissolve, the inhibitions of class and gender are abandoned and the values of money-grubbing, militarism, shooting and fishing are temporarily suspended in an ecstasy of belief, hope and willed naivety, it is a clear statement of Guthrie's theatrical philosophy at its most playfully utopian. In the context of the autobiography, however, *Peter Pan* immediately gives way to the third aspect of Guthrie's account, the rigours of public school and the tortures of adolescence. Describing himself as a 'dreamy, overgrown, morbidly timid but "clever" and rather exhibitionist youth' (p. 10), Guthrie's self-identification is as a Hamlet trapped within an environment which aims to cast him as a Fortinbras, fitting him for the officer class 'leading things called men, beings of a lower social, intellectual, moral and physical status' (p. 6). Offering an outward display of conformity, Guthrie nonetheless had that within which passeth show: 'inwardly I rebelled and seethed with antagonism'; he was 'just at the age when all authority becomes irksome, when all adolescents seethe, when they read Shelley – or now, perhaps, Kafka – and dream mad power-dreams and feel that they are surrounded by evil, foolish, elderly conspirators whose one aim is to thwart innovation and retain the sceptre in their palsied grasp' (p. 9).

Guthrie's main tactic of rebellion against 'the anthill life of the dormitory' which 'demanded absolute social conformity, absolute conventionality' was to fashion a complex interior life as 'energies were withdrawn from the real world and focused themselves upon an imaginary world' (p. 9). But there was also one instance of open revolt, provoked by, of all things, the quality of the food, as, in a single act of defiance, the boys confronted their stern military fathers with a failure of nurturing. The 'night of the rebellion' is reported (with what can only be a conscious sense of historical irony) as having taken place 'in the winter of 1917':

> the margarine was rancid *again* . . . everyone was to leave his pat of margarine untasted, and right after grace . . . the meal ended. Grace was said; and then, instead of filing out as usual, dormitory by dormitory, in alphabetical order, we stood, just stood, five hundred of us, each with his pat of margarine poised on his knife's end. 'What is the matter?' asked the Master in charge. It was our cue. In silence each of us flipped his margarine as high in the air as he could; many pats struck the ceiling with a soft, soul-satisfying, greasy thud. (pp. 7–8)

An insurrectionary moment in which the threat of the knife-wielding mob is tempered by the mundane comedy of the grievance, this is also a piece of pure political theatre, a choreographed demonstration of collective strength and will. Since Guthrie is careful to note the date, the implicit parallel with the revolution that had occurred on the other side of Europe a month earlier can hardly be coincidental. But as Guthrie's account continues, the spectacle of rebellion turns rapidly into a vision of humiliation and horror:

> then followed something I shall never forget. The steward, the stern and dignified individual who was responsible for the catering and upon whom we now all fixed our silent, censuring gaze, suddenly hid his face in his hands and fled from the hall in tears. Our rebellion was a fizzle. We had, like all mobs, found a scapegoat for our wrath; our reward for the ritual slaughter was only to be shocked witnesses of the victim's anguish. (p. 8)

Not only does the revolution achieve nothing (Guthrie concludes: 'the margarine continued to be rancid'); the spectacle of the steward as a broken Coriolanus serves merely as a means of venting spite rather than rectifying a perceived injustice. It is hard not to register an implicit, but profoundly important, political lesson here, in that Guthrie's unease over the incident reflects the ambivalence of his own politics, torn between a recognition of the compelling necessity of

revolution in theory, and disquiet about its consequences in practice.
As a keen student of the relations between the origins of theatre and
ritual (particularly within the framework supplied by Frazer's *The
Golden Bough*), Guthrie would also have been only too aware that the
ritual public sacrifice of the 'scapegoat' steward was closely connected
with the kinds of theatrical pleasures he spent his career investigating.
But it is not until the end of the chapter, when the violence and degradation of the school regime have been left behind, that theatre finally
claims Guthrie for its own. In a full account of the incident which is
compressed in Forsyth's biography, Guthrie documents his experience
at the hands of Gustave Garcia. Sent to the salon of the Maestro to
train the Guthrie Voice, he finds himself inducted into a fetishistic
demi-monde of bizarre relics – 'black cast-iron statuary – naked men
lugging at stallions, stags locked in mortal combat ... singed
photographs of long-dead opera stars; big ladies in white nighties and
long plaits, little ladies in saucy bonnets and high-heeled button
boots, florid gentlemen in tights and waxed moustaches' (p. 11). As
colourfully decadent as his surroundings, Maestro is a cheerfully
volatile mentor; the crucial moment comes when Guthrie finds
himself unable to manage 'an exercise in rapid consecutive fourths'.
Working himself into a violent rage, Maestro screams at Guthrie that
'you have no more music in you than that fender':

> Whereupon he gave the iron fender a most frightful kick. He then
> turned a deep plum colour and began to cough. We were alone in
> the house. Visions of the inquest began to rise. I had certainly been
> stupid, oh criminally stupid, but not to the extent of murder; I
> would not actually swing. But six years for manslaughter ... 'Tea!'
> yelled the corpse, now a much paler shade of plum. 'Go to the
> kitchen and make tea'. (p. 12)

Played for laughs, the narrative is yet again haunted by the shadow of
death and by the prospect of ghosts, although the injunction of this
particular ghoul is not to sweep to some unspecified revenge but
merely to make the tea. When Guthrie has, as the saying goes, 'been
mother' by carrying out this instruction, Maestro orders him to sit
down, announcing, 'I will tell you the story of my life':

> Then followed an hour, two hours, maybe even three, of the most
> high-coloured reminiscence I had ever heard. At the end, we had
> glasses of cognac. Then he made me take off his shoes and tuck him

up on the sofa, under a rug ... One black and bushy eyebrow rose a fraction. 'You will not be much of a singer. But you make a good listener, a good audience. Stick to that'. (pp. 12–13)

It is, of course, this quality of being 'a good listener, a good audience', rather than his tentative and not altogether successful forays into acting, that defines for Guthrie his distinctive role within the theatre as a shaper of performance rather than a performer himself. The general point – that this was when Guthrie's destiny as a director was confirmed – is clear enough. But the passage also implicitly associates the assumption of the directorial mantle with the performance of what would prove for Guthrie to be two related identities: the psychoanalyst, and the mother. Invited to sit as auditor to Maestro's confessional account, which, one is tempted to speculate, consists of a literally unrepeatable sexual history, Guthrie becomes the silent minister of the talking cure; at the end, the masculine ritual of the shared glass of cognac is followed by a maternal gesture, as the tea-dispensing Guthrie tucks Maestro up on the couch. Evidently a catharsis has been effected, since Maestro slips into a healing sleep.

By the end of the first chapter, 'my fate was sealed' (p. 14). Like that of his biographer, Guthrie's text draws upon the material of childhood and adolescence in order to establish the coordinates whereby, as part of the autobiographical project of self-knowing, the subsequent career is plotted; but, as he himself cheerfully admits (and as the foregoing discussion aims to demonstrate), authorial intentionality is only a small part of the story. Reflecting upon his experience of playwrights' capacity to articulate the significance of their own work, he finds that 'the important part of the work would, without his conscious intention, often in spite of it, have slipped in "between the lines", over and above his conscious intention ... ninety per cent of its meaning lies below the surface of the author's consciousness' (p. 17). Although it would be possible to pursue the investigation of what is hidden beneath the conscious façade of Guthrie's autobiography, my aim in the discussion that follows is firstly to chart the textual unconscious of what is an important narrative source and secondly to indicate some of the biographical contexts within which the work can be situated. The combination of a leaderly persona, instinctive anti-authoritarianism and liberal sympathies formulated at Wellington played itself out in the ambiguous cultural politics of a body of experimental work conducted within the institutional and physical structures of mainstream performance; and as I shall aim to demonstrate below, the biographical fact of Guthrie's close relationship with his mother has a significant bearing upon his own thinking about, and practice of, theatre. Indeed, the autobiography is engagingly explicit when it comes to the relationship between the maternal and the theatrical in Guthrie's own work. Avowedly 'a professional, not a personal, document' (p. 72), *A Life in the Theatre* is at its most intriguing when the boundary between these spheres becomes blurred. This happens, quite startlingly, in the final pages:

> Just as I have gradually abandoned the idea of illusion as the aim of theatrical performance, so I have also abandoned the idea that the theatre has a moral aim: to uplift the public, to instruct it, do it good. For the greater part of my professional life this aim had loomed quite large. It was an attitude which I had absorbed quite unconsciously from earliest youth [from] my mother ... like all sons of good mothers, I still, long, long after childhood, felt 'naughty' when I caught myself disagreeing with my mother, when I found that many thoughts and deeds which seemed good to her no longer seemed so to me. (p. 303)

Within this ensemble of conflicting desires, the competing pressures of cultural philanthropy, moral and political didacticism and theatrical pleasure are negotiated within a framework wherein theatrical illusion and maternal injunction exist in complex interrelation. In this respect, *A Life in the Theatre* conforms to a pattern which feminist theorists of autobiography have seen as typifying the classic male life story: the achievement of an autonomous and authentic masculine identity necessarily entails a repression of identification with the mother-figure.[10] Here, repression is associated with the repudiation of illusion and the picture-frame stage: only when mother has been buried (and it was the death of Guthrie's mother in 1956 that enabled him to write the life) can Peter Pan finally cut the wires and fly free. And yet, Guthrie knew, this could never really happen, for the mother–child relationship remains at the heart of his understanding of theatre. Towards the end of his life, Guthrie drafted a proposal for a series of programmes on drama for the BBC. In his draft script for the first programme, Guthrie summarised a lifetime of reflection upon the relations between theatre, pyschoanalysis and anthropology in an opening sequence showing 'woman playing peep-bo with her baby': by hiding and revealing her face, mother presents her baby audience with 'a very primitive and simple drama': 'Here she is ... Here she isn't.'

She has made an exit ... Now here she is again – another entrance'.[11] In this prototype of the *fort-da* game,[12] in which the dynamics of entrances and exits form the basis for further explorations of visibility and invisibility, convention and illusion, birth and death, the infant's response to maternal presence and absence is the fundamental key to theatrical experience.

If the family romance is one of the shaping circumstances of Guthrie's theory and practice, cultural identity is another. Before concluding this section, I want to focus upon an aspect of Guthrie's own biographical situation which is also central to my reading of his work: his Anglo-Irishness. Throughout his life and after his death, Guthrie's relationship with Ireland and the Irish was considered by himself and others to be pivotal to an understanding of his life, work and social and political convictions; inevitably, however, the function of Irishness as an index of character and temperament was complicated by the divisions and contradictions of the larger political history of Ireland's troubled passage towards a post-colonial national identity. As Forsyth records (p. 8), Guthrie was, from early adolescence onwards, happy to identify himself as an Irishman ('he began to talk ... of "home" and to mean, not "Belmont", Church Road, Tunbridge Wells at all, but "Annagh-ma-Kerrig", Monaghan, Ireland'; in the autobiography (p. 31) Guthrie simply states that his appointment as controller of BBC Belfast at the age of twenty-three was down to the fact that 'I am Irish'. But for others his nationality could be both a matter of key symbolic import, and a subject for more careful negotiation; it could also feature as another element of the Guthrie mystique. In a newspaper profile dating from the early 1950s, for example, Guthrie was described as having 'Irish blood' and (patronisingly) 'the sweetest of Irish addresses'; nonetheless 'his upbringing was correctly that of an English gentleman' (*Observer*, 10 June 1951); but for Stratford Festival producer Michael Langham a few years later, 'you know all you need to know about Guthrie as a producer if you've read Freud – and James Joyce'.[13] When the obituaries appeared, it was apparent that the nature and extent of Guthrie's Irishness could be adjusted to taste. Like Shakespeare, Guthrie had the knack of being appropriated as one of its own by the cultures that took him to heart: according to Ivor Brown's death notice in the *Daily Mail* (17 May 1971), Guthrie was only Irish to the extent that he was the 'owner of a small estate in Northern Ireland' (it is in fact in the Republic), since 'he went to an English public school and to Oxford University'. Conversely, in the country which witnessed Guthrie's last productions, the director was affectionately regarded as the kind of ambassador for clowning, devilment and general paddy-whackery that might also render him an honorary Australian: 'Tony Guthrie was a true Irishman in that he was agin the government on principle and loved thumbing his nose at the powers that be' (*West Australian*, 17 May 1971). In Ireland itself, Guthrie's end was described, in the words of one local newspaper, as the 'death of a distinguished Monaghanman'; while another newspaper reported the funeral address of the Protestant Bishop of Clogher: 'although Sir Tyrone Guthrie was not born in Ireland, he served Ireland well and with strict impartiality ... integrity of character is something that Ireland, all over the country, badly needs and Sir Tyrone gave us a great example of it'.[14]

'Integrity' is a term used by many Irish commentators in relation to Guthrie; in 1971, in the context of an increasingly violent post-colonial conflict whose origins lay in the fifty-year-old enforced cultural and national division, Guthrie's display of it is charged with symbolism, in that it embodies hopes for the reconciliation of national and cultural as well as personal conflicts and contradictions. Guthrie had himself made a number of not universally welcomed interventions into the politics of the Irish situation during the previous decade, including a speech at Belfast City Hall at the fortieth anniversary dinner of the Trinity College Dublin Northern Ireland Association in which he 'described the border as wildly artificial and called upon the students to abolish it' (*The Times*, 17 May 1971). In 1969, in the wake of the escalating violence following the disturbances around the Civil Rights movement, he even went so far as to present a television programme in which he analysed the economic and cultural roots of the current crisis, in order to make a plea for decency and tolerance:

> This is the situation we have inherited – a community cleft by a division, which is not the less dangerous because it is intangible and quite largely, though by no means entirely, imaginary, being based on historical origins and emotive situations, which have, to some extent, but again by no means entirely, ceased to exist ... a division in which the dispossessed, overwhelmingly of Celtic race and Catholic faith, stand on one side of an imaginary boundary. On the other stands the numerically larger and economically superior group ... fanatically Protestant, fanatically 'Unionist', fanatical in support of the solid bourgeois values, which are their buttress against the resentment which they rightly feel envelopes them, like a poison-gas, from the enemy's side of the line.[15]

In this account, the physical and geographical fact of the 'artificial' border between North and South finds its counterpart in the divisions historically constructed and culturally perpetuated, divisions which are imaginary, intangible but nonetheless profoundly damaging. What is of interest is here (apart from the *Hamlet* echoes of 'cleft') is that Guthrie's terminology precisely replicates his critique of the (equally 'artificial') theatre of illusion and the proscenium arch. At one point in *A Life in the Theatre*, Guthrie accounts for the evolution of the picture frame stage as the institution of a 'great gulf' between audience and actors:

> This was only partly a matter of practical convenience. It also marked the social chasm, which separated the predominantly courtly and aristocratic audience in the stalls and boxes and the socially inferior persons who were paid to entertain them. The separation was reinforced by yet another practical and symbolic barrier – of fire, the footlights … gradually, all over Europe there came into force a whole budget of precautionary regulations, including the provision of yet another barrier, the iron curtain, now a world-famous political symbol of separation or *apartheid*. (pp. 176–7)

The elision of theatre history, Churchillian Cold War rhetoric and liberal-leftish distaste for the mechanisms of racist oppression may be more sweeping than it is theoretically rigorous, but it is as good an indication as any of the generally anti-authoritarian character of Guthrie's repudiation of the picture frame. But for the Guthrie who would subsequently compare the sectarian structure of the Northern Ireland state with segregation in the American Deep South, there was a more obvious and personally-felt experience of cultural dislocation immediately to hand: the condition of Irish post-coloniality that he inhabited for much of his life afforded a local habitation and a name in the place of Monaghan itself. Equidistant from Dublin and Belfast, positioned a few miles from the village called both Newbliss and Cuil Darach, and a mere ten minutes' drive from the border, Annah-ma-kerrig occupied the space where sectarian divisions were at their sharpest, and which was, therefore, one of the most economically stagnant areas on the entire island; the space, moreover, where a significant proportion of the population on either side of the line regarded its presence as a monstrous imposition. Seen from the 'socially inferior' space of Monaghan, it is a landscape arbitrarily bisected by a barrier which, by the end of Guthrie's life, had become increasingly fortified and carefully policed, which demands of you as you cross it that you suspend your disbelief in the political legitimacy of the state you are entering; a looking-glass world where postboxes and telephone kiosks change colour and placenames and roadsigns speak a different language. That the situation of Ireland on a local as well as national level mattered greatly to Guthrie is evident not only from his public pronouncements but also from the fact that he spent much of the last decade of his life pouring money, time and energy into the initiative of a local jam factory that eventually fell victim to the antagonisms that it had been intended to surmount.[16] It is not altogether fanciful, therefore, to read his relentless drive to abolish the line between audience and performer and auditorium and stage as another manifestation of this desire to dismantle a national barrier that existed both in the imagination and in physical fact.

III

Partly as a result of his own account of the incident, many people now think of the Guthrie–Olivier Old Vic *Hamlet* which played in the court-yard of Kronberg Castle, Helsingor in June 1937 as the event which, thanks to a happy accident of meteorology, first set the director on the trail that would eventually lead him to the Stratford Festival in Ontario, and the postwar Shakespearean theatre in general to the promised land of the open stage. I shall examine some of the previously unremarked ironies of what has become a mythical moment in the Shakespeare revolution below; first, however, I want to explore another equally important and innovative (and, I propose, related) aspect of the production: its significance as the first professional staging of the play to consciously advance a psychoanalytic reading of its hero.

To begin with, in the professional context wherein Guthrie was working, the basic idea that a Shakespearean production might advance a strong directorial reading of a text (let alone one as potentially contentious as this) was itself potentially controversial, since the commercial sector of the 1930s continued to define the interpretative freedoms of what was still termed the 'producer' within strict limits. As the orchestrator of Stanislavskian subtext and the coordinator of the increasingly complex technologies of the picture frame, the work of the producer is embedded within the modes of theatrical realism and the business practices of the commercial stage; ideally, the producer disappears from view as the play takes to the boards. The figure of the director, however, who was for many English critics a scandalously impertinent, alien interloper, was associated with the reactions against realism that took hold even as the system established itself. Geared towards the elaboration of a distinctive theatrical idiom in which the apparent interests of the play are not necessarily paramount, the work of the director differentiates itself from that of the producer through its emphatically 'authored' identity. By the time he came to direct *Hamlet* during his third season as Drama Director at the Old Vic in 1937, Tyrone Guthrie had been in the professional theatre for the best part of a decade, and had already had cause to reflect upon the nature of the producer's role. Initially, Guthrie conformed to the consensual model of the producer by maintaining that it was his task to serve the play and the playwright rather than to impose his own interpretative schemes upon the work. Introducing himself in the pages of the *Old Vic and Sadler's Wells Magazine* in September 1933, Guthrie had defined the best kind of production as 'generally the most unobtrusive', and had stated that the hand of the good producer 'shows only when poor actors seem to be playing well, when good actors seem better than ever, when a fine play seems even finer' (at the Old Vic, this notion of the invisibly orchestrated performance went hand in hand with an aesthetic of scenic austerity). In this account, the responsibilities of the producer are primarily pragmatic and managerial rather than conceptual, his work a matter of craft rather than conspicuous interpretative artistry. In a lecture given in the mid-1930s, Guthrie enlarged upon the idea that the producer was a custodian of artistic and spiritual values but nonetheless a secondary artist: 'not only is he the builder of an architectural edifice to the author's design; not only is the stage a canvas upon which he must paint the author's picture; but also his is a musical score, his actors are an orchestra and he himself as conductor must make audible the symphony that is latent in the printed words before him'.[17] In the context of the English theatre of the time, this was hardly controversial, although there were those who were quick to pick up on Guthrie's liberties with texts, such as, notoriously, James Agate, who described his 1933 *Henry VIII* as 'too clever by half'.[18]

Professionally successful as he was, Guthrie was not altogether comfortable with the existing conditions, structure, philosophy and working methods of the English theatre. In his polemical first book, *Theatre Prospect* (1932), he had identified the impasse faced by the contemporary theatre as its continuing adherence to the 'bourgeois' form of naturalism, and since 'a reaction from rationalism, a reaction from [the] bourgeoisie are in progress', it was time to make 'the break with naturalism ... with material of unexceptionable quality – the classics'.[19] Citing the experiments of Nugent Monck at the Maddermarket, Norwich, and Terence Gray at the Festival Theatre, Cambridge (where he had worked for a spell at the turn of the decade), as instances of, respectively, scrupulously archaeological and wildly avant-garde attempts to engineer such a break, Guthrie identified the task of the experimental producer (still something of an oxymoron) as that of securing a compromise between the two approaches. In Gray's case, revivals which treated the text as 'mere material upon which the producer may exercise his art' had 'expressed extreme ideas of "décor", but neither the director nor the actors have had sufficient technique to bring these ideas into a significant relation with the play and so to redeem them from a slight taint of impertinence and insincerity'. Moreover,

> It is this lack of technique that has hampered all experimental production in this country. Any attempt to break wholly away from the current naturalistic convention requires on the part of the director, not only sufficient originality to invent a new means of expression, but sufficient executive technique to teach the actors; and requires on the part of the actor sufficient executive technique to make a new means of expression intelligible to the public. (pp. 50–1)

Writing from the standpoint of a theatre professional who, unlike the wealthy and autonomous dilettante Gray, is fully implicated within the dominant, mainstream apparatus, Guthrie ascribes the weakness of the contemporary classical avant-garde to its predominantly amateur status. Espousing a theatrical method and language that is critical and anti-bourgeois (but not inordinately scandalous or subversive) he appears to seek an as yet undefined mode of experimental performance that somehow can be accommodated within the cultural mainstream. This was not just about Guthrie's own personal position and predelictions; what is here formulated as a problem of craft and aesthetics is also a matter of the nature of the producer's role, within the industrial and administrative economy of the commercial theatre during the period. Given that financial and executive power lay largely in the hands of the managers behind the scenes on the one hand and a few star names onstage on the other, the producer's capacity either to make a significant contribution to organisational and artistic policy, or to pursue distinctively innovative work within the profession, was limited indeed. Attempting to establish general principles of Shakespearean production in terms of the practical accommodation of interpretative vision, textual imperatives, the raw human and physical materials and given conditions of performance, and the limits of critical and audience tolerance, Guthrie is also, in effect, seeking to define a new space for the producer as a creative agent within a system which would prefer to keep him or her in place as a technical functionary.

The circumstances of production of the *Hamlet* of 1937 afford a glimpse of the complexities of the theatrical situation within which Guthrie was working. Although it was not in the least a state-subsidised institution in the postwar sense, the high-minded philanthropic and educational ethos of the 1930s Old Vic potentially allowed more room for manoeuvre for the producer than in the rest of the commercial sector on the other side of the Waterloo Bridge; committed to a rhythm of ongoing Shakespearean cycles, the work was, in principle, liberated from the imperatives of the quick hit and the star system. The unwritten rules that governed Shakespearean production at the Vic had roots within Poelite asceticism, a commitment to ensemble values and its original mandate of supplying 'high-class drama, especially the plays of Shakespeare ... suited for the recreation and instruction of the poorer classes of the former County of London'.[20] During the period of the First World War and after, this had taken the form of a rapid turnover of what Ben Greet described as 'carefully arranged "Acting Versions"', performed with stock costumes and scenery, designed to make the plays 'entertaining and interesting to ordinary audiences'.[21] The Old Vic was at this stage 'a good specimen of what they call in America "Family Theatre"', where 'it is jolly for the audience to get to know each other'.[22] By the end of the 1920s, however, cheery populism, the enforced aesthetics of the threadbare, and the evangelical reformism of Lilian Baylis, went along with a new spirit of adventurousness: as the 1929 Annual Report concluded (employing some rather Terence Gray-style rhetoric), the Old Vic was now 'pre-eminently the place for artistic experiment, even if some eggshells of prejudice have to be smashed in the process'.[23] The scope for 'experiment', as pursued by Guthrie's predecessor Harcourt Williams during the 1920s, was for the most part dictated by a lack of time and money that made virtues of speed and scenic austerity, although by the time Guthrie succeeded Williams in 1933, the preoccupation with fluidity had given rise to a pattern of relentless over-production, as the number of plays produced increased year by year (reaching twelve in Williams's final season; one of Guthrie's first moves was to scale this down to seven). The repertoire in the early 1920s had been shaped by Robert Atkins's aim of presenting the entire First Folio; by the end of the decade it had narrowed to a dependable core of frequently revived plays, with *Hamlet* as a central fixture.

As a play whose place on the London stage was more secure than most Shakespeare tragedies (there had been annual productions at the Old Vic from 1914 onwards)[24] *Hamlet* was a safe choice for the 1936–37 season; and in this respect it answered to Guthrie's stipulation that experiment should be conducted on sound textual foundations. But the theatrical *Hamlet* of the 1920s and 1930s was also esteemed as a text which, uniquely within the Shakespearean canon, spoke directly to the condition of modernity, a perception which was most obviously manifested in the modern-dress Birmingham Repertory production of 1925, which was directed by A.J. Ayliff and produced by Barry Jackson. In this regard it seemed to call for the tactics of the avant-garde; perhaps more than any other Shakespearean text, *Hamlet* presented the producer with the potentially contradictory imperatives of working within the established theatrical and cultural tradition, and of reacting critically against it. Recognising that Jackson's intervention had aimed to accommodate a modernist agenda within the limits imposed by the formal character of the text, Guthrie suggested that modern dress was not the solution to this problem. Presented as 'a modern Ruritanian drama', this production

> sufficiently reconciled the discrepancies between modern behaviour and the action of the play, but not those between modern speech, crisp and unemphatic, and the diction of the play. Poetry went by the board and could not be replaced by the racy terseness of good modern dialogue. Also in the matter of scenery, this production illustrated clearly the difficulty of applying the naturalistic method to any form that requires number or variety of settings. The sets, pleasing enough pictorially, were neither wholly in the realistic convention of the dresses nor in the formal and heroic convention of the play.[25]

Guthrie presents the issue as a matter of style, but what is also lacking, more importantly, is a *theoretical* framework capable of containing and rationalising the tensions between action and diction, modernity and 'formal and heroic convention', and able to authorise the producer to place theatrical innovation in a 'significant relation' with the play. It was psychoanalysis, both as a system of thought and as methodology, that offered Guthrie just such a framework; and in its specific application in the 1937 *Hamlet* we can see a first attempt to work through a modernist agenda within what was in other respects a respectably conventional revival. At the outset, the production made two explicit claims to distinction. Firstly, this was Laurence Olivier's first season in the lead at the Old Vic, and, by his own admission, he was determined to 'start with the big one'.[26] As a rising star already as well known as a matinee idol as a stage performer, Olivier's engagement made good box office sense, however much this ran counter to what remained of the ensemble principles of the organisation. Secondly, this was a production which revived the practice of playing *Hamlet* 'in its entirety', a tradition which had been inaugurated as a feature of the Birthday Week festivities back in 1915. Audiences were to get the more or less uncut text of John Dover Wilson's 1934 New Shakespeare edition, an innovation which differentiated the production from the 'Acting Versions' which had been offered at the Old Vic to make the plays 'entertaining and interesting to ordinary audiences'. It is obvious that *Hamlet*'s entirety is more than merely quantitative, in that it signifies scholarly rigour, fidelity and authenticity, reflecting a determination to liberate the play from an established Old Vic tradition of populist educational philanthropy and steer it firmly into the realms of a different kind of high cultural seriousness. This was not a *Hamlet* for the frivolous or faint-hearted.

'In its entirety' also has faint echoes of one of the critical works which Olivier subsequently identified as an influence upon the production: John Dover Wilson's *What Happens in 'Hamlet'*, which appeared in 1935.[27] Wilson's project was a conservative one, and the totalising, expository rhetoric of his title reflects the intent of putting an end to the instabilities that had been generated around the play by a variety of modernist literary and critical practices (as manifested in a range of Shakespearean criticisms but also in the works of, amongst others, Joyce, Eliot and Kafka[28]). In the hands of Guthrie, however, the promise of entirety, of laying claim to what *really* happens in *Hamlet*, also heralds a working through of that which has been evaded, censored or repressed. The idea that playing the text 'entire' would yield up the true spirit of the play recalls Poel's polemics against theatrical cutting and reshaping as much as it anticipates the later rhetoric of the open stage which, contrasted to a picture frame that he characterised as a mechanism whose use 'had been gradually perverted',[29] Guthrie would come to regard as an honest, non-judge-mental, uncensored and intimate zone not dissimilar to the space of analysis itself. It is here that the embrace of entirety evokes the other critical discourse which was at work in the production: the diagnostic psychoanalytic method expounded in Ernest Jones's piece on *Hamlet* in his *Essays in Applied Psychoanalysis* (1923). For Jones, Hamlet's much-debated procrastination is rooted in a buried Oedipal conflict, so that Hamlet delays the killing of Claudius because he unconsciously desires his mother and identifies with his uncle. Thus 'to Hamlet the thought of incest and parricide combined is too intolerable to be borne. One part of him tries to carry out the task, the other flinches inexorably from the thought of it.'[30]

In the event, it was Jones rather than Wilson who exercised the most influence over the interpretation (although the *Observer* [10 January 1937] speculated that Guthrie had 'followed Dr Dover Wilson's sugges-tion that Hamlet's entrance reading in Act II, Scene II should be early enough to let him overhear the plot to "loose" Ophelia to him'). The immediate appeal (and difficulty) of Jones's account was that it enabled producer and actor to substantiate Hamlet's modernity as neurosis rather than as fashion or diction; that is, as a quality that need not, in the first instance at least, be articulated in visual or audi-tory terms. For the guardedly dissident Guthrie, the lure of Jones's work lay in its implicit suggestion that to pluck out the heart of Hamlet's mystery was perhaps also to unearth the fundamental secret of the modern human condition. Psychoanalysis appeared both schol-arly and dangerously provocative – a combination which was directly analogous to the rapprochement between convention and experiment that Guthrie sought in performance. If professional psychoanalysis had officially defined itself as an enlightened scientific method and clinical practice, and as a benign social force, its transmission, appro-priation and reinvention through and within the sensibilities of modernism also suggested a scandalously avant-garde and anti-bour-geois potential: as one account of this cultural moment puts it, 'while the International Association attempted to maintain the frontier between madness and science through an appeal to pathology, Surrealism used psychoanalysis to claim the unconscious as a revolu-tionizing expressive form'.[31]

In England, more sedately, the disseminating activities of the Bloomsbury fraction fashioned a place for psychoanalysis within left-liberal culture: Bloomsbury 'not only popularized psychoanalysis for the British intelligentsia, but also domesticated it by incorporating psychoanalysis within its over-arching liberal ethos of the "free and civilized individual"'.[32] As a Bloomsburyite by temperament, if not by direct affiliation, Guthrie would have found Jones's analysis of the Prince congenial to his own version of moderated modernist practice. Although for Wilson, as for many subsequent sceptics, psychoanalysis in the field of Shakespearean interpretation may have belonged to a discredited tradition of character criticism, it became for Guthrie a key aspect of what he later characterised as a generational sensibility shaped by 'the Economic Creed according to Karl Marx, the Psychological Creed according to Sigmund Freud, the Physical Creed according to Albert Einstein'.[33] For the Guthrie of the 1930s, there was no difficulty in combining Freudianism with the apocalyptic mysticism outlined at the end of *Theatre Prospect*: 'it may well be that the reaction from rationalism will be drastic, invading every department of our civilisation with incalculable results, turning all our existing notions and existing institutions topsy-turvy; ending for ever the theatre as we know it, or giving to it a renascence, with another Shakespeare, another Golden Age' (p. 50). Against the background of a Bohemian avant-gardism which consisted of 'a plethora of hybridised elements' in which 'Freud, Marx, Catholicism, Homer Lane, D.H. Lawrence, I.A. Richards, the Leavises, the Surrealists, Socialist Realism, Documentarism and Epic Theatre ... all jostle in uncoordinated chorus'[34], Guthrie's position was not as eccentric as it might at first appear.

Having absorbed Jones's essay, actor and producer visited the analyst himself for a consultation, as Olivier recalled:

> He had made an exhaustive study of Hamlet from his own professional point of view and was wonderfully enlightening. I have never ceased to think about Hamlet at odd moments, and ever since that meeting I have believed that Hamlet was a prime sufferer from the Oedipus complex – quite unconsciously, of course, as the professor was anxious to stress. He offered an impressive array of symptoms: spectacular mood swings, cruel treatment of his love, and above all a hopeless inability to pursue the course required of him. The Oedipus complex, therefore, can claim responsibility for a formidable share of all that is wrong with him.[35]

Olivier later added: 'there are many signals along the line to show his inner involvement with his mother: one of them is his over-devotion to his father. Nobody's that fond of his father unless he feels guilty about his mother, however subconscious that guilt may be'.[36] Since Olivier and, presumably, Guthrie, appeared to share Jones's view that Hamlet can be treated as a real-life pathological type, the psycho-analytic problematics of the production were therefore framed initially in *acting* terms. Inasmuch as the taxonomy of character traits identified by Jones can be readily accommodated within the broadly Stanislavskian parameters of English Shakespearean acting, this was thus far consistent with Guthrie's formula of the 'unobtrusive' production. Discussing his working relationship with Olivier, Guthrie stressed that the initial work focused upon the cultivation of the central character – 'we lived Hamlet, we ate Hamlet and drank Hamlet, we dreamed Hamlet' – but that this was conducted with due regard for theatrical practicalities: 'we didn't expect the actor ... who played Voltimand to sit around for a month while we fiddled about with textual emendations and mother-complexes and the lighting for the Ghost'.[37] The association of ideas is itself revealing: placing its methods halfway between discrete intervention and spectacular illumination (and the Oedipal scene somewhere between the word and the image), it situated psychoanalysis amidst a repertoire of highly specialised theatremaking activities that are simultaneously indispensable and curiously arcane. It also confines this area of exploration to the mechanisms of preparation, and to the internal dynamics of Olivier's performance. However, as Olivier remarked in a later aside, the problem was how this scheme was to manifest itself on stage: 'I must say I have never yet discovered any means of divulging something that is definitely *subconscious* to an audience, no matter how discerning they may be.'[38] Olivier's conclusion makes obvious sense if one accepts, first, a quasi-clinical view of psychoanalysis as confined to the exegesis of motivation and the development of personality and temperament within a predominantly realist mode of characterisation, and, second (providing the conditions which make this possible) the naturalised model of performance as, ideally, an integration of actor, character, text and setting.

But the Oedipal reading proposed by Jones and *consciously* adopted by Guthrie and Olivier at the level of characterisation took on a rather different character in performance. Reflecting on Jones's account of Hamlet's paralysis and internal restlessness, Olivier found in the character a further dimension, 'apart from Hamlet's involuntary pusillanimity', which would enable him to externalise it: 'his weakness for dramatics'.[39] Although the association of theatrical exhibitionism with 'weakness' (failure, impotence, effeminacy) might well have endorsed what Jones reads as Hamlet's over-identification with the female, it was exhibited in performance in what many reviewers considered an emphatic histrionic display of phallic machismo. Under the tempting title *'Hamlet* at full length: Mr Olivier's Virile Performance', the *Daily Telegraph* (6 January 1937) noted an 'intensely vivid, virile and lively Hamlet'; phrasing that was echoed by the *Sunday Referee* (10 January), which found Olivier 'refreshingly vital and virile'. The preoccupation with Olivier's manhood is important, in that for these critics at least it signalled the end of what Marvin Rosenberg has characterised as a Victorian tradition of 'sweet' (that is, effeminate) Hamlets, the latest manifestation of which had been John Gielgud's portrayal at the New Theatre in 1934.[40] As was discussed in Chapter 1, the nineteenth- and early twentieth-century cult of Hamletism carried with it a legacy of gender indeterminacy, but the insistent physicality and athleticism of Olivier's performance decisively eradicated any doubts about this Hamlet's sexual identity. 'He leaps about the stage in the Player's interlude like a ballet dancer', reported the *Daily Mail* reviewer (6 January), but 'never loses his grip'. For the *Observer* (10 January), this was 'the most athletic Hamlet of my acquaintance. In fencing-bout, in faint at fearful news, or in game of "Hide fox and all after" ... Olivier's performance is magnificently agile. This Hamlet could have had his "Blue" at Wittenberg in any exercise ... Mr Olivier's Hamlet has magnetism and muscularity, and gives a general impression of being "up to snuff".' This was an erect Hamlet with 'more of thistle and sword-grass than of the sensitive plant in his composition ... the dominating impression is of "the flash and outbreak of a fiery mind" and of a steely body too'. James Agate, in the *Sunday Times* (10 January), also praised Olivier's 'pulsating vitality and excitement', invoking 'a well-turned head, a pleasing youthful face, a magnificent voice of bow-string tautness and vibrancy ... good carriage, a springy, pantherine gait, and the requisite inches'.

The performative energy which Olivier rationalised as both a tactic of evasion and an Oedipal symptom, was received as manly vigour, purpose and mastery, and, in the process, effectively superseded the psychoanalytic reading supposedly underwriting the interpretation. Although the *Telegraph* inferred that Olivier presented 'a man held back from his obvious duty by a strange streak of inertia for which he cannot account', other critics suspected that the hyperbolic masculinity expressed as action rather than reflection might not quite square with the text: as the *Observer*'s Ivor Brown put it, 'the weakness here is that you begin to suspect that such a Hamlet would have put through his murderous work without so much self-scrutiny and hesitation'. More damagingly, Ernest Jones himself went along to the production, was not impressed by what he saw, and wrote to Guthrie so say so. Conceding that 'the stage setting and décor were at least quite perfect' and that Olivier at least 'has the cast of face and head, is an admirable actor and has a most beautiful voice' Jones spelled out the deficiencies of the performance:

> It is evident that temperamentally he is not cast for Hamlet and I am not sure if he could ever be brought to play the part properly ... He is personally what we call slightly 'manic' and so finds it hard to play a melancholic part. But by his restless agitation, his cheeriness in greeting friends and his hysterical excitement he quite gets away from the idea of a man *internally* tortured. Everything is converted into external fussiness and all trace of dignity in the noble prince is lost ... It would need a great deal of rehearsal with a literary person, who understood the music and meaning of the words, to train Mr Olivier, and I suppose you found it not worth while for this particular production.[41]

For Jones, the stratagem of attempting to externalise Hamlet's self-divisions in space and movement had clearly not worked (he does reveal a more fundamental anti-theatrical bias by adding that 'you will not of course expect me, who have known Hamlet himself, to be content with human substitute'). Guthrie's response to these criticisms can only be guessed at, although the following week a second missive arrived from Jones thanking him for his 'charming letter' and admitting that 'you are probably right when you suggest that much pruning of Mr Olivier's acting might interfere with its delightful spontaneity'.[42] Guthrie, naturally enough, rose to Olivier's defence here; a year later he expressed a more candid view in a letter sent to his mother during the opening week of his second Old Vic *Hamlet*, which starred Alec Guinness: '*no* business is being done. I think the political situation is the big factor; and of course having no big star personality at the head of the cast. Alec is much *much* better in the part than Larry – but Larry with his beautiful head and athletic sexy movements are what the public wants'.[43]

It was left to Agate to voice the most detailed criticism. 'Mr Olivier does not speak poetry badly. He does not speak it at all'; his Hamlet was 'the best performance of Hotspur that the present generation has seen'. It was also irrevocably contaminated by modernity. This was evident in the traces of Olivier's popular stage and screen identity ('a modern, jaunty off-handedness which is presumably a legacy of parts of the Beau Geste order'), and, more importantly, in the echoes of one of his most celebrated contemporary roles: 'it is not Hamlet, but a brilliant performance of the part such as Stanhope in *Journey's End* might have put up in some rest-interval behind the lines'. The metatheatrical conceit is a telling one, in that it suggests that the relationship between Olivier's performance and the established image of Hamlet was rather more dynamic and complex than schematic distinctions between depth and surface characterisation might indicate. Olivier might not have conveyed that within which passeth show in terms of a poetic sensibility securely anchored within romantic tradition, but, Agate was forced to acknowledge, his Hamlet nonetheless established an unmistakably contemporary validity. As both the embodiment of stiff upper lip Englishness and a man on the brink of self-destruction, the exhausted, doomed military hero of R.C. Sherriff's 1928 trenches drama provides an apt analogue for an outwardly confident and assertive Hamlet almost paralysed by horrors beyond the limits of tolerance; unlike the Hamlet who promises to remember 'while memory holds a seat in this distracted globe', the hard-drinking Stanhope desperately desires 'to forget' because 'You think there's no limit to what a man can bear?'[44] By imagining Olivier as Stanhope (or vice-versa) playing Hamlet in the midst of a war zone, Agate offers a telling vision of an utterly contemporary Hamlet for a decade which was increasingly feeling like a 'rest interval' between outbreaks of slaughter, whilst also indicating that the taste for stage heroics may have become rather more uncertain and volatile than before.

In addition, by highlighting the element of theatrical self-consciousness which forestalled straightforward identification between the actor and the part, Agate's analogy may also suggest something about the relationship between the performance and the production as a whole. The lead actor's dominance of the stage was matched by his column inches, leaving Guthrie's part in the proceedings to be briefly summarised: the *Daily Mail* reported that his production was 'smooth and swift and gripping all the time', the *Sunday Referee* that 'the sequence is film-like in its swift precision', and *The Times* that 'the built-up stage is simple and without affectation; changes of place are clearly indicated by the use of various curtains; and the grouping, particularly in the burial of Ophelia, makes impressive use of different levels'. The *Observer* concurred that this was a 'capitally paced exercise in the grander melodrama, with its grouping finely conceived ... the execution of the Play-scene, in particular, is masterly', and added that the use of steps, 'always a practice carrying risk of affectation, has been discreet, and the soliloquies are wisely delivered from an apron'. Noting that the settings were 'simple and ingenious' the *Daily Telegraph* also recorded an intriguing instance of Noh-style staging that sounds more at home at the Festival Theatre, Cambridge, than at the Old Vic: 'one effect, by which Polonius's house was represented by banners carried on by young women in black, struck me as being a bit too ingenious'. In his memoir of the Old Vic published just over a decade later, Harcourt Williams, who considered Olivier's Hamlet 'a shade too acrobatic ... a brilliant but not a moving performance', singled out Guthrie's handling of the players, in that he presented them as 'the kind that I have seen in Bruges, and years ago in the Midlands, playing in booths of wood and canvas'. The incursion of these itinerants was 'fun', but nonetheless an affront to regal dignity: 'I don't believe such a troupe would have been invited to perform in the castle of Elsinore any more than the ones I saw would be found giving a performance at Sandringham.'[45] Both examples might indicate a dimension of non-illusionistic metatheatricality that connected with Olivier's self-consciously heightened portrayal, although it is risky to assume this on such limited evidence. But these are rare details; more representative is Agate, signing off his review with the observation that 'lots could be said about Mr Tyrone Guthrie's highly imaginative production, but not, I think, at the fag-end of an article'. Since speed, pace, fluidity and thoughtful grouping were already established as Guthrie's trademarks, the reviewers' general comments are helpful only in so far as they confirm a preoccupation with rapid mobility which would later become a basic and necessary rule of open stage choreography; but whether the speed and movement had an interpretative as well as instrumental relation to the play was not a question anyone thought to ask. Indeed, Guthrie's work was valued to the extent that he exercised the discretion of the producer rather than the interventionist tactics of the director. He earned praise precisely because, since neither setting nor direction appeared to impose upon the text, he not only gave Olivier his head but also allowed Shakespeare to speak for itself. To remain within the limits of consensus, the production had to be seen to work in spite of directorial theory, not because of it; thus Robert Speaight later allowed himself a touch of *schadenfreude* when he observed that 'the Oedipan [sic] emphasis, which Guthrie bought lock, stock and barrel from Dr Ernest Jones' failed to make 'the expected impact in spite of Gertrude's kiss wiped in revulsion from Hamlet's face'.[46] The paradox of this production, and of Guthrie's Shakespeare work as a whole during this period, was that its success was commensurate with its adherence to the standards of a medium and an apparatus he already suspected to be theatrically and politically problematic.

Even so, the combination of vision and pragmatism that had been fuelled by professional experience in broadcasting and the commercial theatre, community-based touring with the Scottish National Players, exposure to the outrageous impertinences of Gray, peripatetic work in Ireland, Scotland, Canada and London, and lessons learned from the allegedly risible pedantries of Poel and Monck meant that Guthrie was better placed than most firstly to deliver a generally acceptable compromise between the physical exigencies of the Old Vic proscenium stage and the imperatives of modernist neo-Elizabethanism, and, secondly, to make it make some kind of intellectual sense. In the first respect, Guthrie was afforded general approval for staging the play on a permanent non-representational setting which was described by Speaight as 'an architectural set ascending to the left of the spectator by a broad flight of steps leading to an upper platform, where the levels were again broken, leading on the one side into the wings and on the other forming a deeper platform at the head of the first flight'. On the evidence of the production photographs as well as the reviewers' comments, Olivier's ability to exploit the space as a platform for the display of gymnastic virtuosity was thoroughly complemented by Guthrie's use of it to clarify relationships and hierarchies through grouping and movement; in this respect, at least, the star turn was afforded a context and rationale.

The Play scene, praised by a number of reviewers, offers a representative instance of this. Encircled by supernumerary court functionaries whose ranking was established by their positioning relative to the flight of steps that ascended to the throne, *The Mousetrap* was presented centre stage, on a 'low circular platform with properties and hangings' that the players had brought with them. Far up at the back, perched on the highest platform, sat Claudius and Gertrude, while Hamlet prowled the steps that connected the space of the King and Queen with that of their theatrical analogues. At the climax of the scene 'the King rushed down into the lowest stairway below the stage, and by the time the lights he had called for were brought, there was nothing above but the flare of torches and Hamlet jubilant beside Horatio'.[47] Articulated in such graphically spatial terms, Hamlet's triumphant assumption of the advantage over Claudius could hardly be more clearly put. But even if we accept that Olivier's precipitate occupation of Claudius's space is also a spectacular, if momentary, realisation of Jones's thesis, the extent to which the production as a whole effectively marshalled its stagecraft and its theoretical agenda into what, in Guthrie's terms, would constitute a 'significant relation' to the play is altogether less certain. The uncertainty derives in part from the fact that, at this stage, the production was unavoidably Olivier's rather than Guthrie's: the intellectual impetus derived from Jones that in addition to offering the key to *Hamlet* presented a possible solution to the contradictions of the producer's role had been decisively overshadowed by the histrionic energy which, ironically, that very impetus had released.

IV

It is here that what happened next with the Guthrie–Olivier *Hamlet* becomes significant as the pivotal event which, by his own account, led to Guthrie's eventual repudiation of the picture-frame stage and a crucial moment in his career as a Shakespearean director. Early in 1937, a London-based Danish journalist and publicist by the name of Robert Jorgensen suggested an open-air performance of the Old Vic production in the grounds of Kronborg Castle at Helsingor to the Danish Tourist Association, initially as part of the celebrations of the King's Silver Jubilee, and also to inaugurate a planned series of annual international festival productions. At first, all went to plan. What had been dreamed up by the organisers as a site-specific event exploiting the convergence between the cultural authority of the play and the magic of this 'authentic' location was enthusiastically taken up by the Old Vic and British press commentators as a unique opportunity to experience what the *Daily Telegraph* (4 June 1937) described as 'Hamlet in his own home'. This was romantically evoked by Ivor Brown: 'Kronborg of Elsinore' was 'rose-red without where the great brick bastions sink amid their lilac-purple banks to the reedy moat, and grey within where the huge gaunt courtyard with only one narrow entry so grimly echoes Hamlet's sentiment that Denmark is a prison'.[48] The Special Correspondent of *The Times* (4 June 1937) offered a particularly lyrical evocation of the setting:

> The ghost not only of Hamlet's father but of all the vast and shadowy legend of the Danish prince haunts the green roofs, the fantastic pinnacles, the dungeons, the great embattled strength of

Elsinore. Why did Shakespeare choose for that complex prince so local a habitation and a name, setting him against the background of a castle which was taking its present shape in the same century as he was writing? . . . how sweetly does the name drape those enigmatic shoulders and how appropriate is Elsinore with its curious mixture of the forbidding, the austere, the warlike, and its delightful, gay, Hans Andersenish eccentricities.

If this really was, as *The Sphere* (12 June 1937) claimed, 'the great drama enacted in its rightful setting', it was only so as a result of not a little fudging by all concerned. Strictly speaking, the awkward fact that Kronborg postdated by several centuries the chronology of the twelfth-century Scandinavian legend which was Shakespeare's source meant the link with Hamlet had to be seen as a matter more of authorial inspiration than of the precise location of narrative, although Hamlet's stature as a Renaissance rather than medieval type legitimised the association to a certain extent. Seeking parallels with the current visit, *The Sphere* reported that the Old Vic company was 'the first to visit the castle since the time of Frederick II, who invited English players to perform for him' (in fact, Danish companies had staged *Hamlet* in the castle precincts in 1816 and 1916[49]), and, in a spirit of wild speculation, suggested that 'it is not beyond the bounds of probability that Shakespeare himself was among them and that the sight of the fortress moved him to evolve out of a dim legend the most perplexed and perplexing figure in all literature'. Moreover, like any such heritage site, Kronborg's architecturally hybrid character meant that whatever historic authenticity might be ascribed to it was similarly palimpsestic in nature. Founded in the early fifteenth century and remodelled towards the end of the sixteenth, the castle has been subject to repeated alterations: while the exterior dates from the 1580s, the interior, which had recently been restored at the time of the Old Vic expedition, had been rebuilt after a fire in 1629. But if the setting was at best only approximately authentic this strengthened rather than diminished its appeal. Symptomatically, by unanimously anglicising Helsingor (the place which is variously designated as Elsenoure, Elsanoure [Q1], Elsonoure [Q2, F] and Elsonower [F]) as the stable and singular 'Elsinore' the critics absorbed any potential anomalies into the play's cultural mythology. Still, given that *Hamlet* itself adopts a flexible approach to temporality and location (fusing feudal past and Renaissance present, imagined Denmark and the immediacy of London), most were prepared to put up with a willing suspension of disbelief for the sake of good theatrical and international relations.

In the historical circumstances of the time, the event called for goodwill of another kind. The unique package of culture, landscape and architecture offered by the Kronborg venture was only the latest initiative in a concerted, and largely successful, campaign by the Danish tourist industry during the 1930s to promote Denmark as a destination for sophisticated international travellers. Trading upon an established image of the country as a place of architectural and scenic splendour, of order and clean living, and of historic tradition (enlivened here and there, as Ivor Brown picked up, by Hans Andersen quirkiness), Denmark laid claim to a peace and tranquillity that defined itself in marked contrast to the increasingly turbulent scene elsewhere in Europe. Had they had to time to think further than the immediate pressures of the work, the spectacular scenery and the inclemency of the weather, the Old Vic entourage and its attendant press corps might also have seen signs of trouble in a nation-state which was in an increasingly vulnerable economic and strategic position. The reality was of an agricultural economy massively dependent on the United Kingdom and Germany as its sole export markets, and a social-democratic government which had very recently been the target of violent protests by discontented elements in the farming community, largely fomented by a Danish extreme right closely linked to the Nazi party. The previous years had also seen terrorist attacks, again organised with covert Nazi help, and increasingly blatant incursions into Danish territorial waters by the German Navy. Elsewhere in Scandinavia, there was open speculation about Denmark's impending fate as either a 'vassal state' or as the victim of invasion, but, mindful that the survival of its carefully-preserved but increasingly fragile neutrality lay in its staying on speaking terms with the Third Reich, the Danish state authorities colluded with a carefully muted news media to keep critical or dissenting voices out of the public arena. As part of this effort, in the year following the Old Vic visit, the second Kronborg festival made its own contribution to Danish–German *entente cordiale* by hosting Gustaf Gründgrens's production of *Hamlet* from the Staatliches Theater, Berlin, which (according to Mander and Mitchenson's account) expressed 'the back-to-the-primitive "alt deutsch" style in its treatment of the costumes and settings and the iron will-to-power of the "master race" in its treatment of Hamlet'.[50] If this were not blatant enough, there were plenty of other indications that Danish hopes of preserving its sovereign neutrality were cruelly misplaced.

Unsurprisingly, none of this was openly addressed either in contemporary or subsequent discussions of the Old Vic adventure. Understandably in the circumstances, those involved sought the eternal consolations of great art rather than the brutal immediacies of politics; such that the report in *Old Vic and Sadler's Wells Magazine* (September–October 1937) that the local officials had been so cooperative that they had 'even stopped the castle clock – the local Big Ben – so that it should not interrupt the action' seems almost too perfect a metaphor for a general collusion in the suspension of history. But, as we know, history has a habit of returning where it is least desired or expected. Consider this paragraph from *The Times* review:

> 'Scene 1. Elsinore. A platform before the Castle.' So are the stage directions and so it is. Here is Elsinore and here is Barnardo challenging Francisco and receiving the counter-challenge in return. True, the high walls of the great courtyard of the Kronborg Castle shut out the ramparts on which Francisco stands at his post, but were the eastern wall miraculously removed, there would they be and there would be Francisco's modern counterpart pacing up and down with rifle and fixed bayonet, gazing across the Sound at the Swedish coast.

The combination of vivid reportage and imaginative flight of fancy that places time, place, text and sentiment in a temporary alignment of almost hallucinatory intensity promises to lift the burden of history for a moment of transcendence, but what actually swims into view is something more sinister and immediate: an image of armed watchfulness that reflects the reality of modern warfare rather than the fantasy world of Shakespearean tragedy – although, at this moment, the anxious scrutiny of a Danish sentinel might have been better directed not across the Sound but further south. (In any case, thanks to the efforts of the Luftwaffe, RAF Bomber Command and, eventually, the United States Air Force, the next few years would provide ample opportunities to contemplate the sudden removal of walls, buildings, and even entire cities.) The castle is 'permeated with history' nonetheless: 'heroism on the winding staircases where defenders ... contested their ground step by step'. Olivier's Hamlet was of this heroic breed, readily envisaged as 'the inspiration of the defence in that year when Kronborg fell to the Swedes'. Here, at least, is a hint, however coded, that the political situation of *Hamlet* was in this context more than usually resonant.

For Guthrie and his cast, there were more immediate practical problems to occupy their time and attention. The composite set from the Old Vic production had been reconstructed before audience seating of 2500; floodlighting and sound amplification had been installed, a crowd of extras drawn from a Corps of Officer Cadets billeted in the castle had been supplied; and an audience of luminaries had been invited, including, without any obvious sense of irony, the Danish royal family. Efforts were made to integrate the stage with the environment, in that the assembly of steps and platforms was painted to appear as if constructed out of monumental stone blocks, matching the grey slabs and flagstones of the inner courtyard. But, as the publicity shots showing actors costumed posing around the grounds of the castle (rather than on set) demonstrated, it was already evident that the photo opportunities provided by the combination of the castle architecture and mocked-up moments from the play allowed for a far more convincing identification of performance, characters and setting than the stage platform itself. On the evidence of the press photographs and the album of snapshots taken by Phyllis Hartnoll (lodged in the Theatre Museum), the juxtaposition with the crushingly indifferent neo-classical façade of the castle's inner walls makes the set look oddly stranded, open-ended and incomplete, like a model for an unfinished Escher sketch. If the dynamic quality of the production (and in particular Olivier's performance) had in London arisen partly from the tension between the gymnastic potentialities of the set and the constricting matrix of the Old Vic's proscenium arch, the duplication of the set stripped of wings, frame and proscenium walls left the performance cruelly exposed, its tightly focused energies threatening to dissipate into the open air.

The attempt to reconcile theatre, culture and architecture was difficult enough, but in the end it was the intervention of nature that set the event on the course that would, according to legend, alter the course of Shakespearean theatre history. Alongside the communication problems, the necessity of working through the night (the castle was open to visitors during the day), the untrained extras, and, not least, the tortures of nicotine deprivation (there was a ban on naked flames within the castle precincts, so rehearsals had to be entirely non-smoking), the brief rehearsal period was haunted from the outset by worries about the weather. On the afternoon of the first performance, it began to rain. Guthrie recalled:

> The performance was at eight; at seven-thirty the rain was coming

down in bellropes. Miss Baylis, Larry Olivier and I held a council of war. It was out of all question to abandon the performance, indeed the special train had already steamed out of Copenhagen. To play in the open air was going to be nothing but an endurance test for all hands.[51]

The story has all the characteristics of a rattling good cliffhanger, with its half-hour deadline and crisis-point decision-making, the cross-cutting to the train steaming relentlessly towards the moment of destiny (one pictures *Hamlet* as a *Perils of Pauline* heroine, lashed to the track). The account of the incident given by Baylis's assistant Annette Prevost in the pages of the Old Vic magazine reveals a certain amount of compression on Guthrie's part for the sake of melodramatic effect: the Kronborg performance had been abandoned by the early after-noon, and 'even had the weather changed, the costumes would have been ruined by the wet, and the set far too slippery to be safe'.[52] 'Like a general in the field', according to Forsyth[53] (by now the military metaphors will come as no surprise), Guthrie reached a decision: 'we would give the performance in the ballroom of the hotel. There was no stage; but we would play in the middle of the hall with the audience seated all around as in a circus. The phrase hadn't yet been invented, but this would be theatre in the round.'[54] Again, Guthrie simplifies for rhetorical effect: other reports confirm that there was a narrow cabaret stage at one end of the ballroom at the Marienlyst Hotel, whereupon cane chairs represented the thrones of Denmark; the staging combined the use of this with the floor, and the audience were seated on three sides rather than 'all around'. But to admit this would be to compro-mise the simplicity of the opposition between the claustrophobic frontality of the picture frame and the radical spontaneity of a mode of performance so early in its infancy that it yet lacked a name. And it was, according to the director, an essentially intuitive move: 'I should never have suggested staging this rather important occasion as we did if I had not already had a strong hunch that it would work.'[55]

Temporarily reverting to actor-manager tradition, Guthrie handed responsibility over to his lieutenant, Olivier, who 'conducted a light-ning rehearsal with the company, improvising exits and entrances, and rearranging business' (p. 170) as he press-ganged newspaper critics and hotel staff into the task of arranging 870 chairs around the playing space. An hour behind schedule, prefaced by a brief speech from Guthrie announcing 'the strangest performance of *Hamlet* that could ever have been given by a professional company' (*Daily Mail*) the show went ahead. At the end of the first act, Olivier later revealed, Guthrie went backstage: 'Thought this was just going to be a joke. Thought we'd do just one act and apologize, give everyone a glass of champagne and send them home, but everyone's taking it *far* too seriously, we'll have to go through to the end.'[56] By the finish, according to Guthrie, 'the audience thought it a gallant effort and were with us from the start; actors always thrive on emergency and the actors did marvels. But ... after two hours of improvisation the actors became exhausted and a little flustered. The finale was a shambles, but not quite in the way the author intended.'[57] The *Daily Telegraph* (3 June 1937) supplied additional details: 'in some scenes, the actors made their entrances and exits through the audience, and in others they had to go through the rain to reach the stage. The lighting consisted of a spotlight which had been hastily contrived.' For Bishop, it had been 'a remarkable experience'; other notices were polite, if circumspect. The *Daily Mail* (3 June) applauded the 'plucky gesture' of 'playing *Hamlet* in such awkward surroundings', while *The Times* correspondent (3 June) similarly noted 'a very gallant and much appreciated act', but concluded that 'it would be absurd to offer a serious criticism of the performance'. Attention inevitably shifted to the second night, which saw the performance, restored as a large-scale event, go ahead in the castle courtyard, which received generally positive reviews: *The Times* particularly admired the way that 'the colour of the costumes and the lighting allied to Mr Guthrie's grouping continually created pictures which will long remain in the mind', adding that 'his crowd scenes gave the impression that they were about to get out of control, but actually they were under perfect discipline'; for the *Sunday Times*, 'in the artificial light towards the end the massed effects of the crowd scenes will remain among one's enduring memories'; the *Daily Telegraph* concluded that 'on a chilly evening the great tragedy ... held the audience spellbound for well over three hours'.

Fairly soon, however, word began to spread that the ballroom improvisation had been an event of uncommon significance. Writing several months afterwards, Annette Prevost hyperbolically referred to 'our now practically world famous performances [sic] in the hotel ballroom, which put the whole of Denmark at our feet', and to 'an artistic achievement ... probably familiar to everyone even remotely interested in matters theatrical'. For Prevost 'the show went through without a hitch, an inspired and inspiring performance'; but, more importantly, it had quite accidentally created the authentic relationship with the play that the performance at Kronborg was officially intended to produce: '*Hamlet* was played in a theatre as intimate as that for which Shakespeare wrote' (albeit a 'theatre' whose crudeness was alleviated by the delicate bourgeois gentility of a 'somewhat incongruous background of pink curtains with cream net frills').[58] In the November issue of *Theatre Arts*, Ivor Brown underlined the point:

> The players, showing great spirit and willingness to oblige, went down to their hotel and improvised a *Hamlet* as a 'cry' of Tudor players might have done ... This production, which had no more preparation as far as lighting and stage-craft were concerned than a charade at a house-party, was, in my opinion, a great success. It was close, intimate, enthralling. We were all part of Claudius's court. The final duel was so much in our midst that we feared for our own safety as well as Hamlet's.

Having had time to reflect upon the implications of this, Brown concluded that the performance 'made me wonder more than ever why we make such a fuss about lights and atmosphere and all the rest of it when presenting Shakespeare'. The experience had a knock-on effect on the following night. Although it started well enough, 'naturalism died at nine-thirty':

> When day waned and the artificial light was turned on, the castle itself became artificial. Pour flood-light on the most natural of trees and you immediately turn it into an unnatural outline and a piece of scenery. The same is true of castle-walls. Arc-lamps raking their façade make even granite seem insubstantial and give it a thin and lurid air of painted canvas.

As far as Brown was concerned, the confrontation between the raw immediacy of the ballroom performance and the technological sophistication of the courtyard production suddenly drained the latter of the authenticity which is its *raison d'être*, returning it to the unconvincing shoddiness which it is intended to transcend. This was an isolated view, but, as time went on, the first night began to acquire a legendary status. Recalling (inaccurately) that 'the company, without any rehearsal at all, just started off', J.C. Trewin rated it 'the most exciting performance of *Hamlet* I've ever seen'; Olivier that 'it is amazing how many people now think they were there ... some say it was the best thing they'd ever seen'.[59] It is not my place here to question the validity of these reports, or the reliability of the reporters (they were there;

I was not): the concern is not just how and why the event 'worked', but what lessons were drawn from it, what it very quickly came to mean in the story of the revival of the open stage. The answer to the first of these questions is readily available in the eyewitness accounts: liberated from the routine of established and mechanically executed blocking, gestures and entrances and exits, the company were in uncharted territory, forced to improvise, to experiment, and, in the interests of sheer survival, to play as an ensemble; stripped of lighting effects and scenery, the performance seemed to offer an unmediated encounter with the play itself.

It is also, I think, legitimate to speculate that the excitement was fuelled by the perception that the performance was on the brink of falling apart at any moment (as, Guthrie suggests, it did at the end). This is nicely caught by Alec Guinness's recollection of the performance, as conveyed by one biographer. Playing Osric, Guinness was directed by Guthrie to 'be polite to Kings and Queens if they get in your way', and, like some unseasonably sodden Rattigan character, 'make your entrance through the french windows'; but this contribution was slightly marred by 'the schnapps with which his Danish dresser supplied him prior to his "blowing in" ... he smiled rather too much. He rested his sword on the King of Sweden's lap, and blocked the view of at least two crowned heads.'[60] Although Guthrie handled the protocols of the regal encounter rather lightly here, the reality of the situation was that Guthrie and the company were, as cultural ambassadors, in about as exposed a position as could be imagined; ironically, it was a situation that anyone familiar with the Danish climate could have readily predicted. In view of what followed, Guthrie might have found it even more ironic that the terms of engagment of the gala performance as planned were grounded in an illusionistic literal-mindedness in its own way no less extreme than that which unleashed live rabbits to scamper through Tree's *A Midsummer Night's Dream* at the turn of the century; even though no one could have really taken the idea of bringing Hamlet to Elsinore *that* seriously, they took it seriously enough to afford it a sense of occasion that would have turned a theatrical debacle into a public relations disaster on a very large scale. Meanwhile, even though Guthrie had gone along with the exercise with due professionalism, another side of him might well have relished the sight of European monarchs and statesmen, and British diplomatic corps, dignitaries and dowagers, stuffed into a crowded ballroom and forced into uncomfortable proximity to a performance event which, displaced from the castle setting, had been divested of the site-specific qualities that had enticed them to travel to witness it. Guinness's semi-intoxicated interruption of the regal gaze (let alone the close encounter between a property sword and regal genitals) might have constituted a mingling of kings and clownishness that would have earned the disapproval of Sir Philip Sidney, but it also points to a potential for chaos that the performance just managed to keep under control.

What mattered in the long run, though, were the lessons that were drawn from the experience. Asked whether anyone at the time had any sense of what would subsequently be regarded as a fateful and momentous occasion, Olivier's response was: 'it happened and there it was, and I saw it could be done and it was quite good. But I didn't think it was going to transform the shape of the theatre or anything.' Trewin, similarly, recalled that 'we knew this *Hamlet* was special, yet I don't feel any man there would have said, hand on heart, "This is going to be the future of theatre"'; although this is not quite consistent with his claim that he overheard Guthrie confiding to George Bishop that 'this has made me think – look what's happened tonight. Here is the kind of theatre we ought to use.'[61] The comments cited above indicate that the uniqueness of the occasion was at first generally associated with its having unleashed the essence of Shakespeare, but for Guthrie, writing nearly twenty years after the event, hindsight confirmed that its real importance lay in the decision to abandon the end-on configuration: the results 'strengthened in me a conviction, which had been growing with each production at the Vic, that for Shakespeare the proscenium stage is unsatisfactory ... at its best moments that performance in the ballroom related the audience to a Shakespeare play in a different, and, I thought, more logical, satisfactory and effective way than can ever be achieved in a theatre of what is still regarded as orthodox design'.[62] Succumbing to a magically simple logic that would resonate powerfully through the postwar open stage movement, Guthrie concludes that the tensions between the conventions of the text, the existing physical and institutional structure of the theatre, and the expectations of performers and audiences, which had long been evident but which had reached a crisis point at Elsinore, are ultimately reducible to questions of architecture and spatial organisation.

For Guthrie, it was the happy convergence between this insight and the theatrical application of pyschoanalysis – which this production inaugurated – that provided a resolution to what he had previously identified as the problem of the producer's role: quite fortuitously, it seemed, circumstances had produced the prototype for a mode of neo-Elizabethan Shakespearean performance which would combine historical authenticity and avant-garde experiment within the mainstream of professional practice. An important element in all this was the sense that the repudiation of the picture frame was motivated not by dogmatism or pedantry (as was said to be the case with the school of Poel and Monck), but by pragmatism; as a spontaneous, natural and somehow deeply inevitable response to material imperatives, the open stage was, upon Guthrie's intervention, *naturalised* as it never had been before. (Some, half-jokingly, went even further and found a divine sanction for the turn of events: Olivier later wrote that 'it rained, and, because of this, the gods came over to our side'; for Styan, the results were 'miraculous'.[63]) Guthrie also noted that the experience of the Danish trip had another important consequence in that it marked a turning point in his professional relationship with Baylis: previously wary, 'she now thought that I had shown some qualities of leadership in the various emergencies ... she now considered that I was trustworthy'.[64] But, in a small way, Guthrie had also brought about a shift in the balance of power between the manager and the producer. Prevost's narrative suggests that the first stage of the rescue operation had been an executive action: 'Miss Baylis, long used to emergencies, had already spied out the hotel ballroom';[65] but in Guthrie's account the crucial – and conclusive – element is the *artistic* decision to play in the round. Effectively, it is the decision not of a producer, whose remit is defined within the existing chain of command and cultural economy of the proscenium stage, but of a director.

As for Olivier, both the ballroom performance and the subsequent nights at Kronborg saw him consolidate his grip on the role. The presence of Vivien Leigh as Ophelia, the result of a cast change that had taken place since the London performances, was a matter of some consequence. Replacing Cherry Cottrell, Leigh was praised for 'a performance of appealing charm and wistful beauty' (*Daily Telegraph*, 4 June) and for bringing 'grace and an exquisite wistfulness to the character' (*Sunday Times*, 6 June), although *The Times* critic considered that 'her porcelain femininity is in almost too strong a contrast to Hamlet's masculine virility' (4 June). This compared favourably with the notices that had been served on Cottrell, who had been described as 'bizarre' (*Sunday Referee*), 'not quite up to scratch ... authentically mad, but not moving' (*Daily Telegraph*), and, by an Agate unable to resist a pun, as 'unripe' (*Sunday Times*). The best that could be said was that she 'played Ophelia much as the boy actors of Shakespeare's day must have done, with affecting simplicity' (*Daily Mail*). Perhaps it was not that surprising that at the end of the run Cottrell would suddenly become, to use the terminology of one of Olivier's biographers, 'no longer available',[66] but the circumstances of Leigh's acquisition of the role from Cottrell throw a different light on Olivier's performance, as well as, perhaps, on the entire Elsinore escapade. Guthrie later revealed that, at the beginning of the Old Vic project, Olivier had a compelling personal incentive to take on Hamlet : 'Larry was profoundly unhappy at the time. It all had to do with the conflict between his violent, immature love for Vivien Leigh and his more mature, subdued attachment to Jill Esmond ... he wanted to do it because he believed he had a great deal of personal Hamletlike anguish and spiritual paralysis to bring to the part'.[67] His strategy of playing to impress Leigh evidently worked, since she went night after night, convinced, according to Olivier biographer Donald Spoto, that 'her "Larry boy" ... was confronting in this role his own feelings about his mother'. Moreover, 'persuaded that her life was destined to be linked to his, Vivien now longed to play Ophelia to his Hamlet'.[68] Olivier and Leigh had been clandestine lovers for months; in his autobiography Olivier presents the episode as an instance of he and Leigh having to 'accept engagements together'.[69] Spoto tells a rather different story, claiming that when the invitation arrived to go to Kronborg, Olivier went straight to Guthrie to demand that Leigh be given Cottrell's role. When Guthrie, supported by Baylis, refused, Olivier indicated that he would pull out of the production if Vivien were not engaged. The personal consequences of Guthrie's acquiescence were that both Olivier's and Leigh's first marriages were, as the actor put it, 'severed'; equally significantly, the pair managed to utilise the production to promote what was already an established and popular screen partnership (most recently seen in action in Alexander Korda's swashbuckler *Fire Over England*, which was released in May). Mention was made earlier of how the press made use of photographs of the cast members posing against the castle architecture rather than on the set; predominant among these were images of Olivier and Leigh looking like the leads in a romantic melodrama: flirting, canoodling, lunging through ornate gothic archways (a shot which featured in *The Sphere*, the *Daily Telegraph* and *Theatre Arts*). Successfully exploiting the setting and the occasion of the Kronborg performance in the interests of their personal and professional alliance, Olivier and Leigh had evidently learned from (or made use of) a good publicist. Fortunately, they had one ready to hand right from the beginning. By a startling coincidence, and with implications for the Elsinore venture that can only be guessed at, Leigh's publicity agent was none other than the man who had masterminded the Kronborg visit in the first place – Robert Jorgensen.

Guthrie does not mention Leigh's involvement in the production in his autobiography, and Forsyth suggests that the episode would have disturbed him, as the director who returned again and again to *Hamlet* and *Oedipus Rex* 'never liked to see families in upheaval'.[70] There was, however, some consolation to be found in the anecdote with which Guthrie concludes his account of the ballroom performance. In addition to all the problems faced by the cast, there was one entrance ('the most effective one, a double door at the head of a short flight of steps') whose use was strictly, and unaccountably, forbidden. The next morning Guthrie was shown the reason: a pair of blue tits nesting in the architrave. 'If this door had been opened', the head porter informed him, 'she would have deserted her eggs; you wouldn't have wanted that.'[71] Ernest Jones may have been far behind, and, for the time being, largely forgotten, but the capacity of maternity to confuse and complicate theatricality remained undiminished.

4
Revolution in Stratford

I

July 1952: the Toronto *Globe and Mail*'s reporter Bruce West attends a press conference at the Royal York Hotel with 'one of the world's greatest authorities on production of Shakespearean drama'. He expects to meet 'a small, hungry-looking man with great sad eyes, an unruly mop of hair and culture dripping from every pore'. As, indeed, he does: 'I spotted such a type ... the moment I entered the room and lost no time in approaching him with my hand outstretched delicately, in my best cultured manner.' But it is a case of mistaken identity: 'this small man with a large pair of horn-rimmed cheaters was another journalist'. In another corner of the room, the august figure he seeks (who is, of course, Tyrone Guthrie himself) is found, 'drinking plain Coca Cola and evidently enjoying it'. He is 'a great towering man who looked like one of Royal York house dicks, only taller', who also looked 'like a cop' and, for good measure, like 'a rivetter on the 18th floor of a new office building'.[1] Impressed by the director's physical presence and stature, West documents this encounter according to the established rules of the genre of Guthrie anecdotes scrutinised at the beginning of the previous chapter. But he also provides a point of departure for this chapter's discussion of the foundation of the Stratford Festival in Ontario and of the work undertaken there during the first season. The most loaded word in Bruce West's report is, of course, *culture*: styling himself as a plain-dealing man of the people, he handles the term with palpable disdain, characterising it as a kind of unpleasant waste fluid, associating it with things that are feminine, sissy, longhair and unmanly, and identifying the 'cultured manner' with the 'delicately' outstretched hand (or limp wrist?). The surprise is that the Guthrie persona speaks of something different: for West, at least, of the more straightforward, working-class (heterosexual) masculinity readily associated with construction workers, Irish cops and security guards. The Clark Kent/Man of Steel pairing of sad bespectacled wimp and Guthrie juxtaposes the soggy inconsequentiality of the former with an alternative, more muscular, version of culture – a man's man's Shakespeare. Just as significantly, West is mildly surprised (and quietly impressed) by the fact that Guthrie is happily guzzling plain Coke, the quintessentially North American lubricant: further evidence that here is a cultural ambassador who is no alien interloper but a regular guy: a man to trust.

We shall return to West in a moment, but first it is useful to set his remarks in context. Guthrie was in Toronto in 1952 to publicise the foundation of the Stratford Shakespeare Festival, a project which through an accident of nomenclature would become the centre of Shakespearean production on the North American continent. Originally the dream of Stratford businessman Tom Patterson, the Festival afforded Guthrie the opportunity to reshape the architecture of the postwar Shakespearean stage. Much has been written recently about the energetic bardolatry that gave rise to the Stratford Festival and that continues to fuel it: once viewed as a triumphant foundational moment both in Canadian cultural and theatrical history and for postwar Shakespearean production, both its formation and its subsequent history as a purveyor of high culture are now increasingly being subjected to more critical scrutiny. Characterising the venture as a spurious and contradictory amalgam of Old and New World cultures supposedly manifested in an 'essentializing "Canadian-ness"', Denis Salter has described the Stratford stage as 'a decontextualized, ahistorical, pseudo-universal, *un*naturally hybrid space';[2] Dennis Kennedy places Stratford in the broader context of the postwar Shakespearean cultural tourist movement, noting that the Elizabethanism of such festivals is part of the effort of 'clearly mark[ing] themselves as separate from the regular commercial theatre by virtue of their locations, their financing, and their repertory'.[3] In his account of the 1993 season, Richard Paul Knowles dissects the discursive contexts within which the theatrical meanings of its Shakespearean performances are made, concluding that the Festival's written discourse is 'universalist, individualist, essentialist, and literary', that the empty space rhetoric upon which the theatre is founded is merely a 'vacuum ... to be filled by the unquestioned, because naturalized, assumptions of ideology', and that the general thematic content of its work is 'a soft-core and self-congratulatory liberalism'.[4] Writing in *Canadian Theatre Review*, the reviewers of the 1999 season at Stratford underline the point, emphasising that the contradictory quality of the Stratford experience arises in part from its curiously arbitrary positioning: 'the ponderous gesture to an invented Shakespearean tradition remains outside the performance textualities because it is locked in self-referentiality. It has no relationship to locale other than a corporate tradition of naming.'[5]

Hailed by the contradictory messages that emerge from the theatre's uneasy negotiations between art and commerce, the Stratford theatre-goers of the twenty-first century are 'constructed by the productions as unsophisticated, but by the theatre's publicity discourse as the Friends of High Culture', and 'positioned ambivalently as worshipful tourists and critical collaborators'.[6] This ambivalence was written into the enterprise from the very outset, as a consequence of its genesis within the particular conditions of Canadian postcoloniality in the postwar years, in that the uncertain identity of the implied Stratford spectator (and, indeed, performer) effectively mirrors the divided and provisional status of national self-definition during the same period. In 1951, the Report of the Royal Commission on National Development in the Arts, Science and Letters had argued that 'an autonomous nation needs an equally autonomous cultural industry, and suggested that public funding of culture is no less a national imperative than military spending'.[7] But the identification of these imperatives could not be disentangled from the question of what kind of modern capitalist nation Canada could be, or wanted to be – which raised yet further questions about Canada's dual anglophone/French identity, and its multiple orientations towards the cultures of the Old and New Worlds, Europe and the United States. As many cultural commentators have recognised, Canadian national identity has historically been characterised by anxious self-scrutiny and critical interrogation: 'to be Canadian is to live in the space between certainties, to dwell in the gap that separates conviction from speculation ... to exist in a state of constant becoming'.[8] One manifestation of this, writes Alan Filewod, has been that 'the definition of Canada, as a nation and an historical experiment, has always been an imperative project of the drama and theatre', but the definitions that have resulted have been contradictory:

> The evolutionary patterns of the theatre and the drama in the twentieth century can both be seen as the expression of a post-colonial

impulse that failed to transcend the contradictions of colonialism. In both cases, Canada was perceived as an occupied culture struggling for autonomy and selfhood, but the critics who proposed these analyses were themselves implicated in the colonialism they resisted.[9]

These were not the terms in which Guthrie and his Canadian collaborators regarded the Stratford Festival. As far as Guthrie was concerned, the Canadian dimension of the project was straightforward and unproblematic: 'the project must be demonstrably a Canadian one, carried out not merely by Canadian initiative, and with Canadian finance, but by Canadian actors';[10] however, Guthrie's successor, Michael Langham, later asserted that there was 'never anything Canadian about Stratford ... that was a diplomatic thing Guthrie cooked up'.[11] For Guthrie, the value of the Stratford project resided in the potential of theatrical art to ameliorate the excesses of capitalism: 'if Canada is honourably to fulfil its destiny, it is not enough just to be rich and powerful. Canada must not in the councils of the world use the cracked brash accents of millionaire adolescence, but must speak with maturity.'[12] Shakespeare would provide the example and the means for Canadians to grow up, and speak up, properly, and with confidence; as Guthrie's collaborator at Stratford, Robertson Davies, concurred: 'as a nation, we Canadians do not speak well; it is as though we had no ears to hear whether the sounds we make are pleasant or harsh, clear or slovenly ... [Shakespeare's English] was our language as every Canadian could speak it if he chose'.[13] As in much of the contemporary discussion of Stratford's role in the life of the nation, a crucial component of this ideal for national identity is Canada's cultural distinctiveness from the United States. Guthrie's attempt to transplant a supposedly universal conception of Shakespeare into the Canadian context has been read as a neo-colonial manoeuvre willingly abetted by the forces of anglophile nostalgia; at the same time, for many Canadians in the 1940s and 1950s it seemed that 'the British connection remained the only defense against American cultural expansion'.[14]

Despite the confident optimism and idealism propounded by the Massey Report, there was, then, a degree of uncertainty about how and where Shakespeare might be located within the Canadian context; moreover, apart from the Royal Alexandra in Toronto, there was no established theatre building or theatre company in the whole of Canada. Although the sceptical journalist is won over (largely by

Guthrie's charisma), the suspicion that Bruce West voices was widely shared. In his autobiography, Guthrie records that he was repeatedly told that 'Canadians just hate Shakespeare';[15] the broadly sympathetic press coverage of the development of the Festival repeatedly noted the doubts, misgivings and hostility to the project that were registered both on a local and a national scale. Since the dearth of professional theatre in Canada meant that many of the journalistic commentators on the progress of the project were all-purpose hacks press-ganged into the task of theatre reporting or reviewing, the archive is more indicative of popular opinion than is usually the case. A notice in the Toronto-based *Farmer's Advocate and Canadian Countryman* (25 July 1953) may be considered representative. In this account, Shakespeare traditionally signifies 'a dismal business of long incomprehensible speeches in a kind of Never-never language, orated from a distant stage'; a fellow theatregoer confides that 'I can't stand Shakespeare myself', guiltily adding, 'I know I ought to like it . . . but I don't, really'. Yet by the end of the performance, scepticism has been allayed: pausing to admire 'a bumper crop of really distinguished actors and actresses', the reporter records that 'the entire audience was on its feet, shouting and clapping until our hands hurt. Including me, and my friend who couldn't stand Shakespeare' and exhorts his readership: 'even though you're one of the people who looks upon Shakespeare as more punishment than pleasure, it's worth investigation. That hoarse voice at the final curtain may well be your own.' It is in the mixture of suspicion, insecurity, raw pain and adulation that the extent of Canadian ambivalence towards Shakespeare may be truly measured.

Not everyone was won over. Alec Guinness records an incident during a performance of *Richard III*: 'a hefty young man in the front row . . . rolled up his copy of *Playboy* or *Cute* early on and whacked his mother across the head with it, shouting "Shite! I've had enough of this fart arse stuff!" and waddled out of the theatre muttering obscenities. Only his mother dutifully followed him.'[16] As Guinness retells it, the corpulent porn afficionado's combination of grotesque physicality, anal obsessiveness and simultaneous dependency upon and hostility towards the maternal betrays a strain of resistance to Shakespeare that provides material for any number of Oedipal scenarios; it is sufficient to the purpose here that, alongside Bruce West's jocular characterisation of traditional Shakespearean culture as in some way queer or feminine, it can be seen as symptomatic of larger forces within postwar Canadian cultural and political life. The mistrust of Shakespeare is a manifestation of the deeply utilitarian and pragmatic orientation of Canadian culture during the period: while support for the liberal arts flourished in the belief that cultural education contributed to the general economic well-being of the nation, 'men's work' was still prioritised in terms of a heavy investment in knowledge and skills directly related to professional and industrial needs.[17] This retooling was part of the rapid remasculinisation of Canadian working life that accompanied the return of the war veterans and the reversal of the sudden influx of women into paid work that had been necessitated by the war years; in this respect, Canada's experience shadowed that of its nearest neighbour, which, in the period of the Cold War and Korean War, McCarthyism and a resurgent Republicanism, witnessed a similar reassertion of masculine values.

The cultural ramifications of this promotion of a newly anxious masculinity in the United States were far-reaching, but in the cultural sphere were represented pre-eminently by the renaissance of the Western, the genre wherein the enabling myths of an idealised past, the open territory of the frontier landscape, and the iconic figure of the gunfighter, afforded space and opportunity for play within and around complex politicised gender identities. 'In watching a Western', writes Richard Slotkin, 'we are asked to think of ourselves as looking across the border that divides past and present in order to recover a "genetic" myth which displays the (putative) origins of our present condition and by so doing suggests ways of understanding and responding to that condition.'[18] It is a remark which is applicable, with modifications, to the Stratford Festival, situated as it is on an imaginary boundary between Old and New Worlds. For the Canadian theatregoers of the 1950s (and the border-crossing Americans who supplied much of the Festival's audience), talk of horses was an acceptable counterpoint to horse operas; in the Bosworth Field of 1953's *Richard III* or the vasty fields of France of the 1956 *Henry V* could be found both an alternative and a complement to the deserts and mountain ranges of *Red River* and *Rio Bravo*; for John Wayne, Henry V or Coriolanus; for the potency of the six-shooter, the equally emblematic rapier. In this light, it made perfect sense for Guthrie to return to Stratford in 1954 to stage – of all things – *The Taming of the Shrew* as a comedy Western (the intertextual chain takes on a further bizarre twist when we consider that two years before John Ford had transported Western icons John Wayne and Maureen O'Hara to rural Ireland to rework *The Taming of the Shrew* as *The Quiet Man*).

It is not difficult to see why the arrival on Canadian soil of a leading foreign authority on Shakespeare should breed misgivings. If that authority looked like a construction worker, so much the better for him, and it was even more to his advantage that the building of the theatre itself was a helpful contribution to a booming construction industry; nonetheless, the sense persisted that the theatrical activities it housed and celebrated properly belonged within the feminine sphere. Ambivalence about the project is reflected in the extent to which questions of Shakespeare, theatre, and, more particularly, the Stratford Festival itself are repeatedly couched within the rhetoric and iconography of gender and sexuality. This was not entirely new (and to some degree recapitulates Poel's experience, as discussed in Chapter 1): Salter cites one of the founding figures of Canadian bardolatry, Wilfred Campbell, to the effect that the cultivation of an appropriately Canadian Shakespearean performance style would be a matter of discouraging the taste for 'the suggestive, the *unnatural*, and the immoral' and promoting the values of a dramaturgy in which 'there is nothing abnormal, nothing disgusting or revolting, but all is largely human and *natural*'.[19] This was in 1907; half a century later, the gender identity and sexual health of the drama continued to preoccupy a wide variety of participants and commentators as they reflected upon the production process, the plays in performance, and, most of all, the stage and physical structure of the theatre itself. I shall be tracing the shape of their rhetoric in more detail shortly; a brief example will suffice here. In the Stratford Festival archive there is a cutting featuring a cartoon printed in an Ontario newspaper at the end of the first Festival season, which provides eloquent and rather touching testimony to this effect. Under the title 'All's Well That Ends Well', it depicts a bow-tied, check-shirted but emphatically butch Mountie, lurking beside an open flap in the tent (labelled 'Stage Door') that houses the 'Stratford Shakespearian Festival'; as the 'Canada' printed on his hatband confirms, he stands metonymically for the nation itself, tentatively and somewhat self-consciously waiting to offer its congratulations to the Festival. With one hand nervously straightening his dickie bow and the other surreptitiously clutching a bouquet (bearing the congratulatory message 'well done!') behind his back, the Mountie's status as a law and order icon of square-jawed Canadian masculinity is subtly, and somewhat tentatively, feminised by exposure to the unexpectedly seductive pleasures of performed Shakespeare.

Guthrie's own account of the adventure positively relishes its gendered and sexualised terminology. On his first arrival in Stratford, Guthrie takes note of the gender composition of the committee that has been set up to inaugurate the Festival. Joking that theatrical management boards usually consist of 'artistic and excitable elderly ladies of both sexes', and thereby conjuring the hermaphroditic spectre of an antiquated campery to be set against 'a sprinkling of businessmen to restrain the artistic people from spending money' (again, for 'artistic', read effeminate, hysterical, possibly queer), he is pleased to discover that 'the males outnumbered the females by about five to one'. Appealing to a vestigial frontier mentality, he persuades them to mount two productions rather than one, because 'it was wise to have a second barrel to our gun. If we missed with the first, we would have another chance with the second.' Admirably united in masculine resolve, the committee carries the venture through a series of funding crises while Guthrie engages the services of Alec Guinness and Irene Worth and collaborates with Tanya Moiseiwitsch on the design of a stage which determinedly 'eschew[ed] *Ye Olde*': 'we were agreed that, while conforming to the conventions of the Elizabethan in practicalities, it should not present a pseudo-Elizabethan appearance'.[20] The revivalist impulse is resolutely modernist: if the emphasis upon 'practicalities' rather than the meretricious fripperies of 'appearance' inscribes an implicitly gendered opposition, it also foreshadows the austere masculinist design aesthetic that would by the end of the 1950s become embedded in the practices of the Royal Court (and, in the 1960s, the Royal Shakespeare Company), as part of the project of, as Dan Rebellato puts it, eradicating the irrelevancies of 'frivolous theatricality' in the interests of 'the disciplining of meanings on stage'.[21] But the briefest of glances at the Festival stage immediately reveals that it is at best only approximately 'Elizabethan' in its configuration of the doors and balcony of the rear wall and in the absence of a proscenium, whereas the arced arena seating and graduated levels of the stage platform owe as much to the Greek theatre as to the Renaissance. As an architectural hybrid, the Festival stage is less an attempt to replicate playhouse or amphitheatre than a bid to map the deep structure of the non-illusionist dramaturgy to which these spaces gave birth – a dramaturgy fundamentally defined, for Guthrie, in terms of the dance of maternal presence and absence, and converging upon the Oedipal scenarios delineated in Sophocles's play and *Hamlet*. Evoking the primal scene of the killing of Laius, the sports-tunnel vomitoria of the Stratford Festival auditorium locate action at a place where two roads meet; points of ingress and egress distributed around the space multiply the possibilities of the *fort-da* game of entrances and exits to and from a maternal body that holds the audience in the secure embrace of a closed circuit, fostering an impression of the intimacy only truly known by the pre-Oedipal infant. Guthrie was keen to stress that the reconstruction of the Elizabethan stage was motivated by 'strictly practical' considerations which would produce in turn 'the best practical results' (*Life*, p. 284): the restitution of an authentic, natural and healthily intimate relationship between players, audience and stage. But the rehearsal process would prove that this was hardly a straightforward matter. Arriving in Stratford to a stage unfinished and the tent not yet delivered, Guthrie starts rehearsals in a wooden shed infested with sparrows. As at Elsinore, the theatrical is again compromised by the ornithological, as 'their love life became most obtrusive. Boy sparrow would meet girl and pursue her all over our stage. They were impervious to fear, or for that matter shame.' Hunting for a metaphor in the sparrows' shameless occupation of the performance space, Guthrie finds a fusion of sexual drive and murderous energy ('these dear little feathered friends would not have hesitated to make away with *their* nephews') that, amidst 'scenes of unbridled bird sexuality' makes 'the life of *Richard III* seem very anaemic and suburban' (p. 294). Confronted with 'natural' intimacies of this kind, the work of rehearsals seems lifeless and insipid, is comically reduced to the epithet which derisively encapsulates petit-bourgeois timidity and repressiveness: the suburban sensibility which is pathetically stranded in the despised hinterland between country and city, instinctive rural physicality and metropolitan daring (since the 1930s, moreover, the landscapes of the English suburb had, like the Stratford Festival itself, been defined by the architectural combination of modernism and mock Tudor). The tent arrived, and was erected under the supervision of the flamboyantly camp 'tent man', strangely-but-truly named Skip Manley, who, Guthrie notes, 'referred to the tent as "she"', and to the hardware 'which would raise "her" from the ground', and who sported 'jewelled rings' on his fingers and favoured as his working dress 'a shirt made of pink and silver brocade – the sort of garment which, in Europe, old ladies wear for evenings' (pp. 295–6). Rehearsals continued with juvenile rubberneckers lurking 'outside the skirts of the great tent ... occasionally, they would lift the skirts and peek ... ' With the onset of electrical storms the metaphorical transformation of the tent into a grotesque female body was complete: 'great canvas tumours would hang down, where water had collected, diseased-looking, ominous ... Manley dash[ed] hither and yon, with a knife attached to a long pole, slashing the tumours.' As if at the scene of a violent and strangely decadent birth, 'there would be a flash of rubies and diamonds, a ripping sound, and then cascades of warmish, dirty water'.[22]

The previous chapter traced the ways in which theatricality and maternity are often in close proximity in Guthrie's writing, and in this respect his gendering of the Stratford stage belongs to his own idiosyncratic personal trajectory. But he was not alone in thinking about it in this way, as is evident from the rationale that was advanced to account for a range of the adjustments to the stage that were made at the start of the 1962 season. Claiming that the Festival's first decade had confirmed that the stage had 'proved itself the most suitable in the world for Shakespearean performance', Michael Langham (who had been appointed Artistic Director in 1956) asserted that it was time for it to change its sex 'from feminine to masculine – more in keeping with the robust nature of most of Shakespeare's works ... a bolder, more spacious, more rugged appearance was therefore planned'. Langham's characterisation of the Festival stage as feminine was not without precedent: during the period of building and in the run-up to the opening productions, press photographs frequently showed the set being modelled either by Moiseiwitsch herself or by female members of the company; while a set of publicity shots for *All's Well* obeys the conventions of the *Vogue* photo shoot with ballgowned actresses arranged tastefully before and among the stage pillars, again raising the question of who, or what, is modelling whom. Often likened to the prow of a ship, the pillared balcony was here inevitably accessorised with female performers positioned as figureheads. Langham felt that the stage until now had been 'more in tune with the spirit of the comedies' (and up to this point the comedies dominated the repertoire); the stern masculinity of the refashioned space would better suit the histories and tragedies. With this aim of toughening up the stage in mind, a range of modifications were carried out, largely in order to ease entry into an apparently overly feminised space, which was characterised as a not altogether compliant woman's body. The two side stairway entrances 'proved ineffectual for strong and dignified entrances', so these were widened and moved further apart; the 'narrowness of the upstage-centre entrance, together with the many slender pillars ... proved cramping for strong entries', so the entrance was widened, and the newly lengthened and swollen pillars reduced in number from nine to five. Finally, Langham's designers demonstrated the vision that was shown by the urban planners of nineteenth-century Paris, transforming the means of access and passage across the stage to facilitate the passage of armed personnel: 'Shakespeare's plays frequently require a clash of opposing forces or characters, a situation effectively exploited on stage if there is a direct diagonal approach from opposing corners leading to the inevitable conflict in the centre. This was planned in the new stage by setting the rear side doors directly opposite the tunnels'.[23] For Ralph Berry, the result was 'an extremely masculine, thrust stage' which calls for appropriately 'robust, even flamboyant production methods'; conversely, Robert Speaight, inadvertently reversed Langham's sex-change, recording the switch as 'from masculine to feminine'. 'At a single stroke', he continues, engagingly oblivious to the double entendre, 'Guthrie had established the "thrust", or open, stage, as an orthodoxy.'[24] If this confusion of gendered terms is any indication, the Festival stage retained its enigmatic hybridity, and its sexual identity remained open to negotiation.

II

This was yet to come, however. In 1953, it might have seemed to Guthrie that the Stratford stage provided a material form for the psychoanalytically-inflected and sexually-charged theatricality that had preoccupied his work since the 1937 *Hamlet*. In an article for *Shakespeare Survey* in 1955, Guthrie pondered the significance of the venture, characteristically stressing the practical advantages of the space. Firstly, there was its seeming neutrality: 'the general visual effect we aimed at was to be strictly "functional"; neither aggressively modern nor antique; a structure that unobtrusively offered to the actors standing-places, seats, and things to lean against, where they needed them; a platform that offered neither too much space nor too little, and which was so placed as to be the focal point of the nearly circular auditorium'.[25]

In attempting to formulate appropriate modalities of performance within this accommodating and ostensibly non-representational space, however, Guthrie is pulled in opposing and contradictory directions. On the one hand, 'theatrical performance is a form of ritual ... the audience is not asked to subscribe to an illusion but to participate in the ritual ... The attraction of the "open" stage, as opposed to the proscenium, is primarily this: that it stresses the ritual as opposed to the illusionary quality of performance.' Guthrie never really explains what he means by 'ritual', although it seems broadly to embrace elements of ceremonial, the non-pictorial, and the non-naturalistic. Its effect is 'for each member of the audience to lose a great deal of his own identity; to allow his personality to become fused with that of other participants, to become lost, rapt, in a collective act of partici-pation'. Yet, Guthrie proposes, theatre in the round affords the simultaneous advantage of an increased 'naturalness': 'conversational scenes are infinitely easier to arrange if the participants do not have to conform to the highly conventional groupings that rule the prosce-nium stage, where "masking" or "upstaging" one's interlocutor are rightly crimes. On an "open" stage masking is inevitable.' In a typical move, acceptance of this inevitability is presented as a victory for the natural and the real over the conventional (associated with rigidity, conformity and rules): the open stage enforces a mobility which is itself the graphic sign of a new freedom.

Moreover, if the fact of masking poses a threat to the bourgeois viewing regime that persists from the proscenium arch theatre, it can be recuperated by a newly redistributive economy of blocking and movement, since 'it is the producer's duty to see that all parts of the house get fair do's – that if Mr X faced East at one important moment, he must face West at the next'. Placed within a scene which recalls not only one of the primary structural principles of the Western (the spaces of civilisation and the wilderness) but also Guthrie's character-isation of the picture frame as an 'Iron Curtain' system trapped within the divisive binaries of the Cold War, the nimble orientation of the ideal open stage actor positions him as an even-handed and highly flexible negotiator of all points of the political as well as geographical compass. Overall, however, what counts is the collective rather than the individual: 'Mr X' is codenamed into anonymity (and, through a happy accident, ascribed a typographic identity which happens to replicate the sign of the crossroads, the Oedipal scene), and 'in prac-tice two things emerge: the naturalness and expressiveness of the group is more important than the face of any single member of the group; a good actor's behind is often just as expressive as his face'.

This expressive equilibrium between face and fundament is a sugges-tive metaphor for the dynamic interchange between high seriousness and the carnivalesque that is at the heart of Guthrie's theatrical vision and practice. But difficulties persist, above all in those elements of the dramaturgy which the illusionist theatre has most thoroughly consti-tuted in individuated terms. For Guthrie, 'the chief difficulty' arises 'in long soliloquies, especially meditative soliloquies where movement "feels" wrong to an actor and tends to disturb the concentration of the audience'. The solution 'is for the actor to keep turning slowly, facing now this, now that, part of the house. With a little practice this soon feels, and looks, perfectly natural. Both Alec Guinness in *Richard III* and Irene Worth in *All's Well* managed long passages of psychological monologue in a way that felt comfortable and natural to themselves and entirely held their audience.' Here Guthrie inadvertently hits upon one of the contradictions of the open stage's compromise between history and modernity. For Guthrie, the problems of blocking, and the actor's sense of feeling *wrong*, are technical challenges which can be surmounted through a modified physical vocabulary of individualised choreography, so that with due effort the appearance of spontaneity can be contrived. But why such movement should feel 'wrong' to the actor in the first place is a question which he does not ask.[26]

Once again, Guthrie's touchstone text, *Hamlet*, looms into view: as the vehicle for the ultimate soliloquiser, the play is, of course, also one of modernity's most compelling documents of selfhood. As Guthrie's frequent reiteration of the term 'natural' might suggest, the instinctive sense of wrongness that attaches to the violation of introspection in repose is an ideological reflex as much as it is a matter of judgement and temperament. The rule of stillness which is learned behind the proscenium arch and before the camera contributes significantly to the naturalistically-inflected soliloquy's project of cultivating the impression of unified, centred and fully interiorised subjectivity, the essence of the private individual, the figure, as Francis Barker put it, 'that is to dominate and organize bourgeois culture'.[27] If the generally accepted understanding of soliloquy as, in Matthew Arnold's formulation, 'the dialogue of the mind with itself'[28] affords *Hamlet* a decisive role in the modern period's co-option of Shakespeare in the service of its own privatised mode of subjectivity, it also dictates the physical logic of movement and gesture within which this talking into existence of inner being must take place. In a version of what Barker characterises as a general occlusion and suppression of the corporeal in order to shore up the claims of a subjectivity 'whose form is that of the unique and intransitive soul, centred in meanings which are apparently its alone',[29] stage tradition dictates stillness and repose, or, at most, minimal and controlled gesture and movement, as the keynote for Hamlet's soliloquies (whether or not these are treated introspectively or as direct address to the audience). Contemporary praise for Irving's portrayal of Hamlet captures this sense, as he made his first appearance 'motionless, making no show of grief, but gazing, it would seem, half pensively, half cynically, not so much into vacancy as into the heart of some oppressing mystery or sorrow'.[30] John Gielgud reported that when he first tackled 'To be or not to be' in the 1930s, he attempted a 'great innovation by walking about in this speech' but when Mrs Patrick Campbell saw the performance she 'implored him to cut out the movement as it distracted from the lines'. He concluded that 'she was quite right and I never did it again'.[31] Peter Hall underscores the point: 'complex thoughts and close-packed imagery cannot be communicated by an actor continually on the move ... try the explicit and still communication of "To be or not to be" with your back to half the audience.'[32]

For most theatre practitioners the issue is a pragmatic one; it takes a performance critic to formulate a theoretical rationale for the convention. In his monumental survey of the stage history of the play, Marvin Rosenberg offers just such an explanation for the equation between self-reflection and physical immobility. From the moment of Hamlet's first soliloquy,

> we will know that the central action of the play is inward, we will always be party to his sensitive inner process when he becomes immobilized in thought. Never entirely immobilized, for the face, at the surface of the boiling within, will betray, if ever so slightly, repressed disturbance ... Recurrent visual gestures, like verbal ones, take on accumulating meaning, signalling that the body, even when stilled to fend off scrutiny, hides an exquisite sensitivity and a mind furiously active. As the body at other times betrays the mask of the voice, now, in soliloquy, the voice opens to us the mind's secrets. The convention of soliloquy makes a transparency of the character.[33]

The Cartesian basis of the division between mind and body is fairly explicit here: for the actor, the philosophical proposition becomes a technical injunction to subordinate movement to thought in order to sustain the sense that the reflective will is embodied but sovereign. It will also be evident that frontal staging is crucial, both as a condition for the cultivation of interiority and as a means of sustaining it: in order for the illusion of transparency to work, the actor needs to be fully available to the stable and singular perspective of an audience that is conceived as a more or less homogenous bloc; conditions that are satisfied, pre-eminently, by the end-on configuration of the picture frame. On the platform stage, however, this dynamic of reciprocity, or Lacanian mirroring, is sabotaged (according to the rule of 'fair do's') by the imperatives of movement and to the multiplication and dispersal of a formerly singular point of view. Even when alone on such a stage, the performer cannot fail to 'mask' herself, at any given moment, from some part of the house. Guthrie acknowledges the difficulty. Reflecting upon the physical configuration of the Elizabethan theatre, he is 'forced' to conclude that 'the soliloquies must have been spoken by the actor either on the move, or rotating on his own axis'.[34] But this has serious implications for 'To be or not to be', which even Guthrie believes 'demands repose and not movement'.

Guthrie attempts to solve the problem pragmatically, recounting an experiment whereby he delivered the speech 'rotating slowly on my own axis'. The challenge was to effect this movement, which the space demanded but for which the techniques of proscenium acting offered little preparation, without it appearing contrived or artificial, or, as he puts it, 'fussy or fidgety'. Success was achieved by means of a technical trick: 'to move the eyes first, then let the head follow, then let the shoulders slowly follow the head, and so on down to the feet'. The segmentation of the body in a process of phased rotation enables the illusion of availability to be at least partially maintained, an intricately plotted corporeal manoeuvre distending the self across an apparently unbroken arc of continuous direct address. From the vantage point of the spectator, what is offered is a seamless succession of bodily strata descending from head to toe, following the lead of the eye (or the I). But it is still a compromise, and the problem of masking is for Guthrie finally resolved through an appeal to 'the greater naturalness which follows if a group of actors can form circular patterns'; although, as conventions which are necessitated by a particular architectural form, perpetual motion and circular groupings are no more or less 'natural' than the architectonic blocking of the traditional picture frame. The abolition of the proscenium arch, and the encirclement of actors by audience, had been conceived in the spirit of egalitarianism and democratic inclusiveness; it now seemed that Guthrie and Moisewitsch had created the conditions for a physically literal state of perpetual revolution.

Guthrie's general reflections upon the theatrical figuration of the relations between space, movement and thought yield further riches when we consider that, on the differentiated Festival stage (and on its cousin in Minneapolis), the rules of motion and stillness are very much determined by where you actually are. Strictly speaking, the principle of rotation applies most fully when the speaker occupies the *platea* area of the main platform.[35] But the division of the stage between the platform and the pillared area beneath the balcony, which (roughly corresponding to an 'inner stage' model of the

Elizabethan playhouse) produces a partially enclosed *locus* space in which the performer *is* visible and available to the entire auditorium, consequently demarcates a region within which repose is possible, desirable, and perhaps even mandatory. Effectively, this semi-interior (and, relatively speaking, semi-illusionistic) space is the realm of secure interiority: it is the frame within which thought may be articulated through speech as opposed to the arena in which it is mapped through bodily movement. The performance of thought is subtly, but crucially, different in the two areas. The dialogic interplay between antiquity and modernity is crucial: what is also striking about this iconography of atrium and galleries (and it retained this quality after the 1962 alterations) is that its creation of a framed space of contemplation mimics the spatial practice of the medieval cloister. The referencing of Byzantine ecclesiastical architecture fashioned a secular corollary of what Mary Carruthers, in her study of the relations between spatial practice and cognition in the medieval period, *The Craft of Thought*, calls 'the pre-eminent space of meditational memory work ... whose shapes provided particularly effective devices for reading'.[36] Coincidentally, the triangular arrangement of the pillars also happened to reproduce the trinitarian form, represented, for example, by the abbey at St-Riquer, built 'in the shape of an obtuse triangle, each of its points marked by a church'; Carruthers quotes the abbot to the effect that the faithful 'should confess, venerate, *cultivate in their minds*, and firmly believe in the holy and inseparable Trinity'.[37] Since the cultivation of ritual belief was, for Guthrie, one of the fundamental tasks of the Festival stage, the precedent seems entirely apposite. But, in the first instance, the visitors to this new site of pilgrimage needed to learn how to read it.

III

In view of the above, and in the light of the ground covered in Chapter 3, it would have been highly convenient for the current discussion had *Hamlet* been the opening production of the Stratford Festival. In the early stages of the project this was, in fact, Guthrie's intention. In September 1952 he wrote to Alec Guinness suggesting a combination of *Hamlet* and 'something in bold contrast': *Measure for Measure*, say ('but only if there's a really luscious lady around for Isabella'[38]). But, as Tom Patterson later recorded, this proposal was the source of what nearly proved to be a disastrous rift between the actor and the director, since it revived the sore subject of their poorly-received 1938 Old

Vic production, and Guthrie only just succeeded in persuading Guinness from pulling out of the venture.[39] When Guthrie repeated the Stratford venture at Minneapolis a decade later, *Hamlet* was the premiere production.[40] Director and actor settled instead upon *Richard III* and *All's Well that Ends Well*, and it is to the second of these that I now wish to turn. Guthrie suggested that the unfamiliarity of the play (which had never been staged on the American continent and was still seen only rarely in London) provided some potentially useful ground upon which the delicate intercultural and professional negotiations between experienced British leading actors and a relatively inexperienced Canadian supporting cast might take place: 'it would make for a better team-feeling between the British and Canadian actors, if one of the two plays were as new to us as to them'.[41] However, given that the play's unfamiliarity was not unconnected with a subject matter which many Shakespeareans had found deeply distasteful, the choice of this play seems highly appropriate to a set of circumstances whose sexual dimensions have already been identified.

In one way, the simultaneous rediscovery of *All's Well* and non-illusionist staging at Stratford offers itself to be read as a demonstration of a quasi-Foucauldian scheme of repression and liberation: Guthrie's production liberated the play which had been closeted and repressed by Victorian prudery, in a dynamic movement from shame and concealment to frankness, openness and visibility.[42] This is the narrative of J.L. Styan's stage history of *All's Well*, which affirms that the play's 'controversial content and ... unusual style' are 'mutually dependent': as the forerunner of a movement which restored the play to what is envisaged as, in a multiple sense, a 'more open stage', Guthrie's production 'opened up the play'.[43] Evidence is not hard to come by of Victorian and early twentieth century unease over the play's content, and, more particularly, over what the editor of the Oxford edition calls '[Helena's] appropriation of the male role as sexual aggressor'.[44] It is not surprising to find F.S. Boas complaining in 1896 that the play deals with 'an abnormal relation' which is only just 'prevented from becoming repulsive' by 'being elevated almost into the tragic sphere', or John Masefield in 1911 describing the bed-trick as 'underhand' and Helena as 'a woman who practices a borrowed art, not for art's sake, nor for charity, but, woman fashion, for a selfish end'.[45] As the overtly moralising scholarship of the nineteenth century was supplemented by a renewed interest in dramatic and stage conventions, feminine guile became part of a comprehensive network of linked indiscretions and malpractices in content, style, tone and form; problematic sexuality became indissoluble from an equally fraught theatricality. Writing in 1929, the editor of the New Shakespeare edition was particularly candid about why the play was not to be trusted. Concluding his introduction, Sir Arthur Quiller-Couch remarked that, like *Measure for Measure* the play left him 'with something of a nasty taste in the mouth'.

All's Well's failure to adhere to decent standards was matched by an even more fundamental (and related) failure of realism, in that it had 'no atmosphere save that of the stage; as most of its *dramatis personae* have none but a stage existence. It is a thing "of the boards" ... no true drama can belong to the boards'. Overt, excessive theatricality is a matter of groundless, meretricious trickery, and as such is implicitly equated in Q's account with the machinations of a dangerously duplic-itous female sexuality that results not only in a shabby bed-trick but, in Helena, 'the modern young woman familiar to us in modern dramas and novels; a heroine of the pushing, calculating sort, that knows its [sic] own mind and will get its own way to its own ends without convenient scruple'.[46] Guthrie's own attitude to the play's treatment of sexuality might be deduced from his attack (in the volume issued to commemorate the second Stratford Festival) upon those 'who allow themselves to be worked into a high state of moral indignation over the supposed impropriety of what conflicts with their own standards not of moral but merely of conventional behaviour'. This is followed by a forthright condemnation of 'moral McCarthyism', which he char-acterises as 'the most illiberal and vicious thinking and action in the name of purity and virtue'.[47]

Within the context of a pairing of *All's Well* with *Richard III* designed to counterpoint the modernity of the one with the medievalism of the other, setting tragedy against comedy, the known against the unfa-miliar, a male-dominated against a female-centred play, Guthrie's production was an attempt to negotiate the theatrical reputation of *All's Well* within the framework of an abbreviated post-Victorian history of sexuality, conceived as an uncertain movement from repres-sion to liberalisation and enlightenment. In the absence of illusionist *mise-en-scène*, costume was the key factor in suggesting this scheme. By contrast to the elaborate period costumes of *Richard III*, those for *All's Well* were nearly unanimously described as 'modern dress'. In actual-ity, the costuming followed a common variant of modern dress which Guthrie had employed for his 1938 *Hamlet* (and which would recur in his Old Vic *Troilus and Cressida* in 1956), which was to situate the action in the fictitious late nineteenth-century middle-European social world popularly known as 'Ruritania'. Originally coined by Anthony Hope in 1894 as the setting for *The Prisoner of Zenda*, and imagined both as a place of romantic intrigue and as a culture locked in the arcane rituals of its past, the term had survived in the lexicon as a synonym for the comically self-important but politically impotent nation-state. As a setting for Shakespeare, this doubly distanced version of the late Victorian epoch reconciles potential tensions between text and *mise-en-scène* by inhabiting past and present: modern enough to establish a direct connection between character and spectator, but archaic enough to contain those elements of belief and social behaviour which would jar with a more immediately contemporary setting. For *All's Well* (with the exception of the war scenes, which adopted the uniforms of the Eighth Army of the desert campaign during the Second World War), Ruritania took the shape of a court populated by young nobles sporting monocles and clad either in stiff shirts and tails or in baroque regimental uniforms, ladies in voluminous ballgowns, and tight-trousered flunkies in tunics. Culturally and geographically, the world of this production was a hybrid, composed, as Styan read it, of 'the *fin de siècle* of Edwardian England, the Kaiser's Germany and *Merry Widow* Paris'.[48] Indeed, the primary referents were dramatic and theatrical. Described by the *Ohio Intelligencer* (11 July 1953) as 'a sophisticated drawing room comedy in stylised modern dress', and by the *Detroit Times* (15 July), less favourably, as a 'heavy-handed compromise between a bedroom farce and a royal comedy of manners', the production was likened to Wilde, Ibsen, and, most of all, 'in the high grace of movement and the exchange of polite barbs' (*London Evening Press*, 15 July), Shaw. If the periodisation paradoxically invoked a naturalistic dramaturgy which the stage itself was designed to transcend, the eclecticism was further compounded by the score, which, according to one, 'strangely alterna[ted] between Sixteenth Century and gently dissonant modernism, neither style seeming to fit the costumes'.[49]

For Styan, the composite achieved the compromise between modernity and history that was also the ultimate rationale of the stage itself, in that the period setting 'was not so modern as to deny the play its timelessness, and just modern enough to take it out of the category of a costume piece'.[50] It also suited the Old World/New World dynamics of the production's situation, in that it suggested a Euro-Canadian axis connecting the past, present and a future which, as I shall indicate below, might be imagined as female. In the light of the play's content and cultural history, however, I want to speculate upon how this *fort-*

da game with history (then-now, then-now) generates further resonances. In the first volume of *The History of Sexuality*, anticipating the 'repressive hypothesis' which he is subsequently to demolish, Foucault offers the resonant phrase 'We "Other Victorians"' as a metaphor for the twentieth-century 'liberated' condition of sexual identity.[51] Invoking Steven Marcus's study of nineteenth-century pornography and sexual behaviour,[52] Foucault wryly repositions the modern sexual subject within the shadowy realms of prohibition from which he (it is usually he) has more recently been released, indicating that we may well imagine ourselves (personally, or as a culture) as simultaneously still 'Victorian' in our struggle with repression, free of inhibition and guilt but kin to the pornographically active 'others' that in imagination and practice contradicted the public façade of Victorian sexuality.

Rather than attempting to trace Foucault's argument that the rhetoric of sexual openness (defined in binary opposition to a discredited epoch of perverse and hypocritical denial) is a ruse of power, not a route to liberation, I wish simply to suggest that the Victorianisation of the play in order to render it 'modern' is a tactic which to a certain extent replicates the claims of 'liberated' sex to define itself against a spectre of repression which it disavows but secretly needs. In general, in responding to costume drama, the spectator is invited to imagine a convergence between a real, present body, that of the performer, and (at least) two others: the Shakespearean persona and its period doppelganger. If, according to common sense ideology, Shakespeare's characters are timeless and bodies and sex have no history (other than in the epochal emergence and disappearance of the mechanisms of repression), the alliance of actor and role will be perceived to be a seamless one: underneath the clothes, s/he is just like me. But the distancing effect of period dress compromises any too-easy identification by maintaining the visibility of difference, in that the clothes themselves signify otherness: s/he is not like me. This operates at the level of style, obviously, in the visual shorthand that allows doublet and hose, knee breeches, frock-coats and crinolines their various functions as markers of period, sensibility, rank and social class; more significantly, for the current discussion, different types of period costume generate their own distinct codes of posture, movement and gesture. In short, as Foucault asserts in another context, 'it is always the body that is at issue – the body and its forces, their utility and their docility, their distribution and their submission'.[53] The ensemble of bodily practices that is shaped by the conventions of period costume may be a more subtle and delicate index of historical difference than the clothes themselves, but is perhaps ultimately an even more suggestive one. In that costume curtails or restricts certain bodily possibilities and determines or enables others, it may be said to operate within the total economy of the Shakespearean theatrical event as a disciplinary mechanism in the sense described by Foucault: in the interests of verisimilitude, its positioning of the body operates within a larger field of power relations which 'invest it, mark it, train it, torture it, force it to carry out tasks, to perform ceremonies, to emit signs'.[54] In this instance, the bodies of the performers simultaneously inhabited and resisted a regime in which stiffness, tight buttons and ramrod posture labelled sex as a guilty secret.

This might have been the impression had the play been envisaged in these terms within a conventional picture-frame stage, but the costuming was afforded a further dimension by the context, in that, as was seen earlier, one of the key principles of the Stratford Festival as a performance space was that it placed a premium upon freedom, ease and 'naturalness' of movement. In this production, the dialectic of repression and liberation was played out through the dynamic tension between the punitive restrictiveness signalled by the costuming and the speed and fluidity of Guthrie's choreography: reviewers praised a performance which 'flows without effort across the apron stage up and down the stairs, through the forest of columns and out of the ports in to the pit', and applauded as 'actors race from tunnels between seating sections on to the stage' and 'actors are as often in the space between the stage and the first row of seats' (*New York Times*, 16 July; *Hamilton Spectator*, 16 July). These were the familiar hallmarks of Guthrie's work, aiming as much to demonstrate the flexibility of the space as to invigorate the play. An examination of the production promptbook reveals something more: it was in its orchestration of space and movement that the relations between sex, gender and theatricality were most fully elaborated.[55] An immediate difference was evident between the masculine blocking of *Richard III* and that of *All's Well*: whereas the one displayed 'solid, colourful masses of pageantry and solemn impressive processions', the other complemented the 'graceful, slender columns' of the stage with 'graceful, weaving ballet-like movements with elegant groupings', wherein 'the costumes of the ladies give the comedy a bewitching, never a bewildering, note of variety' (*Montreal Star*, 18 July).

At the centre was Irene Worth's Helena, a figure described as 'enchanting' (*Boston Herald*, 2 August), a 'strong-willed young lady' who 'could almost have been devised by Bernard Shaw' (*New York*

Herald Tribune, 16 July), and generally invested with the best qualities of the stage itself: she was 'demure, vivacious, light-hearted and pliant', a mixture of 'loveliness, devotion, ceremony and modest guile' (*New York Times*). As the *Herald-Tribune* concluded, aligning physical blocking with the thwarting and gratification of desire, 'only a cad would stand in the way of Miss Worth's getting exactly what she wants exactly when she wants it'. I suggest, simply, that Helena's authority was articulated in equally literal terms, in that it was her progress towards a confident command not only of herself and Bertram but, eventually, of the stage space as a whole that enabled the production to work through a series of thematic antitheses: sex versus death, youth versus age, duty versus desire, love versus militarism. Like *Richard III*, *All's Well* both offered a demonstration of the representational potentialities of the stage space and provided a lesson in how to read them; in both productions, spatial practices of movement and positioning were accented according to gender. In *Richard III* the King's rising and falling fortunes were exhibited through his fluctuating mastery of balcony and platform: opening the evening with one leg hooked arrogantly over the balcony, Alec Guinness's Richard ended it sprawled ignominiously across the steps linking the platform to the auditorium, a liminal and ambiguously-defined *platea* space 'between the stage and the first row of seats' (*Hamilton Spectator*). With the exception of set pieces such as Queen Margaret's aria and Richard's intimidation of Lady Anne, women were confined to the pillared area beneath the balcony as passive spectators of the violent action within the main stage platform, the arena of masculine prowess and achievement; although, according to Brooks Atkinson of the *New York Times* (and foreshadowing the later modifications of the stage) this meant that Moiseiwitsch's 'formalized setting seemed almost too self-conscious' and 'the actors hardly had room enough to play' (how typical of a female theatre designer to cramp the boys' style!).

In *All's Well*, the space was more open to contestation and, provisionally at least, female occupation. The contrast with *Richard III* was defined in the opening moments. In place of Guinness's bravura solo attack delivered, Hitler-style, from the balcony, the entry of Helena, Bertram and the Countess through the pillars beneath establishes this area as a zone of intimacy and domesticity: throughout, Roussillon is figured in terms of a gravitation of grouping and blocking around this upstage space. For the first part of the play, Helena's position within the drama is signalled through her tentative movements within the confines of the stage platform; Bertram, by contrast, almost immediately moves off the platform and down onto the steps as he announces his intention to 'attend his majesty's command' (I. i. 4–5). From the outset, a division is established between male and female rules of movement, entrances and exits, in that for the early part of the play only male characters are allowed access and exits through the auditorium, indicating an easy ownership of fictional and theatrical space. Parolles (Douglas Campbell, who was described as a 'leonine spiv' [*Toronto Star*, 15 July]), similarly, makes his first appearance descending the balcony steps, and underwrites the 'virginity' exchange with Helena (I. i. 112ff) with his swaggering command of the entire platform, before disappearing at a run through the upstage entrance. This display of energy cues Helena to make a decisive running move up the steps and onto the stage balcony for the statement of intent that will take her to the King of France's court, an explosive movement upwards articulating the leap of faith that is voiced in the declaration that 'the fated sky/Gives us free scope' (ll. 219–20). If her fixed purpose and Edmund-like assertion that 'Our remedies oft in ourselves do lie/Which we ascribe to heaven' momentarily links Helena with the pragmatic materialism of Richard himself, it is here refigured as a proto-feminist assertiveness and sexual energy which defines the balcony as a space of optimism, transformation and hope.

When Helena delivers her next big soliloquy, following her shattering rejection by Bertram, she is once more stranded forlornly, immobilised in the trap of the balcony pillars, as 'with the dark, poor thief', she'll 'steal away' (III. ii. 129), the balcony is occupied by the Duke of Florence presenting Bertram and Parolles with drum and colours, reappropriating the space as the scene of masculine bravado. The alternation continues as the balcony is successively used for Helena's seated, intimate dialogue with the Widow, and then as a hiding place for one of the conspirators during the ambush of Parolles (IV. i) – thus providing the opportunity for the first of the many spectacular leaps down from balcony to stage platform at Stratford. Next, in a perverse rearrangement of the traditional iconography of *Romeo and Juliet* into a scene of betrayal, the balcony becomes the location for Bertram's tryst with Diana (IV. ii). Counterpointing Helena's previous declaration of desire with his own anticipation of sexual conquest, 'a heaven on earth I have won by wooing thee' (l. 66), Bertram inverts the pattern of her ascent, through a sweeping run down the stairs, across the platform, and through the auditorium via the left ramp. But when Diana next appears, once more on the balcony, it is with Helena and the Widow: the trick is accomplished, and Bertram's game is up. Reclaimed as the space of the female, the balcony is also now the position from which is made the play's first promise of closure: 'All's well that ends well; still fine's the crown./Whate'er the course, the end is the renown' (IV. v. 35–6).

Helena's exit from this scene is via a ramp through the audience, a move which at this stage in the action she seems naturally entitled to carry out (she is the only woman in the play to be awarded this privilege). As I indicated earlier, however, this freedom of movement has been acquired incrementally, in a graphic demonstration of Helena's movement through and beyond a predefined and circumscribed sexual and domestic role. From the very first moments of the play, the men are afforded an athletic mobility which gives them the freedom of the steps between platform and audience; thus the mass entry of the court of the King of France in the second scene brings with it a confident occupation of every level of the performance space by the stratified ranks of male figures. Helena's first move onto the steps, which literally takes her outside of herself for the first time, is prompted by the Countess's challenge to her to confess her passion for Bertram, and by her inadvertent bodily disclosure of desire:

> Therefore tell me true,
> But tell me then 'tis so – for look, thy cheeks
> Confess it t'one to th'other, and thine eyes
> See it so grossly shown in thy behaviours
> That in their kind they speak it.
>
> (I. iii. 175–9)

At the end of the scene she retreats with the Countess under the balcony and into the house. When she next appears, however, it is in her guise as potential healer of the King, and she makes her entrance through the auditorium stage right and onto the steps (symmetrically, she makes a second decisive entry and identity shift from the auditorium up the left ramp in III. v, when she appears disguised as a pilgrim). If this is to set in motion the complex dance of advance and retreat, evasion, ambush and confrontation that is the narrative of her pursuit of Bertram (described by one reviewer as 'the man Helena ... chases throughout the play and eventually catches' [*Ottawa Evening Journal*, 15 July]), it also introduces a further important element: Helena's relationship with the King.

Here we may focus upon *All's Well*'s single most important prop: the

bathchair to which Alec Guinness's King was confined until his miraculous cure at Helena's hands. Described as 'stream-lined, latticed and
lavish all at once' (*Montreal Herald*, 20 July), the bathchair's usefulness
as a means of bridging the divisions between modern and early
modern was clear enough, in that it was simultaneously a realistic
device, a version of a property throne, and a highly portable metonym
of the King's sickness; moreover, it signified a more general sense of
stultified gentility and aged and reactionary impotence (there were
further associations: with his neatly trimmed white beard, the chair-
bound Guinness also reminded some critics of Monty Wolley in *The
Man Who Came to Dinner*). In practical terms, the use of the bathchair
meant that the King, like the Helena who cures him, is trapped upon
the stage platform (which had to be overlaid with a ramp in order to
smooth the bathchair's access; the alternative might have been an
undignified and potentially farcical bumping from level to level, or
even worse, a disastrous *Battleship Potemkin*-style tumble down the
steps). As I have already indicated with regard to the placing of Helena,
such stage positioning has a thematic and metatheatrical dimension:
the King in his sickness is stuck within the relatively illusionistic *locus*
space of the platform, and confined, moreover, to what might seem
like a rather absurd relic of representational literalism that can only
serve to block and interrupt the free flow of movement across the
stage.

As the King and Helena face each other for the first time, the one
parked centre stage, the other poised on the threshold of the platform,
so do the principal thematic antitheses of the production: male and
female, youth and age, authority and integrity, and, above all, the
paralysis of illusionism and the mobility of the open stage. Until this
point the King has been wheeled around by lackeys as the court
arranges itself in static, hierarchical patterns around him. Alone with
Helena, he begins to maneouvre the chair by himself; throughout their
intense and sexually-charged dialogue, the increasingly confident
heroine circumnavigates the platform, and the King is compelled to
rotate on his axis in order to follow. When the King asks 'Within what
space/ Hop'st thou my cure?' (II. i. 157–8), the implicit answer is the
space of the stage, the performance, itself: Helena's healing art is to
release the theatrical energy that the residual presence of illusionism
continues to keep in check. At the end of the scene, the King surrenders, meekly acquiescing to Helena wheeling him upstage and through
the central pillars; there is a brief interval of a minute and a half (the
dialogue between Clown and Countess [II. ii.] having been cut), and a

brief dialogue between Parolles and Lafeu. Suddenly, in a classsic Guthrie moment, the stage swirls into life, with the massed entry of the court from all directions and at all levels, watching, spellbound, the spectacular vision of the King and Helena, dancing; at the end of the dance, Helena sinks to the floor in a low curtsy and her white ball-gown spreads out a huge water lily.[56]

The applause that erupts from every corner of the stage is readable, just, as located within the fiction of the play (the court acknowledges the King's cure and marvels at his newfound agility), but there is more to it than that. However illusory the flight from illusionism was subsequently to prove, and however compromised by its implication within the nostalgia industry the Stratford Festival was to remain, it is a rare vision of optimism and hope, and a testament to performance's capacity to escape the disciplinary strictures of text, production and stage. In a gesture that exceeds and encompasses the performance itself, the applause of the cast eagerly doubles and anticipates the response both of the spectators within the tent (who, like the King, are at the end of the play brought to their feet), and of the wider world beyond, incorporating not only the polite approval of the cognoscenti but also the acclaim of the farming journalist and his friend who 'hates Shakespeare' – and poising the King's exploratory footwork at the threshold of a new, and as yet unrealised, era of theatrical health, happiness and liberty.

Part III
The Strange Death of Shakespeare's England

5
Seeing through Shakespeare

I

Like most of Edward Bond's plays, *Bingo* has had a mixed reception from its critics. First staged in 1973, Bond's dramatisation of the last days of Shakespeare (subtitled *Scenes of Money and Death*) has since been hailed as 'theatre-poetry of the highest order' and, together with *Lear* (1971) and *The Fool* (1976), acclaimed as part of 'the most potent series in postwar British drama'.[1] Biographical dramas of Shakespeare tend to come and go, but this one has enjoyed greater longevity than most; it has been afforded more professional revivals in the British theatre than any of Bond's more recent plays. *Bingo* was first staged at the Northcott Theatre, Exeter in November 1973, and transferred to the Royal Court in August 1974; with John Gielgud in the role of Shakespeare, the production broke all previous box-office records at the Court. The play was revived at Stratford-upon-Avon at the end of 1976, at the RSC's Other Place, and transferred to the RSC's Warehouse in London in 1977. It was seen as part of a BBC Television Theatre Night season in 1990; and was revived again by the RSC for its 1995 small-scale regional tour, paired with *The Tempest*. Closer inspection of this performance history reveals that the relatively high profile of this play is not a straightforward index of its popularity; indeed, the praise that *Bingo* has attracted has been more than balanced by negative and dismissive judgements. On its Royal Court showing, for example, it was hailed by the *Guardian* (15 August 1974) as 'magnificent' and dismissed by the *Sunday Telegraph* (18 August 1974) as 'boring and banal'; a damning review in *Plays and Players* (September 1974), which concluded that the play was 'monumentally and deliberately degrading', provoked a furious response in the magazine's letters column.

Over twenty years later, the response to the 1995 RSC production showed that the play retained its potential to divide critics: it was, on the one hand, 'smugly absurd' (*Evening Standard*, 3 July), and, on the other, 'a fascinating work' (*Guardian*, 1 July). Such differences are the stock in trade of Bond criticism, but this play's particular capacity for controversy is, largely, an effect of the presence of Shakespeare as a focus for cultural and political preoccupations which are more pressing and immediate than its ostensible subject-matter might suggest. The cultural history mapped here begins against the background of the sudden and spectacular collapse of the postwar settlement, a bipartisan consensus characterised by a Keynesian commitment to full employment and the welfare state; continues through the perceived 'betrayals' of the Labour government of the 1970s and through the formation of the new, specifically anti-consensual project of Thatcherism; and ends amidst the disintegration of that project in the 1990s. Along the way, the play's use of Shakespeare as a focal point makes it an uncannily sensitive register of the social, cultural and political tensions of the period.

In the context of a tradition of Shakespearean biographical fiction (stretching from Shaw's *Dark Lady of the Sonnets* in 1910 to the 1998 *Shakespeare in Love* and beyond) that generally demonstrates more interest in erotic escapades than property dealings, *Bingo* was from the outset destined for controversy, particularly since the play's claim that Shakespeare killed himself is hardly likely to endear itself to bardolators.[2] In his introduction to the play, Bond establishes the relation of his fiction to historical fact, citing his source as E.K. Chambers's *William Shakespeare*, and noting that the Welcombe enclosures (which are the central focus of the narrative) have largely been ignored in accounts of Shakespearean biographies.[3] At one level, then, Bond offers a documentary basis for his account of the events which lead to Shakespeare's suicide, an account which he suggests is deductive rather than speculative: 'the consequences that follow in the play follow from the facts, they're not polemical inventions. Of course, I can't insist that my description of Shakespeare's death is true ... I can only put the various things together and say what probably happened'. Bond points out that he has compressed and concentrated biographical fact 'for dramatic convenience' (p. vi), omitting Shakespeare's other daughter, Susanna, combining the historical roles of several landowners into the figure of Combe, and changing the date of the burning of the Globe from 1613 to 1616. Moreover, Bond concedes that he is 'not really interested in Shakespeare's true biography in the way a historian might be. Part of the play is about the relationship between any writer and his society.' In terms of Bond's own ethical project as a writer, the use of Shakespeare in order to address more general questions of the responsibilities of the political dramatist makes perfect sense, but the problem (as Bond is well aware) is that Shakespeare simply is not 'any writer', but an immense repository of cultural power; indeed, this is the point of using him.

It is in this sense that the play is about much more than the death of the Bard, and the following sections are concerned with tracing the particular significances that Shakespeare's demise has acquired in different institutional and theatrical circumstances. But there is another aspect of the play briefly to be considered: its oblique relevance to its moment of writing. In his introduction to the play, Bond discusses the nature of aggression:

> How can an American drop bombs on peasants in a jungle if, as I said, a sense of human values is part of his nature? It takes a lot of effort, years of false education and lies, indignity, shabby poverty, economic insecurity – or the insecurity of dishonest privilege – before men will do that ... So he drops bombs because he believes that if the peasant ever rowed a canoe across the Pacific and drove an ox cart over America till he came to his garden, he'd steal his vegetables and rape his grandmother – history proves it.[4]

This is one of those rare moments when the specifics of contemporary history intrude into Bond's discursive writing. It has been observed that Bond's prefaces, like Shaw's, are often tangential to the plays themselves, and at first sight this passage is only tenuously connected with the subject-matter of *Bingo*. In actuality it identifies the immediate concerns underpinning the play. In the year in which the play was written, the United States Congress ordered an end to bombing in Cambodia, following years of organised opposition to the Vietnam War, which had acted as a central, unifying issue in the politics of the left. What had become clear was that 'the world's greatest superpower was defeated by a poor but resolutely organised small nation fighting for self-determination':[5] the full might of the military-industrial complex was no match for a dispersed but disciplined rural army. In *Bingo* this is reworked as the struggle between the centralising, technocratic nascent capitalism represented by Combe and the militant peasantry represented by Joan, Jerome and the Son. But if this conclusion to the war offered cause for optimism on the left, it also brought a realisation that the years of protest and opposition on the home front had contributed rather less to the American defeat than might have been hoped. When Bond's Shakespeare repeatedly asks 'was anything done?', he might well be voicing what has been identified as the 'collective guilt on behalf of the left liberal community in the light of its failure to prevent or stop the war'.[6]

If the Vietnam War is one buried strand of the play, it is intertwined with another which runs through much of Bond's work, particularly during the 1970s: a profound aversion to the particularly American brand of capitalism. In conversation with Howard Davies, the director of the 1976 RSC production of *Bingo*, Bond commented upon the character of the Son: 'he, I think, accepts a series of false values, false beliefs, false attitudes. I think he lies. And you've got to place these people in the historical context: it's absolutely true that these groups of people did go off and founded America. And what good was that? I was writing when there was all this fuss about Nixon.'[7] As Bond observes, the play was written in the shadow of Watergate; the end of the Son's self-serving utopia ('I'll go away – where there's still space ... Us'll take nowt bar bible an' plough' [*Bingo*, p. 50]) is military adventurism and economic imperialism, and the corruption and betrayal of bourgeois democracy. At the time of *Bingo*, resistance to the colonising force of American culture could take the form of a reclaiming of national identity by the left; in an interview published in 1975, Bond declared that he was 'as English as Elgar'[8]; while *Bingo* sets the American values of the Son against the Englishness of Shakespeare. As Bond stresses, Shakespeare retains a certain personal and moral integrity which the Son lacks: 'Shakespeare acts fraudulently but he doesn't deceive himself mentally, he judges himself'.[9] Moreover, he has insisted, Shakespeare's suicide is not an act of despair, although it has repeatedly been interpreted as such, but a rational response to seemingly intractable social contradictions. The extent to which critics and audiences were willing or able to register this lesson will be evident from the account of the play in production that follows.

II

The Northcott Theatre is situated at the heart of the campus of Exeter University, occupying a commanding position overlooking Dartmoor. For first-night reviewers descending from the capital in the middle of November, it may well have appeared an appropriately remote and desolate setting for the premiere of Bond's play; especially since, in the midst of the fuel crisis, the fuel-preserving 50 mph speed limit then in force would have extended the normally three-hour trip from London into a heroic trek of epic proportions. The major advantage of the Northcott stage was its considerable size: its open, semi-circular stage with its fifty-foot stage opening, according to the designer, Hayden Griffin, meant that 'for the distancing effects he requires ... you have no trouble placing one actor twenty-five feet away from another'; previous plays at the Royal Court had suffered as a result of the restricted stage space. Bond had a precise sense of the production's visual aesthetic: 'he wanted an image similar to those old varnish-encrusted paintings of Elizabethan England with just a few spots of light and these two old men, so that the whole thing was like a sculpture in space'.[10] This period-minimalist feel worked for a number of reviewers, who variously commended the design as 'modest' (*New Statesman*, 23 November 1973), 'simple, straightforward' (*Financial Times*, 19 November) and 'stark yet supremely telling' (*Stage and Television Today*, 22 November). The staging conformed to the practice established at the Royal Court by William Gaskill (whom Howell had assisted), and was characterised by selectiveness, clarity and simplicity of detail. The stage space was enclosed on three sides by a network of suspended rope (three and a half miles of it, according to the Northcott's press release), prompting the *New Statesman*'s Benedict Nightingale to comment that it located the action 'within what appears to be a forest of violin-strings or the beginning of some massive game of cat's cradle'. The stage was otherwise mainly empty, with sparing use of props or items of scenery creating an emblematic focus for each scene: a hedge and bench for the garden of New Place, the isolated figure of the executed vagrant woman on a wooden gibbet, a background fire for the drinking session with Ben Jonson. The result was a production particularly strong on stark, emblematic visual images, as Michael Anderson wrote in *Plays and Players* (January 1974):

> One of the central scenes in *Bingo* has the stage unfurnished except for a vast white ground cloth, sloping up to a wooden stake on which a girl's mutilated corpse is nailed. A brooding, drunken wanderer lurches into this wintry landscape; black-clad, anonymous figures scurry furtively across; a simpleton (doomed to arbitrary death later in the scene) scoops up snow and gleefully pelts his master ... the disjointed incidents played out against the harsh, uncluttered snowscape form a telling image of Edward Bond's marrow-chilling world-view.

The scene which proved to be the most challenging (which in this account has been conflated with the earlier scene of the gibbeting), as it has been in subsequent productions of the play, was Scene V, which depicts Shakespeare wandering drunkenly in the snow, half-heartedly joining in a snowball fight with the Old Man, and then lapsing into introspective reverie as the Old Man is shot upstage. The major problem is posed by the shadowy running figures (who, it turns out, are sabotaging the enclosure ditches) that appear upstage of the drunk Shakespeare. Malcolm Hay and Philip Roberts record that, even on such a large stage, Howell 'spent three days rehearsing the running figures, and still found it technically difficult'.[11] The 'technical' difficulty is that of creating and maintaining an appropriate distance between the running figures and Shakespeare that will establish a clear double focus, balancing the urgency of their situation (they are running for their lives from armed men) with Shakespeare's self-absorbed obliviousness to it. The image of violence taking place behind Shakespeare's back is central to the play; here, it is particularly appropriate to think of the relation between foregrounded and background figures as one of close-up and long-shot, and one that is not easy even for a stage as large as the Northcott's to accommodate. The difficulty is not just 'technical': the questions of placement, proximity and distance that arise in the staging of this scene are also matters of political perspective and positioning. If, as I suggested at the outset, the violence of the Vietnam War underpins this play, then it is, for the European spectator, *mediated* violence: here, as if in a soundless television image, the running figures engage in obscure acts of violence at the limit of vision, insubstantial yet also desperately close. As Bond put it in his response to Harold Hobson's *Sunday Times* review (which I shall return to below), the problem becomes one of maintaining a sense of reality and authenticity, as the mundane collapses into the apocalyptic, and reported atrocities become empty images or special effects, simply depthless surfaces: 'starving people are only two-dimensional celluloid cut-outs, cries are deadened on tape-machines, H-bomb silos are hidden or look (probably) like supermarkets'.[12]

The dynamics of the real and the fake find their focus in the physical embodiment of Shakespeare on stage; the visual, as well as narrative and thematic, centre of the play is the figure of the writer himself. If the impact of the play partly stems from its intertextual relations with the genres of Shakespearean biography, in performance it is more fully implicated within the visual culture of authorial representation; in this respect, the business of 'looking at Shakespeare' is, in a remarkably literal sense, of critical importance. At Exeter, Shakespeare was played by Bob Peck: equipped with a bald wig and doublet, he was made up to evoke the familiar features of Shakespeare, drawing upon the familiar repertoire of images of Shakespeare within general circulation, in particular the Droeshout and Chandos portraits, and the bust at the Holy Trinity Church in Stratford. As Graham Holderness and Bryan Loughrey have pointed out, the currency of this 'insistently reproduced icon' is based 'on the cachet of high culture ... combined with instant recognisability', whereby the 'high, balding dome' is an 'almost totemic guarantor of the author's unique genius'; moreover, as 'an image that permeates the fabric and texture of every-day common life', Shakespeare's face is 'a symbol, pre-eminently, of British national culture'.[13] At a personal as well as a cultural level, the function of Shakespeare's image as a devotional icon is to provide a focus for contemplation, an opportunity to organise potentially inchoate Shakespearean thoughts and feelings: looking upon his picture, we are nonetheless thinking about his work. I suggest that when that picture goes live, as in *Bingo*, its potency resides in the mobilisation of memories, dreams and hopes of Shakespearean perfor-mance; watching 'Shakespeare', we are indirectly faced with our own experiences of watching Shakespeare.

One of *Bingo*'s basic stratagems is to reframe the visual image of Shakespeare within contexts which problematise its traditional conno-tations. Shakespeare is repeatedly seen clutching pieces of paper: they are not the traces of literary endeavour but legal and financial docu-ments. He sits before a backdrop of casual exploitation, insurrectionary plotting, executions and arbitrary death. Rather than equipping his Shakespeare with the saving eloquence of his own dramaturgy, Bond assigns him to long periods of silence, interrupted by gnomic or brusquely instrumental verbal interventions. For the Northcott reviewers, the cumulative effect was a worrying discontinu-ity between actorly presence, image and referent, as Bond's text and Peck's portrayal undercut the auratic power of the traditional figure. Thus *Stage and Television Today* reported that Peck 'look[ed] very like the traditional Droeshout portrait' but was 'monosyllabic'; while the *Observer* (2 December 1973) saw 'the traditional egghead' but 'the shell ... is hollow'. According to *The Times* (15 November 1973), Peck's Shakespeare had 'rat-like features surmounted by a balding dome'. Benedict Nightingale offered the most detailed account:

Except for some Victorians, who saw it as the face of self-help rewarded, everyone has been appalled by the stolid, pompous figure that juts out of the wall just above Shakespeare's tomb. Could this 'self-satisfied pork butcher', as Dover Wilson dubbed the monument, really be the earthly likeness of the Immortal Bard? ... Actually, Bob Peck's Shakespeare is less like the monster in the Holy Trinity than the Droeshout engraving, and less like that than some wispy, ferrety Warwickshire poacher, the victim of too much rain and too many gamekeepers.

As Shakespeare slips off the pedestal and down the social scale, he is subjected to a process of degradation that transforms him from bourgeois cultural champion to an isolated, marginalised and victimised outsider. Other reviews concurred: Peck appeared 'lugubrious' (*The Times*), 'morose and haunted' (*Observer*), 'spiritually exhausted ... tired, laconic' (*Financial Times*), 'a disillusioned, morose, brooding figure' (*Stage and Television Today*), 'a poet reduced for the most part to a linguistic inadequacy as complete as Len's in *Saved*' (*Plays and Players*).

That this was at odds with the image of Shakespeare as the supremely articulate, dignified and humane artist is obvious; what is more striking is the extent to which these responses project a desperation which the play strenuously contests. The process of projection is as much cultural and political as it is personal; in effect, these readings of Shakespeare's character and physiognomy epitomise a more general process whereby the critics, without acknowledging it, mapped onto the play concerns which were more to do with the contemporary political scene than with the production itself. If the journey to the Northcott in the depths of the winter of 1973 might have evoked feelings of bleakness and desolation, these would have merely reproduced a more pervasive sense of unease. The speed-limiting fuel crisis, which had been triggered by the Egypt-Israel War in October, the subsequent quadrupling of oil prices by the Arab States, and a sudden worldwide rise in commodity prices, was only the latest of a series of economic and political calamities. The 1970s saw an intensification of the long-running and acrimonious saga of the United Kingdom's relations with the European Economic Community; both before and after entry into the community in 1973, the survival of national sovereignty remained a divisive key issue. Since 1970, the Conservative government under the leadership of Edward Heath had pursued a political programme which aimed to unleash the forces of the free market, reduce state spending, eliminate state subsidy to nationalised industries, and, via the Industrial Relations Act which came into force in 1972, to impose draconian limits on union organisation and industrial action. The results of this confrontational approach to industrial relations and economic policy were an escalation of union militancy and a rapid and, it seemed to many, potentially uncontrollable wage and price inflation. In fact, the fuel crisis was only the start of it. The day before *Bingo* opened, a State of Emergency had been declared; it was to be followed by power cuts, a three-day working week and eventually, in the General Election of February 1974, the removal of Heath's government. This was, in short, the period in which the postwar political culture of consensus in Britain, partly as a consequence of its own intrinsic instabilities and partly as a result of the global recession, suddenly and spectacularly disintegrated, when the compromises that had underpinned the existing welfare capitalist settlement reached the point of exhaustion.

Perhaps unsurprisingly in the circumstances, many reviewers attributed to the play, to Shakespeare, and to Bond, a bleakness and desperation which was perhaps more of a response to current anxieties about political and economic breakdown than to the play itself. The majority recorded that the play's picture of Shakespeare and of history was a harsh one, agreeing with *The Times* that it presented 'a time of disillusion, strife and suicide'; but a number of commentators went further. For Michael Anderson (*Plays and Players*), it was 'a magnificent cry of total despair'; while for Benedict Nightingale, the play was directly confrontational: 'How is it (we're to ask) that a man whom we worship for his humanity could have been so cruel? How can we, his descendants, bear to live in a society directly derived from it?' Moreover, Nightingale asserted, Bond's plays 'may be seen as the dramatic equivalents of those insistent Oxfam ads which thrust children with sparrow-legs and pigeon-bellies under our well-nourished noses. Each insists that we face the kind of realities that make us instinctively drop our eyes and change the conversation.' Whoever 'we' are (the general population of the capitalist west or the readership of the *New Statesman*), the sense is that the play has touched a raw nerve of middle-class impotence and guilt.

A rather different perspective was articulated by Harold Hobson in the *Sunday Times* (18 November). Hobson concluded that 'this is a play, memorably poetic and mysterious, in which the despair is total'. Although disagreeing with Bond's reading of Shakespeare (and of Shakespeare's death), Hobson argues that the play 'raises issues which are urgent in society, but especially so in such an institution as that in which *Bingo* has received its first performance, the University of Exeter'. This is the surprising, but nonetheless crucial, aspect of Hobson's reading of the play:

> *Bingo* puts on trial all those students and professors (and me, too) who watched it on Wednesday night, and perhaps without quite realising what they were doing, gave it so thunderous a reception. For it says unmistakably that the values for which Exeter University stands, and Oxford and Cambridge, and Keele, and Sussex, are wrong. Well, as I say, I do not agree with Mr Bond. I would not have the professors sacked, nor the grants of the students withdrawn. I believe it is as inadequate to judge society and civilisation solely by the number of miners who can afford television sets, or by the percentage of the disabled who are equipped with Jaguars, as it is to judge them solely by the architecture of Wadham, or the quality of Exeter University Library.

The 'unmistakable' message detected by Hobson was refuted by Bond in an article for the same newspaper a week later: 'Mr Hobson is wrong when he says I want to close universities. If they are places where the philosophy of the enlightenment is taught side by side with experiments on how to destroy the human race, then I think they should be changed.'[14] Nonetheless, the fact that Hobson feels that *Bingo* 'put on trial' not only himself but the whole university system, and the culture which is enshrined within and perpetuated by it, indicates the nature and extent of the anxiety that the play was capable of generating. Although Hobson's reading restates the basic binary opposition, traceable back to Matthew Arnold, between culture as the privileged repository of spiritual values and the anarchy of a materialist mass culture, and despite his sturdy defence of the consolations of art (which Hobson characterised in a follow-up article as 'an end in itself, like robust health or a warm and sunny summer's afternoon'[15]) there is a sense that 'society and civilisation' may be in even deeper trouble than he wants to admit. Hobson was wrong in one respect: subsequent history would prove that the new right, not the left, would be the ones to ensure the sacking of professors and the cutting of student grants; but he was right to identify (however inadvertently) the traditional university ethos with the culture of consensus that was about to come apart. At the very least, making jokes about miners with television sets at a time when that very group of workers was, against a background of growing public support, engaged in a course of industrial action that would lead in a few months to the collapse of a government, signals either breathtaking complacency or, as jokes will, genuine unease.

III

Nine months later, in August 1974, the play was seen again, again directed by Jane Howell, in a recast production, scaled down for the Royal Court stage. The transfer was not an entirely happy one, as Hayden Griffin recalled: 'Howell ... was nervous about the different company for the Court and we took the wrong decision in trying to recreate, on that little stage, the space we had in Exeter. I knew it was going to be a disaster at the second run-through.'[16] Although the reviewers did not seem to share Griffin's sense that the disparity of scale was disastrous, there is a discernable shift of emphasis in the general response, away from the strongly visual, image-centred readings of the Exeter production. For the most part, reviewers' comments on the staging of the Court production are sketchy. The *Financial Times* (15 August 1974) recorded that 'the designs are simple, showing no more than the minimum required, the clothes being of no particular period, half modern, half period countryman'; the *Educational Theatre Journal* briefly noted that the play was staged 'with minimal scenery and only the suggestion of Elizabethan dress'.[17] Whereas at Exeter the play had presented viewers with some memorably emblematic images, its visual iconography now attracted little comment.

The difference indicated a shift in the terms upon which the play was being read. The key factor was the casting of Sir John Gielgud as Shakespeare. The obvious risk was that the play would be reduced to a mere star vehicle: the production had shrunk, the central character expanded and, given the difficulties of scale discussed above, this could well have been deeply problematic. However, when it was suggested in a 1975 interview that 'Gielgud obtruded into the orchestration, a solo instrument too far forward', Bond proposed that this gave him an almost Brechtian quality: 'I don't mind star actors as long as they're good. And I don't mind the fact that one knows them because this, in a way, makes them serve the performance more objectively, almost in the sense of a waiter serving it you on a tray.'[18] Bond has also expressed his admiration for Gielgud's handling of language, and for his intellectual approach: 'when you listen to Gielgud ... you hear the brain and not just the voice'.[19] But it is, of course, as a voice that Gielgud has been largely identified in the English theatre; as the voice of a revered lyrical tradition of Shakespearean verse-speaking, but also, perhaps, as the voice of Shakespeare himself. As one of Gielgud's biographers puts it, he is a member of 'the English theatrical aristocracy' whose talent seems 'deliberately bred and not the result of an accident of birth. Few actors in the almost unbroken English tradition which has lasted over five hundred years can have had such a splendid pedigree.'[20] Or, as another admirer suggested, Gielgud's 'silver authority and the patrician tones' are part of a style which is 'bred of a natural elegance of mind'.[21]

To a substantial degree, the framework of expectations generated by the established Gielgud persona determined the initial terms upon which the Royal Court production was to be viewed. Both the pre-publicity and many of the reviews endorsed the appropriateness of the casting; thus, typically, Nicholas de Jongh wrote in the *Guardian* (6 February 1974) that Sir John would 'crown a lifetime of Shakespearean performances ... by taking the role of William Shakespeare', while the *Evening Standard*, a week before the opening night, acompanied a rehearsal photograph of Gielgud-as-Shakespeare with the comment that this 'Shakespearean actor extraordinary' was 'in a role for which he is a natural' (7 August). The casting seemed to promise that *Bingo* would confirm, rather than challenge, settled views of Shakespeare, an impression that would have been reinforced by some of the advance comments in the newspapers (based on the Royal Court press release). According to the *Guardian*, the play was 'a swansong work in which an old and grieving Shakespeare looks back over his life and grim times'; the *Daily Telegraph* (6 February) predicted that it would show Shakespeare/Gielgud 'reviewing his life's achievements'. Bearing in mind that Gielgud at that moment was completing a run as Prospero in *The Tempest* – the final National Theatre production at the Old Vic – the scene was set for a sentimental valedictory.

The consideration that the play itself confronts rather than confirms the expectations generated by this conjuncture did not impress some reviewers. J.C. Trewin combined a dismissive review of the play with praise for its star, concluding that 'to listen to [Gielgud] ... is to know the true authority of a most sensitive artist ... what *Bingo* would be like without Sir John, I cannot begin to imagine' (*The Lady*, 29 August). Elsewhere, however, the confrontation between the institutionalised Bard identified with Gielgud and the Shakespeare of *Bingo* provoked diverse responses. As in the reviews of the Exeter production, Shakespearean portraiture provided an obvious point of reference. For the *Guardian* (15 August), Gielgud's 'grey beard, sad eyes, domed head' made 'no attempt to embody the Droeshout engraving', a view countered by the *Financial Times*, which suggested that the 'short grey beard and moustache' gave 'an uncanny suggestion of Shakespeare, despite the evident difference in the features', by the *New York Times* (24 August) which considered that 'with a little tufted beard he even looks like Shakespeare', and by the *Evening Standard* (15 August): 'his high dome and neat beard measuring almost exactly our preconceptions of Shakespeare's facial features'. Evidently, looking like Shakespeare can operate at a deeper and more persuasive level than the merely iconographic: Sir John was a successful lookalike partly because his baldness was of an earned kind rather than a cheeky rubber prosthesis, but more importantly because for the best part of a century he effectively had been the voice and face of Shakespeare. According to J.C. Trewin, 'Sir John, with that incorrigible nobility and without worrying about any Droeshout or Janssen likeness, cannot help suggesting a man who is not Mr Bond's waxwork ... Rather, he is someone who could very well have written the plays' (*Illustrated London News*, October 1974). Gielgud simply inhabited a different order of authenticity to Peck, and accordingly decisively shifted the tone of the play; as *The Times* (15 August) concluded: 'Shakespeare was given a rat-like performance by Bob Peck, who left you in no doubt that property had always been his main goal. With Gielgud, needless to say, the figure regains heroic proportions.' The most striking aspect of Gielgud's performance, however, was its deliberate denial of expectations. Ronald Bryden wrote in the *New York Times* (25 August) that Gielgud would have been forgiven 'if he tried to soften it, make it more palatable to the audiences Bond has clearly learned to live without. But he is too fine an actor for that'; Richard Cave pointed out that 'for much of *Bingo* Shakespeare is a silent, watching presence. With Gielgud in the role the audience were deliberately frustrated in their expectations of hearing his famous, musical voice.'[22] As the voice of Shakespeare, Gielgud was silent, impassive: he 'achieves his finest effects in silence' (*Observer*, 18 August); 'his restraint is compelling' (*Listener*, 22 August), and his face was an 'inexpressibly sensitive mask' for a text which 'expressly forbids him to give away anything by movement or facial expression' (*Times Literary Supplement*, 30 August).

Yet in this silence and stillness volumes of pain could be unearthed. Again, the figure of Shakespeare carried the projections of his interpreters, exhibiting a blank impassivity which was not dissimilar to the attentive detachment of the analyst in the psychotherapeutic setting. Just as Freud recommends that the analyst 'should be opaque to his patients and, like a mirror, should show them nothing but what is shown to him',[23] Gielgud's Shakespeare offered a compelling focus for the transference of cultural anxieties which had, if anything, intensified since the play's premiere nine months earlier. The *Guardian's* Michael Billington, who had thought the play 'remarkable' at Exeter, now hailed it as 'magnificent ... full of suppressed agony'; the *Daily Express* (15 August) reiterated the verdict of Harold Hobson by identifying Shakespeare as 'a man almost paralysed by self-disgust' in a play 'projecting chill pessimism and despair'. Benedict Nightingale, who in 1973 had seen in *Bingo* the horrors of the Third World, now found its critique even more insistent, even closer to home: 'If a man whom we worship as superhuman could feel so helpless and inadequate, how should we mere mortals feel, surrounded by the cruelty, callousness and avarice of 1974?' (*Harper's Bazaar and Queen*, August 1974). Bond's answer might have been that this was not meant to be an Osborne-style lesson in feeling; and in his commentary upon the play he attempts to present a cooler view: 'the contradictions in Shakespeare's life are similar to the contradictions in us'. Nonetheless, it seemed difficult, in the circumstances, to register the force of these contradictions without verging on the apocalyptic: Shakespeare was a '"corrupt seer" and we are a "barbarous civilisation"' (*Bingo*, p. xiii). What is captured in many of the reviews is a sense of the paralysis of liberalism amidst the disintegration of the postwar welfare capitalist settlement; read within this framework, Shakespeare's suicide enacts fears of the imminent demise of decency, tolerance, even social democracy itself. Peter Hall, the director of Gielgud's *Tempest*, put it more directly: 'each age writes about Shakespeare in his own image. No surprise therefore that [*Bingo*] shows a man who sold out to the bourgeoisie and no longer stood up for the progressive currents of his time.'[24]

The sense of period which had been a strong feature at Exeter seemed largely to have evaporated. Although the staging was pretty much the same as it had been at the premiere, it had seemingly acquired a veneer of contemporaneity in its new context, with many reviewers reading the *mise-en-scène* and costuming as modern dress. This was in part an effect of the theatrical and institutional setting of the Royal Court, the home of radical new drama and the house of anger. The play's ability to resonate with contemporary concerns is indicated by its capacity to provoke responses which, initially, seem oddly tangential or irrelevant to its ostensible subject-matter; but which actually touch upon the hidden history of the text in unexpected ways. A largely positive review in the *Listener*, for example, elicited a furious exchange of views in the magazine's letters column which linked the play with the failure of contemporary American democracy. Identifying himself as 'an American schoolteacher on sabbatical leave', one correspondent attacked the *Listener*'s reviewer, John Elsom, Bond, Gielgud and the Royal Court for 'so mean-spirited an undertaking and understanding', and countered these with the proposition that Shakespeare, while not 'a democrat or a socialist', took 'a tragic view' and was 'one of the true makers of our heritage, our commonwealth – who formed of the sweet English tongue the *public thing* of our republic'; concluding, bizarrely, that 'Nixon's E *pluribus unum* is, unwittingly, a tragic slogan'.[25] This earned a riposte from another correspondent, who scornfully invoked the 'American dream of a society where money, properly earned, earns the landowner a right to dispossess his tenants when it suits him and where self-questioning is "mean-spirited"'.[26]

Rather more spectacular was the row stirred up by Garry O'Connor's *Plays and Players* notice. O'Connor condemned Bond's work as typifying 'a kind of new "brutalism" in the theatre, which takes unlimited freedom for granted, and which also takes for granted a completely amoral society'; it was 'a celebration of humiliation' as Shakespeare 'is led through a guignol of sordid, unredeemed, social, and personal misery'. Identifying Bond's version of Shakespeare with Bond himself, 'now masochistically brooding over the violence he committed in the name of art', he decides that *Bingo* is, ultimately, 'monumentally and deliberately degrading', and signs off his review by invoking Shaw's comment that 'it would be a positive relief to dig up Shakespeare and throw stones at him'. In effect, O'Connor implies, this is what Bond is doing in this play. It is a telling fantasy image, not only because it transfers the violence of the notorious baby-stoning scene in *Saved* to *Bingo* and thus characterises Bond as a cross between jeering tomb raider and inarticulate yob from his earlier play, but because it luridly imagines the grotesque resurrection and defilement of a sacramental corpus better hidden from view; by staging Shakespeare's body at all, *Bingo* seemed to participate in an act of cultural violation tantamount to blasphemy. The shortcomings of O'Connor's review were quickly seized upon by correspondents, in particular by the dramatist Pam Gems, who not only mounted a passionately freewheeling defence of Bond ('the best we've got') and *Bingo* ('the enactment of the character of a brilliant, impassioned, tender, articulate, complex man') but also answered O'Connor's corporeal rhetoric in kind:

There isn't a day that the newspapers don't record somebody

spitting, charring, bursting another human being (all defending liberty to a man, if not the liberty of said spitted, charred exploding jam on a Belfast street, or some airport full of charter passengers to Costa Polluta, or nuns, or gold smugglers, or middle-class American ladies spending their husband's life insurances). Only last week there were the pictures of the charred bodies being dug up in Cyprus, and yet another print of the little girl flying towards the camera alight with napalm, the camera focused at her vagina.[27]

Gems's evocation of the disinterment of incinerated corpses strangely echoes O'Connor's Shavian nightmare of Shakespeare ripped from the grave; equally striking is the reference to the well-known photograph of nine-year-old Phan Thi Kim fleeing from a napalm attack (an iconic image which 'controlled understanding of the war'[28]): was this association the result of condensation, the running figures from *Bingo*'s Scene V fused with the open-mouthed woman on the gibbet in Scene III? For Gems, this was what was really at stake in Bond's portrait: looking at Shakespeare brought no relief from the horrors of the contemporary world. In 1974, to dramatise the death of England's Shakespeare was to draw attention to the fact that England itself was in terminal decline.

IV

The next production of *Bingo* in England was at the Royal Shakespeare Company's The Other Place, in November 1976. This corrugated-iron hut offered an appealing context for the play: for the first time, it was staged in a Shakespearean performance space. The Other Place had opened in 1974, under the direction of Buzz Goodbody, with the aim of bridging the widening gap between the RSC's main-house work on Shakespeare and contemporary drama.[29] Dennis Kennedy writes that The Other Place was both physically and philosophically 'in remarkable contrast to the traditions of the main house'; as regards Goodbody herself, 'her own background, a combination of leftist politics and radical theatre work, led her to attempt a change in attitude at Stratford that was realized in the drastically remodeled style imposed by the small space'.[30] The theatre rapidly attracted acclaim for its small-scale, poor-theatre Shakespeare productions, including Goodbody's 1974 version of *King Lear*, retitled *Lear* (in a homage to Bond), and her 1975 *Hamlet*, and Trevor Nunn's *Macbeth* in 1976. According to Colin Chambers, *Bingo* had been on the cards for The

Other Place from the outset: Goodbody 'wanted to stage [the play] in Stratford for obvious reasons, in that it had 'obvious irony for the RSC'.[31] The most pressing incentive was, of course, location; as Irving Wardle pointed out in his review of the production, the fact that The Other Place was only 'five minutes up the road' from New Place itself (*The Times*, 12 November 1976) created fertile conditions for the telling of home truths about Shakespeare in his place of birth and death. In this respect, questions of the relationship between the play's use of the biographical Shakespeare and its interrogation of the politics of the Shakespearean theatre experience became particularly acute. The primary rationale for The Other Place was that it offered an alternative to the alarming trend towards conspicuous and wasteful expenditure and large-scale spectacle, tendencies which for many commentators went hand in glove with directorial autocracy. The occupation of the studio space was at one level an attempt to restore a sense of directness and immediacy to Shakespearean production, and thus, it was hoped, to recover the essential experience of the plays themselves. This was to be achieved by means of the poor-theatre conditions of the space, but also through a dialogue between Shakespeare and contemporary writing. These concerns were, however, caught up with the equally tricky question of 'relevance', which was, for Goodbody, a political as well as artistic imperative. Although it was in part addressed through the contemporaneity of the productions themselves, there remained the more fundamental problem of what kinds of audiences the RSC was addressing, and what kinds it wished to attract and cultivate. As Goodbody had complained in 1973, the RSC's audience was 'largely drawn from the upper and middle classes' and unless a concerted attempt was made to broaden the appeal of the company's work to attract new audiences (young and working class), 'classical theatre will become like Glyndebourne'.[32] The intention was that The Other Place was to be simultaneously more experimental, more democratic and accessible, and more purely, authentically Shakespearean than the main house. The difficulty was that these imperatives may well have been antagonistic rather than complementary or mutually supportive.

In practice, the work of The Other Place was less of an alternative to that of the main house than Goodbody's radical aspirations might have suggested: indeed, the work on Shakespeare subsequently offered a triumphant vindication of the company's foundational ethos of, in Alan Sinfield's term, 'Shakespeare-plus-relevance';[33] a formula which in the main house had by this time been tried and tested almost to breaking point. In this context, *Bingo* provided the opportunity for a critique not only of the traditional view of Shakespeare and his work but, more pointedly, of the institutional and cultural role of the RSC itself. Chambers writes that the production showed 'the dilemma of the great dramatist to be much more cruel and relevant – he cannot reconcile the justice he promotes in his plays with the injustice he is involved in as an accomplice of land enclosures'.[34] The cruel relevance for the RSC of the 1970s was that, as a purveyor of Shakespearean culture, it found itself engaged in a territorial struggle for the scarce resources of state funding – largely at the expense of the small-scale counter-cultural fringe theatre companies whose energy and radicalism The Other Place was attempting to emulate.[35]

The presence of Gielgud as Shakespeare at the Royal Court had allowed at least the hope of a more sympathetic perspective upon Shakespeare himself, but this revival took a harsher, more uncompromising and ultimately much more pessimistic line. To a large extent, this was the result of deliberate directorial emphasis, as was signalled in a discussion between Bond and the director, Howard Davies, recorded just before the production opened. Davies appeared to be prompting Bond to offer a more severe judgement of Shakespeare than he had hitherto offered; not only does he suggest that the Shakespeare of the play is 'the hangman's assistant', he also hints that he regards him as 'a bad artist' whose work 'actually amounted in the end to nothing'.[36] Although this is an unusual stance for an RSC director to adopt, it is consistent with what was then Davies's own position within the company. Like Goodbody, Davies had joined the RSC from a background in fringe theatre; unlike his directorial colleagues, he had no desire at the time to direct Shakespeare and reportedly felt at odds with the prevailing RSC culture dominated, as he saw it, by a '"Cambridge clique" who always seemed to be quoting Shakespeare to each other'. Davies's attitude to conventional RSC pieties, and to Shakespeare, had already been clearly signalled in his production of John Downie and Penny Gold's *I Was Shakespeare's Double* at The Other Place in June 1974. Chambers refers to this piece as a 'mixed-media' show which 'failed to please some of the governors once they got round to seeing it'.[37] On the evidence of the promptbook (there were no reviews), it is not difficult to see why. An attack on the academic, theatrical and touristic Shakespeare industries, it is an uneasy mix of agitprop, cabaret-style satire, and documentary drama; the piece, which follows the adventures of a Candide-like Shakespeare scholar called Stanley as he wanders around Stratford-upon-Avon, features Shakespeare's ghost, a Maoist Anne Hathaway, and twisted parodies of Olivier and Gielgud, the latter presenting his '1929 performance of ... er Hamlet'.[38] *Bingo* was an obvious follow-up.

Davies's critical frame of mind was evident in the production's (anti-) design aesthetic. He recorded that he and the designer, Chris Dyer, saw the play as 'a series of Chinese boxes':

> There are people enclosed in the land, and Shakespeare is involved in it too, there are people who are putting up fences and ditches to keep other people out of quite large spaces and to deprive them of the access to control their own lives; then there is Shakespeare himself who is putting up hedges round his own garden, then locking himself in a room, then locking his thoughts inside his own head and not talking to anybody.[39]

Davies and Dyer visualised this theme of enclosures by framing the performance space within a rectangular scaffolding box, which remained in place for both exterior and interior scenes, and which represented emblematically the hedges of Shakespeare's garden, the walls of the tavern and finally, Shakespeare's bedroom. With the audience seated on three sides of this semi-enclosed area, the back of the playing space was marked by a series of painted flats, presenting two-dimensional indicators of locale. Whereas the Northcott and Royal Court productions had featured quasi-realistic hedges and snowscapes, this production used flat green backdrops for the exteriors (white for the snow scene), wallpaper flats for the final scene, and a painted fire for the tavern scene. Davies remarked that 'we didn't want to have three-dimensional hedges or things like that. We wanted to get into a Hockney-like flat surface to try to get people to think about the image and not to be concerned with its actuality on the stage';[40] although among the meanings of the image might have been memories of the screens that had featured in Goodbody's *Hamlet* a year before. The construction-site ambience also provided a salutory contrast with the magic-circle setting of Trevor Nunn's good-versus-evil *Macbeth* of the same season. The emblematic method also guided the work of the actors; as *The Times* (10 August 1977) noted, the cast 'create without makeup older characters and convince through posture and characterisation rather than disguise'. Making a virtue of necessity, the committed Brechtian Davies also conscientiously exposed the mechanisms of the staging, so that, as *The Times* reported, 'stagehands visibly construct the gibbet and help a young woman to take the position of one dead'. Avoiding the illustrative literalism of illusionistic pictorial staging, the screens and scaffolding established a visibly temporary and self-consciously theatrical space which aimed to foster a sceptical and thoughtful response, in that it asked the spectator to see through Shakespeare's world just as the play asked them to see through Shakespeare; it also signalled a strong directorial reading of the play itself.

In Howell's production, design had served the play; here, reflecting the difference between a revival and a premiere, it actively commented upon it. This was most strikingly apparent in the final scene, where Davies's view of Shakespeare diverged from Bond's. Whereas the author regarded Shakespeare's suicide as a rational act, Davies condemned it as 'a cop-out ... he should have opened the door, and not kept it locked. I felt it was a ridiculous action and to keep on hiding and hiding inside this Chinese puzzle, behind locked doors, was paranoiac and obsessive behaviour.' In the play as written, and as seen at Exeter and London, Judith and her mother remain offstage, unseen behind the solid door of Shakespeare's bedroom. For Davies, this arrangement meant that 'you only saw it from Shakespeare's point of view, whereas I felt that they had good claim upon him'. Adding a scaffolding door to the downstage left corner of the frame, Davies brought Judith and the Old Woman onstage for the final scene, so that Judith's account of her mother crying, falling down and tearing her clothes was acted out before the audience. This shifted the emotional balance of the final scene: Judith's lines, now addressed to the Old Woman herself, were less obviously readable as a blackmailing performance for Shakespeare's benefit. According to Davies, Bond approved of the change: 'when he came to see the play, he said something like "You've probably re-written it better than I wrote it." He was quite happy with it.' Bond guardedly confirmed this: 'I was quite happy not to have the door ... because it was an interesting new way of looking at it ... Some people found it hard to take, for other people, it worked. It worked for me.'[41]

The costuming seemed to elicit parallels which were both localised and more generic. Suggesting that the location of the production meant that 'scenic realism is as superfluous as bardolatry to this revival', Irving Wardle wrote in *The Times* (12 November 1976) that the non-illusionistic sense of immediacy was reinforced and intensified by the production's use of modern dress. Thus Shakespeare (Patrick Stewart) appeared in 'sports coat and flannels'; 'you see Frances Viner wearing knee socks, being put down by an affable, business-suited magistrate (Paul Brooke) and climbing on to the gibbet to position herself as a corpse out of Goya; likewise the transformation of Judith Shakespeare into a smartly-tailored country girl with monied inflexions (Meg Davies), and Ben Jonson into David Waller's bowtied old pro'. As Wardle interpreted it, the transposition into a contemporary idiom meant that, like the versions of modern-dress Shakespeare also seen at The Other Place, the play gained in directness and immediacy whatever it lost in historical specificity: 'written in a timeless vernacular, *Bingo* lends itself as easily to modern as to period costume. And the combination of modern dress and minimal staging at once dispenses with the irrelevant biographical element and intensifies the sense and social horror of the play.' This was echoed in Ned Chaillet's *Times* review (10 August 1977) of the Warehouse transfer: 'losing none of its evocative power ... it certainly gains more in immediacy than most modern-dress productions of Shakespeare's plays'. Read thus, the contemporary costuming positioned *Bingo* within the theatrical conventions of modern-dress Shakespeare, and although this is seen as a strength by these two reviewers, it also implicated the production within the contradictions inherent within that tradition which have been addressed in previous chapters.

The imperative of immediacy (which was informed by the physical logistics of the studio space, but also determined by the constraints of tight production budgets) had been central to the modern-dress Shakespeare productions at The Other Place that had preceded *Bingo*. The combination of scenic minimalism, the proximity of performers to the audience, and modern dress in Goodbody's productions, for example, has been claimed as integral to a 'cultural intervention which manifests an explictly political challenge';[42] within the context of the RSC of the 1970s, however, modern dress was readily amenable to incorporation into the universalising and aestheticised version of 'relevance'. Putting *Bingo* into contemporary costume, although consistent with the house style of The Other Place, and probably entirely necessary in pragmatic terms, ran the same risk of making the topicality that was largely implicit in earlier productions of the play not just explicit but paramount, and possibly undermining Bond's own tactic of establishing a sense of historical distance and difference between the events of the play and the world of the audience. Davies himself pointed out that, since *Saved*, Bond had 'never written another contemporary play except for some one-act plays ... what he allows you to do thereby is actually to look at the play objectively and not feel that this is part of my everyday life which is dispensable, disposable, habitual and therefore something I can take for granted'.[43] It seems, however, that Davies was not trying to attempt anything so banal as updating the play to present Shakespeare as 'our contemporary', but that the modern dress was intended to work analogically rather than pictorially: Shakespeare, Jonson and the rest were still to be understood as seventeenth-century figures, with the contradiction between costume and historical situation producing a dialectical tension between past and present rather than a closure of the gap. In effect, Davies had introduced into one of Bond's more straightforwardly historical plays the anachronistic techniques of *Lear* and *Early Morning*, where feudalism is armed with rifles, and Queen Victoria hears news of rioting cinema queues – although to less nightmarish, wrenching effect.

The figure of Shakespeare, as before, provided a focus for these contradictions, here complicated even further by the fact that 'the unadorned person of Patrick Stewart' (Wardle's phrase) resembled the Shakespearean portraiture only in his baldness. For Wardle, the biographical dimension had simply become 'irrelevant':

> Mr Stewart sets aside completely the idea that he is playing the dying Shakespeare: instead of Gielgud's emotional cadenzas and mute intensity, he offers a mild smiling presence, delivering even the harshest passages with a bemused relaxation that enforces attention to what is being said. As a result, the echoes of Lear and Timon become increasingly insistent, together with the central character's property-owning relationship to the landless peasants. (*The Times*)

The technique is, evidently, Brechtian: cool, detached, and relaxed, Stewart's presence is more evocative of Shakespeare's dramaturgy than he is of the author himself. Stewart himself recalled the performance slightly differently, recording that his portrayal of Shakespeare at Stratford was a largely introspective one, but that when the production transferred to London, it underwent a significant shift: 'I had been ... concerned with a man in isolation. The man I played here ... was a man who was firmly in the world, alive and aware and perceptive of everything and reacting to it. Before, it put him too much in isolation intellectually and emotionally and as soon as I brought myself into the world, it changed everything. He became always inquisitive, right to the very last moment of the play.' The move from Stratford and London, which seemed to embody a shift from bleak pastoral alienation to metropolitan self-awareness, produced a Shakespeare who was, as Stewart intended, 'less sympathetic to the audience'; the play as a result became 'crueller, harsher, uglier'.[44] According to the *Observer*, 'Saturn himself could hardly be more saturnine', and Stewart was 'strong while establishing his despair, monotonous when reiterating it' (14 August 1977). *The Times* (10 August) suggested that Stewart 'brings to Shakespeare an actor's quality, certainly not an unfitting way to portray him ... Mr Stewart's voice is practised and expressive. But, except for a few startling and powerful sudden breaks, including his death, he seldom uses his expressive range, maintaining an impassivity which verges on arrogance, not introspection.' Davies, and Stewart, clearly did not want the audience to warm to Shakespeare, but to judge him.

The fullest and most eloquent critical response was John Peter's description of Stewart's Shakespeare as 'a trim, rugged man on the brink of disintegration, his body held together by constant physical effort. You can almost see his tendons and sinews stiffen; his mouth and chin, rigid with all the terror that an egomaniac can feel, send out ripples of palpable anxiety' (*Sunday Times*, 14 August 1977). Rather than the famous Gielgud voice, it is the alarming physicality of the performance that compels attention: the disinterred Shakespearean body is this time not just muzzled but threatened with dismemberment. It is not hard to see the anxious body that threatens to disintegrate as a metaphor for the body politic; amidst sinew-stiffening echoes of *Henry V*, Stewart's incorporation of the fissiparous state of the nation reflects a climate in which the 'break-up of Britain' was being widely canvassed as a serious possibility. When *Bingo* opened at Stratford towards the end of 1976, the contract between organised labour, employers and government which had been precariously established by the Labour Party in 1974 was in serious trouble; as the decade stumbled towards its close, cuts in public expenditure, rising unemployment, and accelerating inflation contributed to a general sense of crisis that was successfully exploited by the cultural and political forces of the right, who proved successful in mobilising petit-bourgeois and popular discontent in support of a firmly reactionary agenda, defined by blatant appeals to naked self-interest, family values, anti-statism, law and order, and attacks on immigration, progressive education and the welfare state.

From the standpoint of left, much of this was the responsibility of a Labour government whose compromises had not only failed to reform capitalism, or even make it work, but had actively intensified its structural contradictions. For some, this was a source of comfort since (against most of the available evidence) it indicated the imminence of revolution; for many others, the signs that the progressivist social and political project of the 1960s was soon to be viciously dismantled were the source of deep anger, chiefly directed at a Labour government which was perceived as having 'betrayed' its programme and its own supporters. The dramaturgy of The Other Place and the Warehouse during the late 1970s was a reliable barometer of the climate of opinion on the left. Preceding *Bingo* at Stratford was David Edgar's *Destiny*, a play which charted the rise of the racist right and attributed much of its strength to the timidity of parliamentary Labourism; the Warehouse opened in 1977 with Howard Barker's *That Good between Us*, a scabrous near-future vision of a pathologically authoritarian Labour government; 1978 saw Howard Brenton's *The Churchill Play* at The Other Place, a 1984-set fantasy imagining a Labour–Conservative coalition given to imprisoning left-wing dissidents in detention camps, and Peter Whelan's *Captain Swing* at Stratford and Bond's *The Bundle* in London, both of which optimistically assessed the prospect of armed revolution. A key player within the RSC's studio counter-culture, Stewart was frequently seen in work of this kind: in *The Bundle* he took the part of the poet Basho, a flawed liberal who is left at the end of the play a blinded, irrelevant and isolated figure; in *That Good between Us* he played Knatchbull, the mild-mannered fascist Home Secretary. Stewart's Shakespeare was turned out from the same mould, a discredited figurehead of the Liberal-Labourite establishment whose suicide was as much as he deserved in a relentlessly unforgiving production.

V

Throughout the period of national history with which *Bingo*'s fortunes on the English stage coincide, the issue of Europe, and the implications of Britain's membership of the European Economic Community, has rarely been off the political agenda. By the end of the 1980s, Europe had become something of an obsession amongst the political classes: in the period leading up to the declaration of the European single market in 1992, worries (mainly on the right) about the weakening of British sovereignty under the rule of Brussels had deepened into fears of the loss of the entire English way of life. The idea that the future of post-imperial Britain might lie within a pan-European federal structure rather than in insular self-sufficiency alarmed those who continued to invest emotionally in Anglo-Saxon supremacism, in that it seemed to threaten not just a reconfiguration of the United Kingdom's economic and military international position but a negation of an increasingly vulnerable and defensive national identity. In the words of one contemporary political commentator, 'to the British, or at least to the English, power is by its very nature unshareable ... Sovereignty is absolute, indivisible and inalienable; to pool it is to lose it.'[45] It was in this climate of nationalist opinion that the BBC Television production of *Bingo* was broadcast on 30 June 1990 (scheduled opposite the World Cup semi-final between Ireland and Italy). This time, the role of Shakespeare reflected the temper of the time through a rather unexpected piece of casting. The part was taken by David Suchet, an actor with an established Shakespearean reputation (he had been one of the stalwarts of John Barton's series *Playing Shakespeare* in 1984) who was, more significantly in this context, best known for his long-running television portrayal of Agatha Christie's Belgian detective, Hercule Poirot. Suchet's screen persona established the terms for his embodiment of Shakespeare, and it presented a noticeable contrast with the impeccable, undisputed Englishness that Gielgud brought to the part. In this version, not only did Suchet/Poirot-as-Shakespeare signal a more hybrid, insidiously Europeanised Englishness; he had also diminished in scale and stature. Suchet also provided a telling physical contrast to previous actors in the role: in contrast to Peck, Gielgud and Stewart, Suchet's Shakespeare is a hunched, diminutive figure, 'little England' personified. Combe, Jonson and the Son tower over him. For Suchet, the matter of Shakespeare's visual appearance was a serious matter but also a bit of a joke. Making himself look like Shakespeare was, he reported, a process which caused his children great amusement: 'Robert teased me unmercifully', he recalled, 'But I just thought, if I'm going to play Shakespeare then I've got to shave my head.'[46] It is an example of another kind of baldness, distinct from the superficial latex fakery of Peck and the earnest eggheads of Gielgud and Stewart, this time achieved through Method-style disciplining of the body to conform with the traditional iconography against which the portrayal was to be authenticated. To become Shakespeare is to accept a kind of punishment, to join ranks with the GI, the surgical patient, the prison inmate and the football fascist.

Suchet's light-hearted determination to get the surface details right was entirely in tune with the spirit of the production. *Bingo* (directed by Don Taylor) was shown as part of the BBC2 Theatre Night season, a Saturday-night series of productions of 'classic' plays presented, for the most part, with few concessions to the demands of the television medium. Positioned as quality broadcasting which is stylistically and culturally distinct from the surrounding schedule, this mode of production conspicuously does not attempt to assimilate its chosen theatrical texts into the normative codes of television drama. Since classic theatre in this context has largely meant naturalistic plays confined to single or few settings, it has usually seemed at odds with the conventional scenic mobility of the medium itself; often the effect is of staginess within an ostensibly realist form. In the case of *Bingo*, according to one reviewer, this tension between the text and the medium created an interesting dialectic which was perhaps unique to the play, which 'hit you at the start with ... bald [sic] visuals and pointed theatricality':

> We were in a three-sided set representing a climateless garden exterior, lit like a hen-house, filled with improbable horticulture, and exited via 'stone' steps that were clearly made out of wood; actors swept in and out from stage left and right with news of interesting-sounding events that we had no prospect of witnessing; and the players were heavy on the use of noisy, stage-strutting gesture. Gradually, though, the klutzy-bombastic look of the piece took on a curious, backhanded appropriateness to the dramatic task at hand. For Bond's play, first staged in 1974 [sic], was setting out to perform a hatchet-job on none other than the founding father of our klutzy-bombastic literary-theatrical tradition – William Shakespeare. (*Listener*, 5 July 1990)

This leads to the conclusion that the formal incongruity of the television *Bingo* ('the shrivelled aural and visual landscape provided by the proscenium-arch-in-a-TV-studio') was not only endemic to its form but 'by accident or design, deliciously apt. It perfectly embodied the shrivelled outlook of the central character himself'. Indeed, the chief impression left by the production is of a scaling-down and domestication of the action within the confines of the screen, with the panoramic scenography of Bond's text reconstituted as a series of dialogues between talking heads. Inevitably, the play's strongest visual effects did not readily translate into televisual terms. Scenes that in the theatre rely upon the sustained juxtaposition of contrasting actions or images (one of Bond's characteristic dialectical strategies) are in the television production mapped via the characteristically televisual unit of the close-up: Bond's synchronic stagecraft is adjusted to the diachronic vocabulary of the television medium.

Two examples will illustrate this. The first is Scene III, which (in a proscenium arch set-up) sets the gibbeted Young Woman upstage against the silent figure of Shakespeare downstage. As Howard Davies observed, 'Bond works those two off against each other ... he presents two very hard, clean and uncluttered, apparently static, and inert objects of thought and then strikes them together in front of the audience'.[47] In the televised version, the relationship between the woman and Shakespeare is mediated through a series of alternating points of view which ultimately cohere within the perspective of Shakespeare himself. The scene begins with the camera trained upon the Young Woman's feet; it tracks up and then in to close up on her head and shoulders. Cut to a long shot revealing the rural scene (obviously a studio set), with the gibbet at the centre, and Shakespeare seated in the foreground right. Cut then to what will be the anchoring shot for the entire scene: a head shot of Shakespeare, with the dead woman visible over his shoulder but out of focus. During the first half of the scene, in which Shakespeare says nothing, recurrent shots of the impassive Shakespeare counterpoint the exchanges between Joan and Jerome and the Son and Wally, which follow the dialogue-driven logic of shot-reverse-shot. In the second half of the scene, after Shakespeare's re-entry, the habit of using the close-up for moments of emotional intensity is deployed in order to focus fairly exclusively upon Shakespeare's face as he delivers his long speeches, not addressed to camera, but internalised. The result is that the Young Woman is seen primarily from the point of view of the agonised and introspective central character, and the spectator actively positioned to empathise and identify with Shakespeare.

Similar strategies are seen at work in Scene V, which is, as we have seen, the most technically (as well as conceptually) problematic scene in the theatre. The key moment here is the presentation of the shooting of the Old Man. At the Northcott, the Royal Court and The Other Place, technical difficulties arose from the disparity between the panoramic scale of the scene as written and the size of the performance spaces; in this version, the problem was side-stepped altogether. Instead of juxtaposing Shakespeare and the shooting within the same scenic space, as the text stipulates, the images are diachronic rather than synchronic, or, to put it another way, sequential rather than simultaneous. Thus where Bond has the dark figures run across far upstage while Shakespeare kneels downstage (*Bingo*, p. 42), the television version cuts from a long shot of Shakespeare kneeling in the snow to a low-angled medium shot of the running figures, apparently somewhere on the other side of the hill. The shooting which follows is seen through a series of close-ups: first of Shakespeare, then (bathetically) of a shotgun, extended from behind a bush and fired; of Shakespeare, who starts as if it is he who has been shot; of a bloody hand scrabbling in the snow; and, finally, of Shakespeare, as he falls forward, exactly mirroring the movements and positioning of the wounded figure. As in Scene III, Shakespeare owns the dominant perspective.

Such moments typified the production as a whole, which ostensibly presented a faithful rendering of the play even as it transposed it into heightened television naturalism. It is, moreover, as much a product of its time as the other productions discussed in this chapter. I have suggested a connection with the question of Britain in Europe, and to the imperilled Englishness that Shakespeare precariously symbolises; more pointedly, the domestic emphasis of the production, and its intensely naturalistic anatomisation of the corrosive effects of money upon personal and familial relationships, pointed towards the specific appeal of the play at the turn of 1990s. Far more thoroughly petit-bourgeois than in any of its previous incarnations, Suchet's scaled-down Bard is a prototypical Thatcherite (as Stuart Hall defines him or her, the 'respectable, patriarchal, entrepreneurial subject'[48]), a surrogate for those who were for the first time experiencing the devastating consequences of the Thatcher era's economic and political adventurism. In this instance Shakespeare embodies the bitterness and the anger of the middle classes who bought into the short-lived 'economic miracle' of privatisation, house price inflation, tax-cutting, and expanding credit during the 1980s only to see it rebounding upon themselves as they increasingly found themselves faced with negative equity, debt and redundancy. It is no accident that the most potent, most fully realised presence in the television *Bingo* is that of the house itself – the 'new place' which, for many of the aspirant, property-owning middle classes of the 1980s, was the dream which would subsequently become nightmare. With their thick beams, heavy furniture, and dense foliage, the houses and gardens in which the play is set form a solid, heavy, relentless environment in which its characters are utterly, hopelessly trapped; as even the exterior scenes are enclosed by the walls of a studio, there is no outside, no alternative, no way out except death.

Almost without exception, the reviewers took a dim view of the production. In any case, the bulk of that night's television audience preferred to watch Ireland playing Italy to Suchet playing Shakespeare;

a consideration which allowed one reviewer at least to combine a verdict of the play with a reference both to Suchet's screen alter-ego and to the current football vernacular: 'despite the obvious quality of the play, all the hurt looks, doom, gloom and relentless misery left me sick as a Poirot' (*Today*, 2 July). The only other positive account, in addition to that in the *Listener*, was that of the *Sunday Times* (1 July), which also noted that the production was 'stagey to the extreme'; and who recognised a teasing topicality: 'Shakespeare is a member of the chattering classes – a one-time yuppie who faintly recalls the passions of his youth but can't quite remember where he left them':

> It is a seductive thought, as any journalist who has interviewed a literary lion in his own lair will confirm; those who rail against the injustices of the world with such eloquence are quite often to be found in the country, spending their private passion arguing with the local council about street lights. Shakespeare, according to Bond, was no different.

The weary fatalism may be an appropriate response to the production (if not the play); it was also, implicitly, a commentary upon Bond himself, and upon his generation of playwrights. This theme was picked up again in Benedict Nightingale's review of the 1995 revival of *Bingo* by the Royal Shakespeare Company:

> The mantra Bond's Shakespeare repeats, 'was anything done?', must rattle round the heads of many responsible dramatists as they seek to justify themselves to themselves. Has their work made a difference to anybody? Have they done anything to change the world, or have they let the world change them? These are of course contemporary rather than Jacobean worries, especially appealing to an angry, unreconstructed socialist like Bond. But they are no less worth airing because they come in as provocative a form as this ... *Bingo* dates from 1973 but, if you think the way Bond thinks, the succeeding 22 years have not exactly made its cynicism less topical. (*The Times*, 1 July 1995)

For Benedict Nightingale, once of the *New Statesman*, these were certainly apt questions: the reference to 'unreconstructed' socialism signals that Nightingale reads the play as a possible epitaph not just for Shakespeare and for the political theatre of the 1960s and 1970s, but for socialism itself.

This was not Bond's view. In an article in the *Guardian* (28 June 1995) published to coincide with the opening of the production, he wrote that as a playwright Shakespeare was 'sweepingly radical', but as a man 'he was frightened and grasping ... as a man he was a Tory':

> I wrote *Bingo* in 1972 [sic] because I felt this conflict in Shakespeare was the beginning of the present conflict in society. Since I wrote it, the conflict between capitalism and conservatism has deepened. Capitalism depends on constant technological innovation. This turns the world upside down and people inside out. But conservatism needs all things to stay the same. That is why it has to return to the values and behaviour of the past. In *Bingo* I credit Shakespeare with self-knowledge, which means he did his own suffering. In my play he kills himself. Our leaders have no self-knowledge and so we will suffer for them ... It is a purpose of *Bingo*, of all my plays, to show that it is a Culture of Death.

If Bond's Shakespeare was now a Tory, he was a man out of time; since this was the period in which the broader political culture in Britain finally turned decisively against the brand of conservatism that had held sway since the RSC had last produced this play, leaving the right united by little more than its core principles of greed and self-interest, and a visceral loathing of all things European. Bond's exposition of the play had little bearing on the production itself, with which he had no involvement. Stating that he 'hadn't seen it', Bond subsequently wrote that he had been 'told the production was bad', that the RSC had 'worked out a style of packaging plays so that they "please" audiences', and that director David Thacker 'realised he couldn't do that with *Bingo* but didn't know what else to do'.[49] Most of the reviewers shared his poor opinion of the production. Presented as part of an RSC regional tour (sponsored by National Westminster Bank), *Bingo* formed part of a double-bill with *The Tempest*; it opened at the Young Vic on 21 June 1995, moved to the Swan in Stratford for a brief run in August, and then toured the United Kingdom and beyond (playing in non-theatrical venues) until early in 1996. Both productions were directed by David Thacker, and were cross-cast: notably, the parts of Shakespeare and Prospero, Caliban and Ben Jonson, Miranda and Judith, and Ariel and the Young Woman.[50] It was not the first time that the RSC had paired a Bond play in this way: the 1982 season had featured linked productions of Bond's *Lear* at The Other Place and *King Lear* in the Royal Shakespeare Theatre; his *Restoration* had formed part

of a season of Restoration plays at the Swan. As with the RSC production of *Lear*, the conjuncture seemed intended to establish a strong intertextual relation between the two plays. Noting the parallels and divergences between them, reviewers generally read the pairing as offering a contrast between the dream and the reality of Shakespeare's final days, with the master-magician Prospero acting as doppelganger to Bond's Shakespeare (and with Paul Jesson giving a virtually identical performance in both roles). In a way, this was an old-fashioned reading of *The Tempest* as covertly autobiographical testament; the added edge in this production was that the juxtaposition with *Bingo* was intended to reframe what was understood to be Shakespeare's version of his own ending. The *Evening Standard* (3 July) felt that the pairing indicated that Shakespeare's 'supposedly autobiographical portrait of himself ... as a benign, colonial ruler, gracefully surrending his island power, is far less truthful than Bond's critical vision'; the *Sunday Times* (2 July) wondered 'if Thacker were asking: "Could this arid, greedy, hard and broken man have written this other complex, generous play? Was it worth ending your artistic life with *The Tempest* if you ended your personal life as a grasping, self-centred failure?".'
The *Independent* (3 July) suggested that 'with Sarah-Jane Holm playing both Miranda and Shakespeare's sourly chiding daughter Judith, bitter at paternal neglect in Bond, you could be forgiven for thinking that the father-daughter relationship in *The Tempest* is the idealised compensatory projection of the guilty dramatist'; while the doubling of Caliban and Ben Jonson, according to the *Times Literary Supplement* (28 July), implied that 'Caliban is Prospero's *alter ego*, who dares to express publicly the jealous hatred which Shakespeare and Prospero keep hidden'.

The general effect of the interaction between the two plays and productions was to define the remit of both within the realms of the interpersonal and the familial. The majority of reviewers found the pairing tendentious, and Nicholas de Jongh in the *Evening Standard* voiced the general view when he wrote that 'there's something smugly absurd about condemning an Elizabethan playwright by the values and standards of a late 20th century old leftist like Bond'. Like Nightingale, de Jongh regarded *Bingo*, the politics it articulated, and the political theatre it represented, as relics of an era that the supposedly post-ideological Britain of the mid-1990s had happily transcended; Bond's critique of Shakespeare was less outrageous than irrelevant. Shakespeare, quite simply, was no longer a figure to be fought over. Symptomatically, there was no attempt to turn Paul

Jesson into a Shakespeare lookalike: sporting a magnificently full head of hair, he had little kinship with Droeshout, Chandos and the Holy Trinity bust, and yet no critic thought this worth commenting upon. Shakespeare was simply 'tetchy, cynical, lethargic' and given to 'peevishness and banality' (*Time Out*, 5 July); 'a mean, disgusted, cowardly figure' (*Observer*, 2 July); 'a tedious if decent burgher with no scrap of authority or genius' (*Financial Times*, 1 July); 'depressive, exasperatingly listless' (*Independent*, 3 July); a presence who (perhaps mindful of the venture's sponsors) exuded 'the glum blankness of a defrocked bank manager' (*Evening Standard*), and who was 'incapable either of the lyricism or of the anger required by both parts' (*Times Literary Supplement*). But for all the dissatisfaction that this generated, there was little sense that a more heroic, tragic, lyrical or active Shakespeare might have stood as a plausible alternative; the unspoken consensus was that this Shakespeare was as good as he could get. In a revealing addendum to her review, Emily Watson of the *Times Literary Suppplement* reported an intervention during the 'Lear-like scene in which Shakespeare is cast out in the snow': 'someone in the audience shouted "Come on, put some life into it!"'; Watson adds: 'it was hard not to sympathize'. Whether or not this exasperated spectator had read Bond's remarks about the 'culture of death', the intervention identified a sense of an absence of vitality that was endemic to the production as a whole. The anomie of Jesson's performance was pervasive: '*Bingo* is presented in a stage world that seems to have signed a unanimous pledge against colour' (*Independent*); the production was 'brown and ochre' (*The Times*); 'austerely staged and bland' (*Evening Standard*). Staged in the round, designed for maximum portability and destined for exhibition in draughty sports halls in wintry provincial towns, *Bingo* adopted a small-scale touring theatre aesthetic that seemed deliberately drained of theatricality. Critics found *The Tempest* equally tired: envisaged as a metatheatrical exercise 'conjured out of Prospero's book' the cast slumbered around the performance space until 'prodded into life' by a 'grubby Ariel' (*Time Out*), who wore 'Glastonbury-esque black nail polish and period dresses ripped to shreds' (*TLS*); Prospero's spirits 'transform themselves into Ferdinand's logs, the contents of Prospero's wardrobe, or whatever else is needed' (*Independent on Sunday*, 2 July). *Bingo* offered no such opportunities for inventiveness or magic, only the execution of a grim duty.

The notices that greeted the double bill at the Young Vic apparently heralded the exhaustion of *Bingo*'s currency as a stage play, at least for the time being. But *Bingo* had another airing, this time at the Swan

Theatre in Stratford, before setting out, probably rather forlornly, on the road which took it from Cornwall to Belfast. I will conclude with this because the single review that survives presents a rather different account of the play in performance to the Young Vic experience. Headlined 'Journey into unmissable passion', the review in the *Birmingham Post* (4 August 1995) was emphatic that this was a 'fascinating play', a 'compelling performance' by Jesson, and a production 'not to be missed'. Unless the writer of this was seeing a production which had been radically reworked since it was witnessed by his London colleagues, something had obviously happened to *Bingo* in its transition from the capital to Stratford. That something was not just that the play acquired new resonances from its return to origins, but that it was performed in the Swan, which for the RSC was the nearest thing possible to an authentically Shakespearean performance space; never mind New Place, this bleached wooden amphitheatre was the real house that Shakespeare built. In a space informed by both the Guthrie-esque values of the open stage and the Styanist poetics of the Shakespearean empty space, the rootless, context-free and studiedly anonymous stagecraft of the production flowered into a different kind of life, just as Shakespeare is meant to do. The contiguity of space and text is absolute: 'dark images of cruelty and selfishness occur constantly and a compelling text, linked to fine performances, free the mind entirely. The imagination does the rest, as Bond intended.' In this account, Bond's play has at last reached the ideal state of Shakespearean performance, as it coaxes the spectator into the limitless liberties of the theatre of the mind. But there is a cruel irony in this, for the vision that emerges is hardly one of shared humanity, joy or hope. To come face to face with Shakespeare in the home of his dreams is to meet neither genius nor magic but bitterness, injustice, and an icy, deadly silence.

6
Ruined Lear

A Friday evening in Sheffield towards the end of a century: the location is the Lantern Theatre, a compact proscenium arch space built at the behest of one of the city's Victorian steel magnates as a present for his daughters. An audience gathers for a one-off showing of the results of a week's practical investigation of *King Lear* by a company who have never before worked in this fashion on any playtext, let alone a Shakespeare play. The small group of invited spectators know what to expect from this group of theatre makers, but for many readers of this book, some scene-setting may be required. Founded in Sheffield in 1984, Forced Entertainment (writer and director Tim Etchells, performers Richard Lowdon, Robin Arthur, Cathy Naden, Terry O'Connor and Claire Marshall) has become established as Britain's best-known and most influential experimental performance group; famously declaring at the outset that they made work which would speak to anyone who had been brought up in a house with the television always on, Forced Entertainment construct shows out of found resources, the scraps, fragments and garbage of media culture and of everyday life, pulling together disparate narratives and relying upon 'intuition, chance, dream, accident and impulse' to create a landscape of 'cities, late-night television, ghosts and half-remembered stories'.[1] Etchells succinctly identifies the performance vocabulary that articulates these concerns:

> For its own part identity onstage is now rarely a fixed point. More often, through actions, choreographies, or even speech the performers are seen as sharing a constituency of texts in which their own part or parts must be worked out, or in which their role is ever fluid ... from this context conventions including verbal game

playing, listing, obvious quotation of imagery or text, partial or flawed character representation, alienated delivery, mediated performance via video or PA systems, identical costuming, frantic costume-swapping or undressing, the construction of stage spaces with internal mirroring or echoing and the ceaseless re-arrangement of objects to produce fictions have passed into common performance language.[2]

Rooted as it is in the unique longevity of the company's collaborative working methods and shared personal histories and preoccupations, the result has been a body of work which, from the 1984 *Jessica in the Room of Lights* to (at the time of writing) 2001's *First Night* has been distinctive and remarkably consistent, and which has returned repeatedly, in a move which is entirely characteristic of postmodernity, to the problematics and failures of performance itself, to 'the inability of the performers to fully inhabit the texts and gestures which they perform ... there's no utterance by anybody that isn't somehow a quotation of something else'.[3]

Borrowed and second-hand identities, stories and scenarios are the bedrock of the work. In *Some Confusions in the Law about Love* (1989), 'the performance of a British Elvis Presley impersonator, either acting out the demise of Presley or enjoying one of his own, is interrupted by a pair of jaded showgirls, by two 16th Century Japanese love-suicides dressed as skeletons, and by a babbling duo named Mike and Dolores who, via "satellite link up" discuss the sex act they intend performing in Hawaii'.[4] *Club of No Regrets* (1993) depicts 'a figure Helen X' who 'orders a series of enactments of scenes by a pair of performers inside a tiny box set, centre stage ... the enacted scenes are replayed many times as though Helen is unsure as to their true order'.[5] *Pleasure* (1997) throws together a pantomime horse, women in wedding dresses, guns, excessive amounts of alcohol, slowed-down gramophone records and a text downloaded from the internet – '*2,334 Filthy Words and Phrases* – a pedant's catalogue of obscenities, slang words and descriptions containing some 500 alternative ways to say masturbate' – to produce 'a kind of late-night radio message picked up on some random scanning receiver – a portrait of a world where it is always after midnight, and where the dawn never comes'.[6]

Lyrical and exhilarating as it is for many, Forced Entertainment's rubbish-strewn world in which 'terrible dancing and exquisitely played bad acting take centre stage'[7] has not been to everyone's taste: reviewing *200% & Bloody Thirsty*, the *Independent* (15 February 1989) declared that 'the whole performance is wholly out of control ... there is nothing to enjoy here and much to regret'; this was a gift for the company, who incorporated this judgement into a subsequent show, utilising it for the closing lines for *Marina & Lee* (1991). Sharing as much (if not more) ground with installation work, fine art, photography, dance and video making as with the drama world, Forced Entertainment's output has taken the form of site-specific and gallery-based projects as well as work conceived for theatre spaces; these include *Ground Plans for Paradise* (1995), in which 'a deserted model city – comprising nearly 1000 balsa wood tower blocks – is laid out in a grid plan ... above are the faces of many people sleeping ... like angels looking after or dreaming of this world';[8] and *Nights in this City* (Sheffield, 1995, and Rotterdam, 1997), which took spectators on a phantasmagoric coach tour, with its drunk and increasingly desperate tour guide finding his wayward narratives of the city slipping from his grasp: 'all the streets round here got named after famous football hooligans from history and all the buildings got named after ghosts and cleaning products and convicted kerb crawlers'.[9]

Even on the evidence of this brief sketch, it will be evident that the work of Forced Entertainment is hardly the most obvious place to go looking for Shakespeare, and as such it provides an anomalous presence within the culture of Shakespearean performance which it has been the task of this book to anatomise. Of course, Shakespearean traces can be unearthed from the work if one looks long and hard enough. In *Some Confusions*, there is (possibly) a vague paraphrase of *A Midsummer Night's Dream*, as a speaker recalls: 'we did a thing quite a while ago now, it was a love show and everyone on the stage drank down a love potion that, er, sent them all off to sleep and when they woke again they were all in love and no one felt sad'. *Pleasure* features a man wearing a pantomime horse's head which is also irresistibly reminiscent of that of an ass, slowly stripping while women in wedding dresses stand by and watch records turning; concerned with 'memory, with the body, with sexuality and its presentation, with romance, with sex', the world of the show, 'obsessively night-time, drunken, disconnected' might be a dark, distorted version of Shakespeare's *Dream*. *Speak Bitterness* (1995) is a durational piece featuring seven performers reading from piles of texts of real and made-up confessions, ranging from 'the largest political crimes to the most banal of daily errors';[10] admitting that they 'stayed up after midnight', 'told long boring anecdotes' and 'dropped atom bombs on Nagasaki, Coventry, Seattle, Belsize, Belsize Park and Hiroshima', they also 'murdered sleep', and 'cut open our bodies to try and find the evil in them', but 'found nothing'. *Emanuelle Enchanted (or A Description of this World as if it Were a Beautiful Place)* (1992; revived 2000) begins with three performers presenting a vast parade of characters by means of quick costume changes, extravagant gestures, and crudely-lettered cardboard signs; alongside FRANK (DRUNK), PRINCESS NOT-SO-BRIGHT and A BLOKE WHO'S BEEN SHOT, we briefly register the presence of BANQUO'S GHOST, A STATUE COME TO LIFE and (in the 2000 revival) A MAD OLD KING. But these are, on the face of it, relics rather than reference points: the Mad Old King is Robin Arthur with a lost expression and a blanket on his head, a wandering derelict from another theatre; the snatches of Shakespearean text no more (and no less) trustworthy as touchstones of meaning than graffiti, advertising slogans or B-movie dialogue. Unlike, for example, the Wooster Group, the New York-based ensemble with whom they have been frequently compared, Forced Entertainment's practice has generally steered clear of the canonical works of dramatic literature. Whereas the Wooster Group have dismantled and rebuilt *Our Town* as *Route 1&9* (1981), *The Crucible* as *LSD (. . . Just the High Points . . .)* (1984), and *Three Sisters* as *Brace Up!* (1991), as part of the project of (as company member Ron Vawter described it) 'replaying the tapes of the twentieth century, of going back over them to see what went wrong', Forced Entertainment have preferred to work on the understanding that 'no one did their homework too well',[11] and that 'no element of the theatrical language might substantially precede any other – so that any element could lead'.[12] To begin from a pre-existing script, let alone from Shakespeare, would seem to be a betrayal both of a company aesthetic and a collaborative ethic of theatremaking.

Even so, within a body of image-based work which is consciously poised on the knife-edge between 'the meaningless and the very highly-charged', the Shakespeare effect cannot be altogether extinguished; indeed, it can suddenly and unexpectedly flare into significance. Etchells isolates such a moment in *Emanuelle Enchanted*: 'there were times when I would look at it and think this is terrible – this is just the empty fragments of 2000 stupid stories colliding with each other – there's no meaning in it, just the noise left in the machine of culture . . . and then FRANK (DRUNK) would take a curious look at BANQUO'S GHOST and meaning would happen, like electricity between two lovers who are kissing goodnight, car alarms ringing, and there'd be nothing I could do to stop that'.[13] Etchells characteristically depicts the brief meeting between wasted but still-breathing representative of English low culture and revenant from another world as both a theatrical accident and yet another chance urban encounter, but also suggests that even the most fleeting of Shakespearean echoes can carry an explosive force entirely disproportionate to its performance context, and that the work knows itself to be haunted by the spectres of a tradition which a shallower postmodernism might claim to have transcended. Paradoxically, in this instance, the Shakespearean presence creates a space in which a kind of grounded meaning is temporarily possible.

Moreover, the appearance of Banquo's Ghost as a specifically *theatrical* figure (and as a figure who, like the Mad Old King, actually stands for 'theatre' itself) among 'the great crowd of some scrappy collective unconscious'[14] points towards a strengthening preoccupation in Forced Entertainment's more recent work with drama and theatre themselves. *Dirty Work* (1998) takes place amidst a half-built setting of scaffolding and ragged drapes: two performers, seated on chairs, verbally conjure up the most immense and impossible stage spectacle never to have happened, in a pure theatre of the mind. At one point (immediately after 'a handsome woman plays a number of popular tunes by farting'), 'Great scenes from Shakespeare are presented':

> The Old Monarch Lear in His Madness On The Heath, The Rude Mechanicals in Their Simplisitic Honest Buffoonery, The Callous and Wicked Macbeth in Bloody Combat with Macduff, The Youthful and Beautiful Juliet Drinking Poison In The Tomb.

Showtime (1996) begins with a ten-minute monologue from a man strapped to a *Road Runner*-style ticking time bomb, in which he coolly evaluates the nature of theatrical convention; later on, '"They don't want this", says one character ... shuddering with sobs, gore and intestines (in the shape of a tin of Heinz spaghetti) pouring from his middle. "They want costumes, a set and a plot, for God's sake."'[15] Here, and elsewhere, the act of theatremaking, and the politics of participation in performance itself (an act which Etchells, emphasising its ethical responsibilities, characterises as 'witnessing' rather than spectatorship), are subjected to sometimes playful, sometimes bruisingly confrontational, scrutiny. In *Showtime*, a long monologue about suicide is followed by a sudden, psychotic outburst (from a female performer costumed as a pantomime tree):

What the fuck are you looking at? What the fuck is your problem? Fuck off! Voyeurs! There's a fucking fine line and you've just crossed it. Where's your human decency? Call yourselves human beings? Why don't you fuck off, piss off, cock off, wankers, voyeurs. Fuck off. Go on, pick up your things, pick up your coats and your fucking bags and bugger off just fucking cocking buggering wank off.

Etchells wryly notes, 'they had this game with the audience, that's for sure', but it was a darkly comic game played at the limits of tolerance, and with a serious purpose: 'your presence at this event had to cost something'.[16]

This, then, was the immediate performance context within which, early in 1999, Forced Entertainment took what was for them the unprecedented and ground-breaking step of tackling *King Lear*. There were manifest site-specific ironies implicit in the choice of the text for the event and the venue. The play traditionally too huge for the stage was offered after a week's workshopping in a space which seemed crowded with its cast of eight. Further, the architectural legacy of the magnanimity of a nineteenth-century patriarch documents a largesse, and a politics of the family, which the forces of de-industrialisation (which, amongst other things, Forced Entertainment's work has striven, obliquely, to comprehend) had turned into ancient, possibly mythical, history. For the company, *King Lear* was neither a mountain to be scaled nor a monument to be disfigured; according to Etchells, in tones which suggest a postmodern blanking of both traditional Shakespearean cultural authority and the politicised theatrical agendas that have attempted to contest it, Forced Entertainment took on *Lear* simply because 'we were curious'.[17] The curiosity initially seemed to focus upon the nature of the encounter between a performance-making method rooted in the assembly of found materials and the most thoroughly canonical work in global dramatic literature – a status which, paradoxically, levelled the status of Shakespeare's play by making it more 'to hand' than any other; as Etchells wrote, it was 'a school play. The one I knew without having to think. The one I wrote punk bands in the margin of. And read aloud in a glass and concrete classroom.' In addition, *Lear*'s stage history, particularly as filtered through the 1983 film fictionalising the demise of Donald Wolfit, *The Dresser*, stood for a histrionic tradition which the company not only regarded with affection (supposedly alien to the sensibilities of the theatrical avant-garde) but viewed as a kind of yardstick against which performance might be truly measured: 'we talk about that film very often. More storm, boy. More storm ... if you're going to do acting you may as well start there.'

The result was *Five Day Lear*, whose workshopping process consisted 'more [of] research than anything else, in which the company invited a few guests to Sheffield for a week during which time we read, edited, made video material and generally mutilated the play'. The outcomes were the work in progress showing at the end of the week, and a forty-minute video of Etchells's brother Mark explaining the plot 'as best he can after a single reading undertaken during that day's journey from Bristol to Sheffield' (another fractured, unreliable narrative). As Etchells recalled, this was legitimate fun, in that 'crudely ... we succeeded in turning the play to rubble', but 'that's the easy part'; more tricky is the task of 'making something new and strong and beautiful in/out of the rubble'. Central to this pounding of *Lear*, as to all of Forced Entertainment's work, are questions of sabotage, of failure, that were written into the project from the outset:

> I guess our question is 'What happens when it all goes wrong? When it doesn't work? When the thing is ruined?' Does something else take place instead? That thing of being in the ruins of something – we're fascinated with that. As if to say 'We may get *Lear* confused, lose track of it, repeat scenes, turn the plot to mush etc, BUT something will stick and MAYBE we'll get closer to the heart of the thing than if we did it A to Z'.

Within a conceptual landscape defined less by the boundaries of narrative than by those of urban topography, the alphabetical trajectory evokes the street atlas, not the dictionary; in this sense, Forced Entertainment's *Five Day Lear* offered a mapping of the play, rather than a reading of it. It is a cartography of devastation, not security: the play is seen from the air and experienced on the ground in terms of bombing and being bombed, of ruination and a desperation in which unexpected truths might yet come to light. These preoccupations with bombing were, so to speak, very much in the air during the brief period in which *Five Day Lear* took shape. On Friday 9 April 1999, at the end of a fortnight in which the corners of living rooms had been haunted by visions of NATO airstrikes in former Yugoslavia (intended to put an end to the Milosevic regime's genocidal policy of ethnic cleansing of Kosovo Albanians), the findings of the week's work were given a single, informal airing. My purpose in the pages that follow is simply to present an account of the at times rather shambolic show that resulted. It is, it must be admitted, a description rather than a reading of the piece. In a sense, this approach is prompted by the nature of the performance itself: as an event which sits comfortably within neither Shakespearean nor postmodern performance, *Five Day Lear* testifies to the recalcitrance of performance itself in the face of performance analysis. The extent to which the piece has any wider resonances in the overall context is a matter I will return to in the concluding chapter.

The show begins with seven men and women (Robin Arthur, Mark Etchells, Tim Hall, Terry O'Connor, Claire Marshall, Sue Marshall and Cathy Naden) walking onto a tiny proscenium arch stage. Five of them take their seats behind a row of tables running across the back of the space, and one of the women moves to the front. Richard Lowdon, playing DJ for the evening, takes up position behind a table stage left, on which sits an old-fashioned gramophone; he begins to cue up records. Upstage there is a portable lighting console, downstage right a video monitor. The set-up is reminiscent of *Speak Bitterness* and, more distantly, the Wooster Group's *LSD*: on the tables are piles of typewritten scripts, the text of *Lear* as print on A4 paper, handwritten placecards (LEAR, KENT, CORDELIA), and cans of strong lager, from which a few of the performers occasionally take discrete pulls. They are dressed in jeans and casual shirts. The performer seated centre (who will play, or rather read, Lear) starts by announcing, a military commander or politician addressing a press conference, that he will be unable to discuss 'any details of last night's air strikes or the specifics of Serbian collateral damage', but is interrupted by the woman standing downstage, who seems to combine the roles of director, prompt and stage manager, and who issues an instruction: 'Start with Act 1, Scene 1, page 1. King Lear's palace.' Still seated, the performers begin a relaxed reading of the first scene, starting with Kent's 'Is this not your son, my lord?' (l. 7), and proceeding smoothly until Lear's entry. As Lear stands and begins to speak, Richard supplies a rasping, over-loud fanfare (he is playing Donald Wolfit's recording of the play), making the King's attempt at an opening address inaudible. Lear strug-gles through five lines and then gives in, and Richard allows the record (now onto voice-over narrative: 'Lear, King of Britain, is old ... ') to wind down to a growling halt, sounding like the lobotomised HAL in Kubrick's *2001*. A pause, and then a second instruction from Director: 'Act 2, Scene 4, page 17. Before Gloucester's Castle. Kent in the stocks. Lear, Regan and Kent.' Twenty lines of dialogue between Lear and Regan follow (beginning with 'Good sir, to the purpose' [l. 176] to 'You

will return and sojourn with my sister' [l. 198]) before a further interruption: 'Act 2, Scene 2, page 12. Before Gloucester's Castle again.'
Pages are turned and scripts re-ordered. Accompanied by a brief spurt
of cocktail-lounge Hammond organ, the performers at either end of
the row of tables read through the first exchange between Kent and
Oswald ('Good dawning to thee friend ... '). The tone is light, off-
hand, playful ('If I had thee in a dark alley I would make thee care for
me'), and, just as Kent reaches the climax of his diatribe (both are now
standing), a directorial intervention orders them back to the beginning
of the scene ('OK, let's do the whole scene again').

There is some throat-clearing and they begin again, still casual, and
the trading of insults is accompanied by Oswald removing his shirt
and Kent his jacket. Oswald walks round to face Kent (who momentarily loses his place in the script) and the action is stopped: 'Let's go
back to the beginning of the scene. Act 2, Scene 4' [sic]. There is a
sound of helicopters; this time Kent gets as far as line 13 ('a knave, a
rascal, an eater of broken meats ... '), and both are shirtless, limbering
up as if for a bout of all-in wrestling. 'OK, OK, OK .... Act 1, Scene 4,
page 10. Claire, could you play the Fool?' A correction from one of the
cast: 'Act 1, Scene 5'. Kent and Oswald sit, dress themselves, Claire
stands to give the Fool's 'Canst tell how an oyster makes his shell?' (I.
v. 25) . Lear and his Fool manage twenty lines ('Keep me in temper; I
would not be mad' [l. 44]) before they are stopped again: 'Act 2, Scene
4, page 17. Goneril, Regan and Lear.' And so it goes on, with the interruptions coming faster, the scene fragments getting shorter, the
reading more perfunctory, the organ more obtrusive. Lear's dialogue
with Kent in the stocks is played, and halted, several times.

The reading stops. Director: 'I think ... we need two things. First of
all, if you could all go and get yourselves some ... costumes' (cast look
down at their clothes with a who-us expression; another audience
laugh), 'And secondly, if we could have an explanation of the plot.'
Video footage rolls, with a head and shoulders shot of Mark Etchells:
'From what I can gather, on a train journey, *King Lear*'s about a king
who thinks he's going to die, or knows he's going to die. He's got three
daughters. I can't remember all the names yet, but I will do as I go on
maybe ... ' Lights dim and performers leave the space, apart from
Director, who sits alone centre, watching the monitor. Mark's account
reaches the end of the opening scene ('all they've got to do is look after
the old man, King Lear, and a hundred knights'), and the video is
switched off.

To the sound of an orchestra tuning up, the performers re-enter and take their seats. They are now swathed in the cast-offs from some tawdry theatrical costumiers: fur robes, greatcoats, dressing gowns. Lear sports a tight knitted woollen cap, Robin and Richard campily fake little beards. (For Etchells, this illuminates 'a fundamental absurdity of theatre, grown men in "Elizabethan-looking" smocks that someone's mum hemmed up. We have a love/hate relationship to all that I guess.') An instruction from Director: 'Let's go back to the beginning. Act 1, Scene 1, page 1. A hall in King Lear's palace.' The record slowly spins, the fanfare crashes: 'Lear, King of Britain, is old. He decides to divide his kingdom between his three daughters ... ' Performers sit, impassive, shuffle scripts, scribble notes, listen to Wolfit's Lear, his delivery sliding frantically up and down the tonal scale as Lowdon jockeys with the record speed. Distorted images of Tim Hall as Lear appear on the video monitor. On cue ('Goneril, our eldest born, speak first'), one stands to answer. She manages two lines before corpsing; Robin swiftly steps in and whisks through the rest of the speech. The exchanges between King and daughters that follow are played as a sequence of duets (or duels) between live and recorded performance, playing upon the disparity between Wolfit's actorly relish and the jokey colloquialism of the cast. Suddenly, there is a moment of unexpected stillnesss, as Claire stands as Cordelia. She is visibly, heavily, pregnant; her response ('Nothing, my lord') is quiet, unemphatic, dignified. For an instant, Wolfit's orotund mannerisms create pathos as well as broad comedy, and then the record grinds to a halt once more. 'Act 3, Scene 4. The heath outside the palace.' Cocktail-lounge music starts up again, and Lear interjects: ' I'd just like to underline the fact that the reports of the downing of the F16 fighter are totally and wholly unsubstantiated ... ' Then Kent: 'Here is the place, my lord ... ' After less than a minute ('Poor naked wretches ...'), it is back to 'Act 2, Scene 2, page 12', to Oswald's stripping and 'filthy-worsted-stocking knave', then forward: 'Here is the place, my lord.'

The opening lines of III. iv are delivered four times and the storm scene begins. A performer stands, moves to the lighting board, and flicks switches; the lights brighten and dim and storm sound effects are heard. The scene stops, rewinds, starts again. Lear stands and rails, the curtains close, the clamour continues behind them. Director parts the drapes a little and we catch a glimpse of flashing lights and movement. The curtains open. Lear is now on the monitor, giving a full-out, ranting rendition of the King on the heath ('more storm boy, more storm ... if you're going to do any acting you may as well start there'); the biggest piece of acting in the show boxed and isolated in a corner of the space, while the next scene is set up. Robin places a chair centre, sits, and is secured to it with thick black gaffer tape. The video ends ('O, 'tis foul'), and it is 'Act 3, Scene 7. The Blinding of Gloucester.' Gloucester's beard is a joke-shop goatee, which Regan pulls off, pantomime-style ("tis most ignobly done/To pluck me by the beard' [III. v. 35-6]). It gets a laugh. Upstage, behind the tables, two men strip to their underwear, assuming their roles as silent, malevolent comedy doubles of Poor Tom. The scene stops, reverts; the beard is stuck back on. Goneril, Regan and Gloucester begin again; the beard is pulled off again. This time the audience laughter is more sporadic. They begin again; this time there is no laugh: reactions are being tested, played with. The boxer short men, co-opted as servants, move round and lower Gloucester's chair backwards to the floor; Gloucester watches them blankly, trustingly. The blinding (a simple covering of Gloucester's eyes with gaffer tape) is flat, emotionless, quiet. The sequence is run through again, accompanied by the sound of helicopters: this time Gloucester's eyes are sealed with the gaffer tape that was used to bind him to the chair. And, then, a small, plaintive cry from Robin (which earns another laugh): 'I can't see'. Unable to read his script, he is fed his lines by other members of the cast: his 'I have no way and therefore want no eyes ... ' is played as a line-by-line repetition, with exaggerated emphasis, of Director's stage-whispered cues.

With Gloucester seated alone centre stage, Mark appears on the video again: 'Gloucester got tied to a chair and had his eyes poked out ... ' After a brief reprise of Act 4, Scene 1, during which muzak plays and Lear places flowers on the floor, Lear invites Sue to say 'a few words about the current refugee crisis'. She begins, haltingly:

> Forty thousand refugees have gone missing. Thirteen thousand of them are reported to ... be ... fine. Ten thousand of them are still ... it is still unknown ... of their whereabouts ... the United States will take –

She is silenced by a loud burst of recorded applause. On video, Mark resumes the story of Blind Gloucester and 'Mad Pete or Mad Bob or whatever his name was'. Then it is 'Act 5, Scene 3. The British camp near Dover.' The soothing, elevator-style muzak plays briefly as the tables are cleared to the sides and chairs are placed in a circle. The lights dim: performers stand or sit, heads bowed over scripts and commence a reading of the final scene (from 'Help, help, O help' [V. iii. 220]) that is conducted barely above the level of a whisper.

Freighted with emotions withheld and contained rather than indulged, it is quietly, oddly moving. Robin, eyes masked, stands downstage and smokes. Claire, as Cordelia, stretches out at the front, her hand protective on her stomach. Lear squats on his heels behind for his last closing speech; on 'Look there, look there' he calmly lays his script aside and lies down to die beside her, curled in a foetal position, hunched inside his furs.

With Edgar's final words the monitor comes to life for the last time, revealing the bloodied face of Gloucester, soundlessly mouthing. Music swells, a crooning, string-heavy ballad (George Harrison from the Beatles' *White Album*):

> Now it's time to say goodnight
> Goodnight, sleep tight ...

As the lights fade, the performers leave the stage one by one, Robin stumbling blindly through the auditorium, the others into the wings. The song ends, and there is one final audio cue: a sound, as it were, from beneath the rubble of the play, and the provocation for a last laugh that is composed in equal measure of warmth, surprise, and relief.

It is the cry of a newborn baby.

Conclusion

The field of enquiry addressed by this study is just over a century of performance activities which has seen a more rapid pace, and variety, of change in the practice of Shakespearean theatremaking than in any previous period in history. The landmark Shakespearean events of that period have been thoroughly documented; more recently, the culturally-inscribed historicity which was formerly elided in the search for the elusive ideal or essence of Shakespearean performance has begun to be more carefully identified and evaluated than ever before. If part of the project of this book has been to shed a new light upon the larger histories of performance which provide the context for the localised encounters that it discusses, it is also concerned to problematise the assumptions which, to a certain extent, continue to determine not only what we consider Shakespeare in performance actually is, can be, or should be, but also the ways in which it can be thought or written about. We may now be rightly suspicious of the narrative schemes which retrospectively impose a trajectory of development upon events and materials that are characterised by chance, contingency and opportunism, and shaped by cultural forces far larger than a modernising impulse which seeks to return the future of Shakespearean theatre into an idealised past by the 'revolutionary' imposition of performance conditions and textual imperatives which previous generations were held to have abused or ignored. We may also consider that the old arguments between the literary and theatrical Shakespeares have been amicably settled, with performance safely installed within the disciplines of scholarship as a legitimised area of study, and with the text fully respected as the product of the theatrical medium for which it continues to be destined.

That this book exists at all, and in the form it does, is itself testament to the security of a consensus around Shakespearean performance that will no doubt be maintained well into the century that is to come. Writers and readers (of this book, of others) will continue to enter the vicarious arena of theatre history because it offers a way of seeing cultures, or because of the rich panorama of human ingenuity and folly it affords, or even because it offers new, and often immensely pleasurable, ways of thinking and feeling about the plays themselves. But, at least as far as this study is concerned, it is the last of these considerations that is, ultimately, the most problematic. The legitimacy that has been accorded to the theatre, the authority which has been vested in performance and, to a lesser extent, in the writings which document and explicate it, reflect the perception that Shakespearean theatre is worth making, and theatre scholarship worth doing, because they enlarge understanding of the texts which stand behind them. It is an attitude which has deep roots in the paradigmatic alliance between scholarly endeavour and pedagogic stage practice engineered by Poel; and although the work itself (as discussed in the first chapter) has been firmly put in its place by theatre history, what remains of the stage-centred movement within the critical profession has retained a residue of the founder's evangelical sense of responsibility. There is, moreover, an appealingly symmetrical quality to the model of the relationship between Shakespeare and the performance medium which understands contemporary theatrical practice to be, in a fundamental sense, partnered with its early modern prototype. Extended and, to a certain extent, distended, 'performance' can be taken to designate a domain in which all may be possible but, importantly, that which is permissible is finally arbitrated on the grounds of the security of that partnership.

For a long time, as these pages have attempted to demonstrate, the convergence between the imperatives of the Shakespearean avant-garde and a revivalism which cultivated authentic theatrical intervention as a variant of theatrical modernism meant that the claims of past and present remained in a dynamic, mutually beneficial balance. Posterity may take the view that Poel got it wrong in practice even if, debatably, he was right in principle; but Granville Barker, Guthrie, Goodbody, and, in the end, Sam Wanamaker succeeded in hammering the elusively perfect Shakespearean stage into a working material form. In this sense, the modernist legacy is still very much with us as a mental as well as literally material architecture of performance, but it is also evident in the continuing adherence to the notion of the Shakespearean 'performance text', viewed as both the authoritative repository of theatricality as history and the motor of all future innovation.

It is an attitude glimpsed in the slightly naive form of the example which marks the opening of this book but which is chronologically situated at the close of the period under consideration: the opportunistic and paradoxical convergence in the Red Shift *Hamlet: First Cut* between textual fundamentalism and slam-bang sartorial modernity is in a sense a rehearsal of the conflicts between text, performance, contingency and principle that are mapped throughout. However apparently iconoclastic the method engaged in this revival may appear by the standards of the mainstream Shakespearean stage, what is in the end a dutiful relation to textual and cultural authority keeps it within the legitimate realms of pertinence, taste and sense. As I hope to have shown, performance is often at its most interesting (if not its most 'successful') when that customary relationship is challenged or otherwise put under strain, deliberately or otherwise. Although performance appears to be haunted by the presence of admonitory textual ghosts, and regulated by institutional and discursive constraints, which together comprise what I understand to be the Shakespeare Effect, the opportunities for remaking Shakespeare (something far larger than the texts of the plays, as the chapter on *Bingo* aims to reveal) are themselves well in excess of the critical and ideological mechanisms that would seek to administer them.

Here the Red Shift production, regarded as one kind of postmodern Shakespeare, may be set alongside the Forced Entertainment project with which it is contemporaneous, and which is the subject of my final chapter. I am well aware that although some readers may find the work amusing or intriguing, many others will be dismayed or irritated by such a flagrantly inconsequential and irresponsible venture, one which is uniquely resistant to being read within the larger frame of performed Shakespeare inhabited by the book as a whole. So be it: if the recurrent preoccupations of this study have been the entropic tendencies within performance and its potential to create effects and meanings which escape the remit of the Shakespearean, then *Five Day Lear* provides something of a limit case against which may be viewed the eccentricities and conformities of the work discussed elsewhere. Restricted in scope and significance as it may be in one way, the example of Forced Entertainment nonetheless poses larger questions about the potential for performed Shakespeare to encounter vocabularies – and politics – of performance which call for a far more drastic dismantling of long-standing protocols of textual and theatrical authority than those attempted in the epoch of modernism. In effect, if Shakespeare is to survive within Anglo-American culture (and I suspect that Gary Taylor's hope, as outlined in the introduction, that his demise is imminent reflects an exaggerated sense of his mortality), it may need to return to the tactics of adaptation, reinvention and cultural appropriation that sustained the plays within the public sphere before the proponents of authenticity ruled them out of order, and which are in any case more genuinely representative of

Shakespeare's fortunes in world culture than is the revivalist tradition. Whatever happens, it will not be a story of progress, but a further stage in a history of change which, if the lesson of the previous century is anything to go by, will be nothing if not unpredictable.

Notes

Introduction

1. Mentioned in Bryan N.S. Gooch and David Thatcher (eds), *A Shakespeare Music Catalogue*, 5 vols (Oxford: Clarendon Press, 1991).
2. Graham Holderness and Bryan Loughrey (eds), *The Tragicall Historie of Hamlet Prince of Denmark* (Hemel Hempstead: Harvester Wheatsheaf, 1992). Although it is not acknowledged, this was clearly the edition used for the production, in that the comments in the programme by Sam Walters and Christopher McCullough are taken verbatim from the introduction. The Shakespearean Originals series has generated a great deal of (mostly rancorous) debate: for a summary of the charges levelled at them by their critics, and a response, see Graham Holderness and Bryan Loughrey, 'Shakespeare Misconstrued: the True Chronicle History of *Shakespearean Originals*', *Textus*, 9 (1996), 393–418.
3. Maeve Walsh, *Independent on Sunday*, 23 January 2000.
4. Ann Thompson, 'The Non-Canonical *Hamlet*', unpublished paper delivered to the London Renaissance Seminar at Birkbeck College, University of London, 13 January 2001. I am grateful to Ann Thompson for supplying me with a copy of this paper.
5. W.B. Worthen, *Shakespeare and the Authority of Performance* (Cambridge: Cambridge University Press, 1997), p. 3.
6. Ibid.
7. See Susan Bennett, *Performing Nostalgia: Shifting Shakespeare and the Contemporary Past* (London: Routledge, 1996).
8. See Ania Loomba, '"Local-manufacture-made-in-India Othello fellows": Issues of race, hybridity and location in post-colonial Shakespeares', in *Post-Colonial Shakespeares*, ed. Ania Loomba and Martin Orkin (London: Routledge, 1998), pp. 143–63; John Russell Brown, *New Sites for Shakespeare: Theatre, the Audience and Asia* (London: Routledge, 1999).
9. Gary Taylor, 'Afterword: the Incredible Shrinking Bard', in *Shakespeare and Appropriation*, ed. Christy Desmet and Robert Sawyer (London: Routledge, 2000), pp. 197, 199.
10. Ibid., p. 202.
11. Quoted in *The Daily Chronicle*, 3 September 1913.
12. Quoted in Dennis Kennedy, *Looking at Shakespeare: a Visual History of Twentieth-Century Performance* (Cambridge: Cambridge University Press, 1993), p. 84.
13. See Barbara Hodgdon, 'Looking for Mr Shakespeare after "The Revolution": Robert Lepage's Intercultural *Dream* Machine', in *Shakespeare, Theory, and Performance*, ed. James C. Bulman (London: Routledge, 1996), pp. 68–91.
14. See Robert Shaughnessy, 'The Last Post: *Henry V*, War Culture and the Postmodern Shakespeare', *Theatre Survey*, 39 (1998), 41–62.

15. Johannes Birringer, *Theatre, Theory, Postmodernism* (Bloomington: Indiana University Press, 1993), p. 221.
16. Michael Cordner, 'Repeopling the Globe: the Opening Season at Shakespeare's Globe, 1997', *Shakespeare Survey*, 51 (1998), 206.
17. Raymond Williams, *Marxism and Literature* (Oxford: Oxford University Press, 1977), p. 124.
18. Thomas Clayton, 'Theatrical Shakespearegresses at the Guthrie and Elsewhere: Notes on "Legitimate" Production', *New Literary History*, 17 (1986), reprinted in *Shakespeare: the Critical Complex: Shakespeare in the Theater*, ed. Stephen Orgel and Sean Keilen (New York: Garland, 1999), p. 533.
19. Stanley Wells, *Shakespeare in the Theatre: an Anthology of Criticism* (Oxford: Oxford University Press, 1997), p. 1.
20. Peter Holland, *English Shakespeares: Shakespeare on the English Stage in the 1990s* (Cambridge: Cambridge University Press, 1997), p. 19.
21. Richard David, *Shakespeare in the Theatre* (Cambridge: Cambridge University Press, 1978), p. 18.
22. Alan Read, *Theatre and Everyday Life: an Ethics of Performance* (London: Routledge, 1993), p. 2.
23. Peggy Phelan, *Unmarked: the Politics of Performance* (London: Routledge, 1993), p. 146.
24. George Bernard Shaw, Foreword to *Cymbeline Refinished*, in *Geneva, Cymbeline Refinished, and Good King Charles* (London: Constable and Company, 1946), p. 133.
25. See in particular Kennedy, *Looking at Shakespeare*; and Jonathan Bate and Russell Jackson (eds), *Shakespeare: an Illustrated Stage History* (Oxford: Oxford University Press, 1996).

1. The Last of the Pre-Raphaelites

1. For discussions of Poel, see Robert Speaight, *William Poel and the Elizabethan Revival* (London: Heinemann, 1954); Arthur Harris, 'William Poel's Elizabethan Stage: the First Experiment', *Theatre Notebook*, 17 (1963), 111–14; Charles Glick, 'William Poel: His Theories and Influence', *Shakespeare Quarterly*, 15 (1964), 15-25; Stephen C. Schultz, 'Two Notes on William Poel's Sources', *Nineteenth Century Theatre Research*, 2 (1974), 85–91; 'William Poel', *Shakespeare Quarterly*, 28 (1977), 334–50; J. L. Styan, *The Shakespeare Revolution: Criticism and Performance in the Twentieth Century* (Cambridge: Cambridge University Press, 1977), pp. 47–63; Cary M. Mazer, *Shakespeare Refashioned: Elizabethan Plays on Edwardian Stages* (Ann Arbor: UMI Research Press, 1981), pp. 49–84; Rinda F. Lundstrom, *William Poel's Hamlets: the Director as Critic* (Ann Arbor: UMI Research Press, 1984); Peter Womack, 'Notes on the "Elizabethan" Avant-Garde', in *Shakespeare and the Twentieth Century*, ed. Jonathan Bate, Jill L. Levenson and Dieter Mehl (Newark: University of Delaware Press, 1998), pp. 75–84; Martin White, 'William Poel's Globe', *Theatre Notebook*, 53 (1999), 146–62. The most comprehensive account, to which the current chapter is heavily indebted, is that of Marion O'Connor, *William Poel and the Elizabethan Stage Society*

(Cambridge: Chadwyck-Healey, 1987). O'Connor has recently supplemented this study in '"Useful in the Year 1999": William Poel and Shakespeare's "Build of Stage"', *Shakespeare Survey*, 52 (1999), 17–32; and 'William Poel to George Bernard Shaw', *Theatre Notebook*, 54 (2000), 162–76.

2. Kathleen O. Irace (ed.), *The First Quarto of Hamlet* (Cambridge: Cambridge University Press, 1998), Introduction, p. 23. Irace refers to productions by Ben Greet's company at the Rudolf Steiner Hall, London, 1928, at the Nottingham Playhouse in 1983, at the Orange Tree, Richmond (directed by Sam Walters) in 1985, for Shakespeare in the Park at Fort Worth, Texas in 1992 (director: Michael Muller), by the Medieval Players in the same year, and at the Oregon Shakespeare Festival in 1994. To these may be added the Red Shift production (1999–2000) discussed above, pp. 1–5.

3. Dutton Cook, 'The *Hamlet* of 1603', in *Nights at the Play: a View of the English Stage* (London: Chatto and Windus, 1883), pp. 454–5.

4. Sir Henry Bunbury, Bart. (ed.), *The Correspondence of Thomas Hanmer* (London: Edward Moxon, 1838), p. 80. The volume also contained *The Merchant of Venice, The Merry Wives of Windsor, A Midsummer Night's Dream, Troilus and Cressida, Romeo and Juliet, 1 & 2 Henry IV, Henry V, Richard II* and *The Two Noble Kinsmen* ('with MS corrections of the text').

5. *The First Edition of the Tragedy of Hamlet* (London: Shakespeare Press, 1825).

6. See Edward Malone, *The Plays and Poems of William Shakespeare*, vol. 3, ed. James Boswell (London: F.C. and J. Rivington, 1821), p. 298; R.A. Foakes and R.T. Rickert (eds), *Henslowe's Diary* (Cambridge: Cambridge University Press, 1961).

7. Samuel Timmins, 'Bibliographical Preface', *The Devonshire 'Hamlets'* (London: Samson, Low, Son and Co., 1860). The legend on the title page, 'Looke heere on this Picture, and on this', may have been incorporated to encourage objective and even-handed scholarly evaluation, but it may well also call to mind the invidious comparison between Old Hamlet and Claudius: it is not difficult to guess which text would be identified with the honoured father and which with the reviled interloper.

8. F.J. Furnivall, 'Foreword', in *Shakspere's 'Hamlet': the First Quarto, 1603* (London: Shakspere Society, 1880).

9. Michael Twyman, *Lithography 1800–1850* (London: Oxford University Press, 1970), p. 253.

10. John Tagg, *The Burden of Representation: Essays on Photographies and Histories* (Basingstoke: Macmillan Press – now Palgrave Macmillan, 1988), p. 11.

11. Roland Barthes, *Camera Lucida*, trans. Richard Howard (London: Jonathan Cape, 1981), p. 76.

12. Gary Taylor, 'General Introduction', in Stanley Wells and Gary Taylor, *William Shakespeare: a Textual Companion* (Oxford: Clarendon Press, 1987), p. 4. Taylor describes the Praetorius facsimiles as 'unreliable' (p. 62n).

13. Lady Elizabeth Eastlake, 'Photography', *Quarterly Review*, March 1857, reprinted in *Classic Essays on Photography*, ed. Alan Trachtenburg (New Haven, CT: Leete's Island Books, 1980), p. 64.

14. William Poel, *Shakespeare in the Theatre* (London: Sidgwick and Jackson, 1913), pp. 203–4.

15. *Mr Wm Poel's Shakespeare Reading Class*, undated pamphlet (probably

c. 1900) in the Theatre Museum, London.

16. William Poel, *Shakespeare in the Theatre* (London: Sidgwick and Jackson, 1911), p. 60.
17. Letter to Furnivall, 1 February 1881.
18. Herbert A. Evans, Introduction to *Romeo and Juliet, by William Shakspere. The First Quarto, 1597* (London: New Shakspere Society, 1886), pp. vii–viii.
19. Richard Proudfoot, *Shakespeare: Text, Stage and Canon* (London: Arden Shakespeare, 2001), p. 48.
20. Nina Auerbach, *Private Theatricals: the Lives of the Victorians* (Cambridge, MA: Harvard University Press, 1990), p. 8.
21. Russell Jackson, 'Actor-Managers and the Spectacular', in *Shakespeare: an Illustrated Stage History*, ed. Jonathan Bate and Russell Jackson (Oxford: Oxford University Press, 1996), p. 113.
22. Henry Irving, 'Shakespeare as a Playwright', in *The Henry Irving Shakespeare*, ed. Henry Irving and Frank A. Marshall, Vol.1 (London: Blackie and Son, 1888), pp. xvii, xxi.
23. Quoted in Norman Marshall, *The Producer and the Play*, 2nd edn (London: Davis-Poynter, 1962), pp. 145–6.
24. Simon Shepherd and Peter Womack, *English Drama: a Cultural History* (Oxford: Basil Blackwell, 1996), p. 106; Edward Dowden, *Shakspere: a Critical Study of his Mind and Art* (London: Kegan Paul, 1875).
25. O'Connor points out that Poel's production photographs are 'unique as records of theatrical performance at the time. Made at photo calls, they show players posed, in costume and as if enacting a particular moment in production, on whichever stage was being used for it. By contrast, most theatrical photography through the 1890s is studio work ... often with the photographer's stock items' ('Useful in the Year 1999', p. 29).
26. Hugh Grady, *The Modernist Shakespeare: Critical Texts in a Material World* (Oxford: Clarendon Press, 1991), p. 28.
27. Reprinted in *Shakespeare in the Theatre* (London: Sidgwick and Jackson, 1913), pp. 156–76.
28. R.A. Foakes, *Hamlet versus Lear: Cultural Politics and Shakespeare's Art* (Cambridge: Cambridge University Press, 1993), pp. 13–15.
29. Clement Scott, *Daily Telegraph*, November 1874, reprinted in *Shakespeare in the Theatre: an Anthology of Criticism*, ed. Stanley Wells (Oxford: Oxford University Press, 1997), p. 107.
30. Dowden, *Shakspere*, p. 157.
31. Quoted in H.H. Furness (ed.), *Hamlet*, New Variorum Edition, vol. 2 (Philadelphia: J.B. Lippincott & Co., 1877), p. 36.
32. Poel, Letter to Furnivall, 23 October 1880; *Academy*, 12 February 1881.
33. O'Connor, *William Poel*, p. 19.
34. Raymond Mander and Joe Mitchenson, *The Lost Theatres of London* (London: Rupert Hart-Davis, 1968).
35. *Era*, 7 January 1900, quoted in Mander and Mitchenson, *Lost Theatres*, p. 443.
36. O'Connor, *William Poel*, p. 20.
37. See Diana Howard, *London Theatres and Music Halls 1850-1950* (London: The Library Association, 1970), p. 210.
38. Lundstrom, *William Poel's Hamlets*, p. 19.

39. Marvin Rosenberg, *The Masks of Hamlet* (London and Toronto: Associated University Presses, 1992), p. 156.
40. Robert Hapgood, *Shakespeare in Production: Hamlet, Prince of Denmark* (Cambridge: Cambridge University Press, 1999), p. 38.
41. Hapgood, *Hamlet*, p. 102, quoting the *New York Evening Post Magazine*, 20 December 1919.
42. Shepherd and Womack, *English Drama*, p. 117.
43. Speaight, *William Poel and the Elizabethan Revival*, p. 60.
44. Sale catalogue for the auction of Elizabethan Stage Society property, July 1905, quoted in O'Connor, *William Poel*, p. 28.
45. *Daily Chronicle*, 13 September 1913, quoted in Mazer, *Shakespeare Refashioned*, p. 56.
46. Kennedy, *Looking at Shakespeare*, p. 39.
47. Mazer, op. cit., p. 58.
48. *The Times*, 11 July 1899, quoted in O'Connor, *William Poel*, p. 69.
49. Lundstrom, op. cit., p. 58.
50. Programme held in Theatre Museum Archive.
51. Quoted in Dorothy Thompson, *Queen Victoria: Gender and Power* (London: Virago, 1990), p. 136.
52. Ibid., p. 119.
53. Speaight, *Elizabethan Revival*, p. 101. O'Connor records the following breeches parts: Balthazar in the 1890 *Much Ado*; Claudio in the 1891 *Measure for Measure*; Valentine, Proteus, Thurio and Eglamour in the 1892 *Two Gentlemen*; Romeo, Mercutio and Benvolio in the 1895 *Romeo and Juliet*; Trebonius, Messala, Lucius, Metellus Cimber, Cinna the Conspirator, Flavius, Titinius, Messenger and Servants in the 1896 *Julius Caesar* (*William Poel*, p. 64).
54. Poel, *Some Notes on Shakespeare's Stage and Plays* (Manchester: Manchester University Press, 1916), p. 61.
55. Poel, *An Account of the Elizabethan Stage Society* (London, 1898), pp. 6–7.
56. Edward Vining, *The Mystery of Hamlet* (Philadelphia: J.P. Lippincott and Co., 1881), pp. 54, 48.
57. Quoted in Marjorie Garber, *Vested Interests: Cross-Dressing and Cultural Anxiety* (Harmondsworth: Penguin, 1993), p. 38; and in Foakes, *Hamlet versus Lear*, p. 25. Raymond Mander and Joe Mitchenson record the following nineteenth-century female Hamlets: Mrs Bartley in New York (1819); Charlotte Cushman (1851); Julia Glover at the Lyceum (1821); Mrs Bandmann-Palver (from 1895); Clara Howard at the Imperial Theatre (1899). See *Hamlet through the Ages: a Pictorial Record from 1709* (London: Rockliff, 1952), p. 24.
58. Sally Ledger, 'The New Woman and the Crisis of Victorianism', in *Cultural Politics at the Fin de Siècle*, ed. Sally Ledger and Scott McCracken (Cambridge: Cambridge University Press, 1995), p. 22.
59. Womack, 'Notes on the "Elizabethan" Avant-Garde', p. 75.
60. Kerry Powell, *Women and Victorian Theatre* (Cambridge: Cambridge University Press, 1997), pp. 70–1.
61. *The Times*, 3 March 1900, quoted in Styan, *Shakespeare Revolution*, p. 27.
62. Poel, *What is Wrong with the Stage: Some Notes on the English Theatre from the Earliest Times to the Present Day* (London: George Allen and Unwin, 1920),

pp. 4, 10; *Shakespeare's Profession* (London: London Shakespeare League, 1915), pp. 15, 3.

63. Address to Annual General Meeting, 10 July 1899, Elizabethan Stage Society Annual Report 1899, p. 4.
64. Speaight, op. cit., pp. 257, 70.
65. Carol J. Adams, *The Sexual Politics of Meat: a Feminist-Vegetarian Critical Theory* (New York: Continuum, 1998), p. 30.
66. Elisee Reclus, 'On Vegetarianism', *Humane Review*, January 1901, quoted in Nick Fiddes, *Meat: a Natural Symbol* (London: Routledge, 1991), p. 130.
67. William Poel, *Monthly Letters*, ed. A.M.T. (London: Werner Laurie, 1929), pp. 42, 45, 42–3.
68. Lynne Vallone and Claudia Nelson, 'Introduction', in *The Girl's Own: Cultural Histories of the Anglo-American Girl, 1830–1915* (Athens and London: University of Georgia Press, 1994), p. 3.
69. Anna Jameson, *Shakespeare's Heroines*, revised edition (London: Bell, 1891), pp. 117-18, p. 114; William Hazlitt, *Complete Works*, Vol. 4, ed. P.P. Howe (London: Dent, 1932), p. 251; cited in Philip Davis, 'Nineteenth-Century Juliet', *Shakespeare Survey*, 49 (1996), 131–2.
70. Edward Dowden (ed.), *Romeo and Juliet*, The Arden Shakespeare (London: Methuen, 1900), Introduction, p. xxiii
71. Kimberley Reynolds, *Children's Literature in the 1890s and 1990s* (Plymouth: Northcote House, 1994), p. 3.
72. Cook, *Nights at the Play*, pp. 453, 4–5.
73. Tracy C. Davis, *Actresses as Working Women: their Social Identity in Victorian Culture* (London: Routledge, 1991), pp. 139-40.
74. Speaight, op. cit., p. 41.
75. Jill L. Levenson, *Romeo and Juliet*, The Oxford Shakespeare (Oxford: Oxford University Press, 2000), p. 81.
76. William Poel, *The Stage-Version of Romeo and Juliet* (London: London Shakespeare League, 1915), pp. 25, 26.
77. Speaight, op. cit., p. 197.
78. *Pall Mall Gazette*, 2 December 1912, quoted in Speaight, *Elizabethan Revival*, p. 192.
79. O'Connor, 'Useful in the Year 1999', p. 29.
80. O'Connor, *William Poel*, p. 14.
81. *Monthly Letters*, p. 95; *Notes on Some of William Poel's Stage Productions* (London: A.W. Patching and Co., 1933), no pagination.
82. Quoted in Speaight, *Elizabethan Revival*, pp. 87–8.
83. William Poel, 'The Functions of a National Theatre', *The Theatre*, May 1893, quoted in Jackson, 'Actor-Managers and the Spectacular', p. 124.
84. Poel, *Some Notes on Shakespeare's Stage and Plays*, pp. 3–11.
85. See Robert Shaughnessy, 'Shakespearean Utopias', *Shakespeare Survey*, 53 (2000), 233–43.

2. Cambridge Irish

1. Robert Morley, *Around the World in Eighty-One Years* (London: Hodder and Stoughton, 1990), pp. 32, 34, 33.

2. Léon Moussinac, *The New Movement in the Theatre: a Survey of Recent Developments in Europe in America* (New York: Benjamin Blom, 1932), p. 128.
3. Norman Marshall, *The Other Theatre* (London: John Lehmann, 1947), p. 69.
4. A.C. Sprague, *Shakespeare's Histories: Plays for the Stage* (London: Society for Theatre Research, 1964), p. 11; Robert Speaight, *Shakespeare on the Stage* (London: Collins, 1973), p. 163.
5. Richard Allen Cave, *Terence Gray and the Cambridge Festival Theatre* (Cambridge: Chadwyck-Healey, 1980), p. 75. See also Graham Woodruff, 'Terence Gray and Theatre Design', *Theatre Research*, 2 & 3 (1971), 114-32; and '"Down with the Boot-Faced": Public Relations at the Festival Theatre, Cambridge', *Theatre Research International*, 1 (1976), 114–25; Steve Nicholson, '"Nobody Was Ready for That": the Gross Impertinence of Terence Gray and the Degradation of Drama', *Theatre Research International*, 21 (1996), 121–31.
6. Andrew Davies, *Other Theatres: the Development of Alternative and Experimental Theatre in Britain* (Basingstoke: Macmillan Press – now Palgrave Macmillan, 1987), p. 86.
7. Kennedy, *Looking at Shakespeare*, p. 119. See also Styan, *Shakespeare Revolution*, pp. 153–4.
8   Cave, *Terence Gray*, p. 53.
9. Gordon McMullan (ed.), *Henry VIII*, The Arden Shakespeare, 3rd Series (London: Arden Shakespeare, 2000), pp. 44, 48.
10. Harold Ridge, *Stage Lighting* (Cambridge: Heffer and Sons, 1930), p. 111.
11. Marshall, op. cit., p. 54.
12. Ridge, op. cit., p. 114.
13. Terence Gray, 'I Look to the Audience', *Theatre Arts Monthly*, vol. 15, no. 10 (1931), p. 818.
14. Terence Gray, 'This Age in the Theatre', *The Bookman*, vol. 32 (1932), 11.
15. Gray, 'I Look to the Audience', p. 818.
16. Terence Gray, *Festival Theatre Review*, vol. 4, no. 64 (1930), 3.
17. Bertolt Brecht, 'The Literarization of the Theatre (Notes to the *Threepenny Opera*)', in *Brecht on Theatre*, ed. John Willett (London: Methuen, 1964), p. 44.
18. For a discussion of the relations between theatre, fire and safety, see Alan Read, *Theatre and Everyday Life*, pp. 228–36.
19. Woodruff, '"Down with the Boot-Faced"', p. 123.
20. Marshall, op. cit., p. 57.
21. Terence Gray, 'Who are the Critics: a Reply', *Festival Theatre Review*, vol. 2, no. 30 (1928), 10.
22. Gray, 'I Look to the Audience', p. 817.
23. Francis Mulhern, *The Moment of 'Scrutiny'* (London: Verso, 1979), p. 28.
24. Raphael Samuel, 'Theatre and Socialism in Britain (1880–1935)', in *Theatres of the Left 1880–1935: Workers' Theatre Movements in Britain and America*, ed. Raphael Samuel, Ewan MacColl and Stuart Cosgrove (London: Routledge, 1985), p. 44.
25. Steve Nicholson, 'Nobody Was Ready for That', pp. 124–30.
26. Quoted in Sarah Stanton, 'Theatre of Pleasure', *CAM: the University of Cambridge Alumni Magazine*, Michaelmas Term 1995, 27.

27. Christopher McCullough, 'The Cambridge Connection: Towards a Materialist Theatre Practice', in *The Shakespeare Myth*, ed. Graham Holderness (Manchester: Manchester University Press, 1988), p. 14.
28. Terence Hawkes, 'Entry on Q', in *Shakespeare and Appropriation*, ed. Christy Desmet and Robert Sawyer (London: Routledge, 1999), p. 41.
29. E.M.W. Tillyard, *The Elizabethan World Picture* (London: Chatto and Windus, 1943); *Shakespeare's History Plays* (London: Chatto and Windus, 1944).
30. E.M.W. Tillyard, *The Muse Unchained: an Intimate Account of the Revolution in English Studies at Cambridge* (London: Bowes and Bowes, 1958), pp. 77, 94.
31. Terence Gray, *Cuchulainn: an Epic-Drama of the Gael* (Cambridge: Heffer and Sons, 1925).
32. Andrew Sanders, *The Short Oxford History of English Literature* (Oxford: Oxford University Press, 1994), p. 495.
33. Terence Gray, *Dance-Drama: Experiments in the Art of the Theatre* (Cambridge: Heffer and Sons, 1926), pp. 6–13.
34. Declan Kiberd, *Inventing Ireland* (London: Jonathan Cape, 1995), p. 274.
35. David Cairns and Shaun Richards, *Writing Ireland: Colonialism, Nationalism and Culture* (Manchester: Manchester University Press, 1988), p. 71.
36. Gray, *Dance-Drama*, p. 13.
37. Edward Gordon Craig, *On the Art of the Theatre* (London: William Heinemann, 1911), p. 138.
38. Terence Gray, 'The Future of the Drama', *Festival Theatre Review*, vol. 1, no. 15 (1927), 3.
39. Gray, *Dance-Drama*, pp. 26–7.
40. Annabel Farjeon, 'Choreographers: Dancing for de Valois and Ashton', in *The Routledge Dance Studies Reader*, ed. Alexandra Carter (London: Routledge, 1998), p. 24.
41. Kiberd, op. cit., p. 274.
42. Ibid., pp. 269, 280.
43. *Evening Mail*, 6 July 1911, quoted in Robert Hogan, Richard Burnham and Daniel P. Poteet, *The Abbey Theatre: Rise of the Realists 1910–1915* (Dublin: Dolmen Press, 1979), pp. 132–3.
44. See Richard English, 'Shakespeare and the Definition of the Irish Nation', and Michael Cronin, 'Rug-Headed Kerns Speaking Tongues: Shakespeare, Translation and the Irish Language', in *Shakespeare and Ireland: History, Politics, Culture*, ed. Mark Thornton Burnett and Ramona Wray (Basingstoke: Macmillan Press – now Palgrave Macmillan, 1997).
45. Micheál Ó hAoadha, *Theatre in Ireland* (Oxford: Basil Blackwell, 1974), pp. 118–19.
46. Woodruff, 'Theatre Design', p. 126.
47. Marshall, op. cit., p. 64.
48. Terence Gray, *Festival Theatre Review*, vol. 3, no. 4 (1926), 6.
49. Sybil Rosenfeld, *A Short History of Scene Design in Britain* (Oxford: Blackwell, 1973), p. 183.
50. Terence Gray, 'The Presentational Treatment of Shakespeare', *Festival Theatre Review*, vol. 2, no. 32 (1928), 6.
51. Wodruff, 'Theatre Design', p. 114.

52. Gray, 'Presentational Treatment', p. 6.
53. John Collick, *Shakespeare, Cinema and Society* (Manchester: Manchester University Press, 1989), pp. 26–8.
54. Moussinac, op. cit., p. 125.
55. Terence Gray, 'Historical Drama', *Festival Theatre Review*, vol. 1, no. 4 (1926), 6.
56. Alistair Cooke, 'The Cambridge Festival Theatre: Ten Seasons of Dramatic Experiment', *Theatre Arts Monthly*, 15, 11 (1931), p. 901.
57. Cave., op. cit., p. 52.
58. Robert Weimann, *Shakespeare and the Popular Tradition in the Theater: Studies in the Social Dimension of Dramatic Form and Function*, ed. Robert Schwartz (Baltimore: Johns Hopkins University Press, 1978).
59. Woodruff, 'Theatre Design', pp. 131–2.
60. Davies, op. cit., p. 105.
61. Donald Rackin, *Alice's Adventures in Wonderland and Through the Looking-Glass: Nonsense, Sense and Meaning* (New York: Twayne, 1991), p. 63. It is not accidental that it was in the late 1920s that the *Alice* books were first afforded serious critical attention, partly as a consequence of the growing interest in psychoanalysis. Oddly enough, one of Carroll's diary entries records his rapture at Kean's production of *Henry VIII*: 'I almost held my breath to watch; the illusion is so perfect, and I felt as if in a dream all the time it lasted ... I never ... felt so inclined to shed tears at anything fictitious, save perhaps at that poetical gem of Dickens, the death of Little Paul [sic]' (Entry dated 22 June 1855, *The Diaries of Lewis Carroll*, Vol. 1, ed. R.L. Green [Westport, CT: Greenwood Press, 1971], p. 54).
62. Terence Gray, *Festival Theatre Review*, vol. 3, no. 55 (1929), 12.
63. Woodruff, '"Down with the Boot-Faced"', p. 122.
64. Marshall, op. cit., p. 66.
65. Cooke, op. cit., p. 902.
66. Marshall, op. cit., p. 67.
67. Ibid.
68. Vsevolod Meyerhold, 'The Actor of the Future and Biomechanics', in *Meyerhold on Theatre*, ed. Edward Braun (London: Methuen, 1969), p. 199; Bertolt Brecht, 'A Dialogue about Acting', in *Brecht on Theatre*, p. 27.
69. Speaight, *Shakespeare on the Stage*, p. 164.
70. Sigmund Freud, *The Standard Edition of the Complete Psychological Works of Sigmund Freud, Volume VIII: Jokes and their Relation to the Unconscious*, ed. James Strachey (London: Hogarth Press, 1960), p. 175.

3. Hamlet and Oedipus Biggs

1. 'Tyrone Guthrie', in *International Dictionary of Theatre, Volume 3: Actors, Directors and Designers* (London: St James Press, 1996), p. 335; Denis Salter, 'Acting Shakespeare in Postcolonial Space', in *Shakespeare, Theory, and Performance*, ed. James C. Bulman (London: Routledge, 1996), p. 120.
2. Tyrone Guthrie, *A Life in the Theatre* (London: Hamish Hamilton, 1959), p. 313.
3. Peter Brook, *The Empty Space* (Harmondsworth: Penguin, 1968).

4. James Forsyth, *Tyrone Guthrie: a Biography* (London: Hamish Hamilton, 1976).
5. Sigmund Freud, 'Address Delivered in the Goethe House in Frankfurt', *The Standard Edition of the Complete Psychological Works of Sigmund Freud, Volume XXI: the Future of an Illusion, Civilization and its Discontents, and Other Works*, ed. James Strachey (London: Hogarth Press, 1961), p. 211.
6. Ibid., pp. 471–2.
7. Forsyth, op. cit., p. ix.
8. Liz Stanley, *The Auto/biographical I: the Theory and Practice of Feminist Auto/biography* (Manchester: Manchester University Press, 1992), pp. 155, 8.
9. Guthrie, *Life*, p. 13.
10. Sidonie Smith, *A Poetics of Women's Autobiography: Marginality and the Fictions of Self-Representation* (Bloomington and Indianapolis: Indiana University Press, 1987), pp. 53–4.
11. Tyrone Guthrie, outline draft script for a series of programmes on drama (1969), p. 1 (TS held in the Theatre Museum, Covent Garden).
12. Sigmund Freud, 'Beyond the Pleasure Principle', *The Standard Edition of the Complete Works of Sigmund Freud, Vol. XVIII*, ed. James Strachey (London: Hogarth Press, 1961), pp. 14–15.
13. Quoted in Barbara Moon, 'Why Guthrie Outdraws Shakespeare', *Maclean's*, 6 August 1955.
14. Unidentified newspaper cutting in the Guthrie papers at Annagh-ma-kerrig.
15. Guthrie, draft television script, 4 June 1969, p. 20 (TS held in the Guthrie papers at Annagh-ma-kerrig).
16. See Forsyth, *Tyrone Guthrie*, pp. 284–305.
17. Untitled and undated manuscript in the Guthrie papers, Annagh-ma-kerrig; references to Soviet and Expressionist theatre and to the technicalities of film would seem to place it at some time in the mid-1930s.
18. *Sunday Times*, 12 November 1933.
19. Tyrone Guthrie, *Theatre Prospect* (London: Wishart and Co., 1932), pp. 62, 48–9.
20. 1891 Order of Council for RVHA, quoted in George Rowell, *The Old Vic Theatre: a History* (Cambridge: Cambridge University Press, 1993), p. 109.
21. Winifred Isaac, *Ben Greet and the Old Vic* (London, 1964), quoted in Rowell, *Old Vic*, p. 99.
22. Ibid., p. 98.
23. Ibid., p. 115.
24. Between 1930 and the outbreak of the Second World War there were fifteen productions in London, as many as of *Othello*, *Macbeth* and *King Lear* combined. At Stratford-upon-Avon there were four revivals of *Hamlet* as compared to three of *Macbeth* and *King Lear* and one of *Othello*. In London, the frequency of productions was matched in this period only by *Twelfth Night* (fourteen in London) and *A Midsummer Night's Dream* (twelve).
25. Guthrie, *Theatre Prospect*, p. 50.
26. Laurence Olivier, *Confessions of an Actor* (London: Coronet, 1984), p. 109.
27. John Dover Wilson, *What Happens in 'Hamlet'* (Cambridge: Cambridge University Press, 1935).
28. See Martin Schofield, *The Ghosts of 'Hamlet': the Play and Modern Writers*

(Cambridge: Cambridge University Press, 1980).
29. Guthrie, *Life*, p. 180.
30. Ernest Jones, *Essays in Applied Psychoanalysis* (London: Ernest Benn, 1923), p. 70. The essay was revised and expanded as *Hamlet and Oedipus* (London: Victor Gollancz, 1949).
31. Lyndsey Stonebridge, *The Destructive Element: British Psychoanalysis and Modernism* (Basingstoke: Macmillan Press – now Palgrave Macmillan, 1998), p. 8. The term 'Bloomsbury fraction' is taken from Raymond Williams, who (as Stonebridge notes) contends that 'the different positions which the Bloomsbury Group assembled, and which they effectively disseminated as the contents of the mind of a modern, educated, civilized individual, are all in effect *alternatives* to a general theory' (*Problems in Materialism and Culture* [London: Verso, 1980], p. 167).
32. Stonebridge, op. cit., p. 10.
33. 'After Ten Years', BBC Radio talk recorded on 29 July 1949 (TS in the Guthrie papers, Annagh-ma-kerrig).
34. Keith Williams and Steven Matthews (eds), *Rewriting the Thirties: Modernism and After* (London: Longman, 1997), pp. 2–3.
35. Olivier, *Confessions*, p. 109.
36. Laurence Olivier, *On Acting* (London: Weidenfeld and Nicolson, 1986), p. 48.
37. Quoted in 'The Producer's Job: Discussion between Tyrone Guthrie and L.A.G. Strong', *The Listener*, 20 March 1941.
38. Olivier, *Confessions*, p. 113.
39. Ibid., p. 109.
40. Marvin Rosenberg, *The Masks of Hamlet*, p. 119.
41. Ernest Jones, Letter to Tyrone Guthrie, 8 January 1937.
42. Jones, Letter to Guthrie, 14 January 1937.
43. Tyrone Guthrie, Letter to Norah Guthrie, October 1938.
44. R.C. Sherriff, *Journey's End*, in *Plays of a Half-Decade* (London: Victor Gollancz, 1933), p. 108.
45. Harcourt Williams, *Old Vic Saga* (London: Winchester Publications, 1949), pp. 143–4.
46. Robert Speaight, *Shakespeare on the Stage* (London: Collins, 1973), p. 155.
47. Ibid.
48. Ivor Brown, 'The Very Spot', *Theatre Arts Monthly*, November 1937, p. 877.
49. See Neils Hansen, 'Gentlemen, you are welcome to Elsinore', *Shakespeare and his Contemporaries in Performance*, ed. Edward Esche (Aldershot: Ashgate, 2000).
50. Mander and Mitchenson, *Hamlet through the Ages*, p. 61.
51. Guthrie, *Life*, p. 170.
52. Annette Prevost, 'The Lighter Side of Elsinore', *Old Vic and Sadler's Wells Magazine*, September–October 1937, p. 6.
53. Forsyth, op. cit., p. 159.
54. Guthrie, *Life*, p. 170.
55. Ibid., p. 172.
56. Quoted in Alfred Rossi, *Astonish Us in the Morning: Tyrone Guthrie Remembered* (London: Hutchinson, 1977), p. 96.
57. Guthrie, *Life*, pp. 170–1.

58. Prevost, op. cit., p, 6.
59. Quoted in Rossi, *Astonish Us*, p. 34; Laurence Olivier, *On Acting*, p. 55.
60. Garry O'Connor, *Alec Guinness: Master of Disguise* (London: Hodder and Stoughton, 1994), pp. 33–4.
61. Rossi, *Astonish Us*, pp. 96, 34.
62. Guthrie, *Life*, p. 172.
63. Olivier, *On Acting*, p.55; Styan, *Shakespeare Revolution*, p. 184.
64. Guthrie, *Life*, p. 171.
65. Prevost, op. cit., p. 6.
66. John Cottrell, *Laurence Olivier* (London: Coronet, 1975), p. 130.
67. Quoted in Thomas Kiernan, *Olivier: the Life of Laurence Olivier* (London: Sidgwick and Jackson, 1981), p. 139.
68. Donald Spoto, *Laurence Olivier: a Biography* (London: Harper Collins, 1991).
69. Olivier, *Confessions*, p. 108.
70. Forsyth, op. cit., p. 158.
71. Guthrie, *Life*, p. 171.

4. Revolution in Stratford

1. Bruce West, 'The Bard has Hefty Emissary', *Globe and Mail*, 17 July 1952.
2. Denis Salter, 'Acting Shakespeare in Postcolonial Space', in *Shakespeare, Theory, and Performance*, ed. James C. Bulman (London: Routledge, 1996), pp. 120–2.
3. Dennis Kennedy, 'Shakespeare and Cultural Tourism', *Theatre Journal*, 50 (1998), 177.
4. Richard Paul Knowles, 'Shakespeare, 1993, and the Discourses of the Stratford Festival, Ontario', *Shakespeare Quarterly*, 45 (1994), 211–26, pp. 213, 218, 219.
5. Maria DiCenzo, Alan Filewod, Ric Knowles, Harry Lane and Ann Wilson, 'Cultural Tourism at Shaw and Stratford: the Shaw Festival and the Stratford Festival 1999', *Canadian Theatre Review*, Spring 2000, 86.
6. Ibid., 87.
7. Alan Filewod, 'Regionalism after Meech Lake: the Unmapping of Canadian Theatre', *Journal of History and Politics/Journal d'Histoire et de Politique*, 9 (1991), pp. 12–13.
8. Geoff Pevere and Greig Dymond, *Mondo Canuck: a Canadian Pop Culture Odyssey* (Scarborough, Ont.: Prentice-Hall, 1996), p. viii.
9. Filewod, 'Regionalism', p. 12.
10. Tyrone Guthrie, *A Life in the Theatre* (London: Hamish Hamilton, 1959), p. 284.
11. Quoted in Carol Corbeil, 'It's Very Strange to be Back', *Globe and Mail*, 24 July 1982, cited in Salter, 'Acting Shakespeare', p. 121.
12. Guthrie, *Life*, p. 299.
13. Robertson Davies, 'The Players', in Tyrone Guthrie, Robertson Davies and Grant MacDonald, *Renown at Stratford: a Record of the Shakespeare Festival in Canada 1953* (Toronto: Clarke, Irwin and Co., 1953), p. 102.
14. Filewod, 'Regionalism', p. 13.
15. Guthrie, *Life*, p. 288.

16. Alec Guinness, *Blessings in Disguise* (Harmondsworth: Penguin, 1997), p. 88.
17. Paul Axelrod, 'Higher Education, Utilitarianism, the Acquisitive Society: Canada, 1930–1980', in *Modern Canada 1930–1980s*, ed. Michael S. Cross and Gregory S. Kealey (Toronto: McLelland and Stewart, 1984), pp. 179–206.
18. Richard Slotkin, *Gunfighter Nation: the Myth of the Frontier in Twentieth-Century America* (New York: Harper Collins, 1992), p. 352.
19. Wilfred Campbell, 'Shakespeare and the Latter-Day Drama', *Canadian Magazine*, November 1907, quoted in Salter, 'Acting Shakespeare', p. 119, emphasis Salter's.
20. Guthrie, *Life*, pp. 282–6.
21. Dan Rebellato, *1956 and All That: the making of Modern British Drama* (London: Routledge, 1999), p. 99.
22. Guthrie, *Life*, pp. 284, 294–8.
23. Festival Theatre Press Release, 1962.
24. Ralph Berry, *Shakespeare in Performance: Castings and Metamorphoses* (Basingstoke: Macmillan Press – now Palgrave Macmillan, 1993), pp. 50–1, Robert Speaight, *Shakespeare on the Stage* (London: Collins, 1973), pp. 237–9.
25. Tyrone Guthrie, 'Shakespeare at Stratford, Ontario', *Shakespeare Survey*, 8 (1955), p. 128.
26. Ibid., pp. 129–31.
27. Francis Barker, *The Tremulous Private Body: Essays on Subjection* (London: Methuen, 1984), p. 35.
28. Matthew Arnold, 'Preface to the First Edition of *Poems*', in *The Poems of Matthew Arnold*, ed. Kenneth Allot (London: Longmans, 1965), p. 591.
29. Barker, op. cit., p. 36.
30. Edward R. Russell, *Irving as Hamlet* (London, 1875), p. 22.
31. Mary Z. Maher, *Modern Hamlets and their Soliloquies* (Iowa: University of Iowa Press, 1992), pp. 10–11. In Guthrie's production at the Old Vic in 1938, Alec Guinness played key soliloquies seated, on a stool for 'O that this too too solid flesh', on the floor for 'O what a rogue and peasant slave'. Ben Kingsley, who in Buzz Goodbody's 1975 production at the RSC's Other Place punctuated his delivery of the 'rogue and peasant slave' speech by leaving the theatre building, played 'To be or not to be' rooted to the spot: 'he brought a chair in from the wings, banged it down, sat astride it' (pp. 23–4, 82).
32. Quoted in J.C. Trewin, *Shakespeare on the English Stage, 1900–1964* (London: Barrie and Rockliff, 1964), p. 249.
33. Marvin Rosenberg, *The Masks of Hamlet* (London and Toronto: Associated University Presses, 1992), p. 205.
34. Guthrie, *Life*, p. 187.
35. See Robert Weimann, *Shakespeare and the Popular Tradition in the Theater: Studies in the Social Dimension of Dramatic Form and Function*, ed. Robert Schwarz (Baltimore: Johns Hopkins University Press, 1978), pp. 73–85.
36. Mary Carruthers, *The Craft of Thought: Meditation, Rhetoric, and the Making of Images, 400–1200* (Cambridge: Cambridge University Press, 1998), pp. 272–3. I am grateful to Allen Fisher and Joe Kelleher for suggesting this connection.

37. Ibid.
38. Guthrie, Letter to Alec Guinness, September 1952.
39. See Tom Patterson and Allan Gould, *First Stage: the Making of the Stratford Festival* (Toronto: McClelland and Stewart, 1987).
40. For an eyewitness account, see Alfred Rossi, *Minneapolis Rehearsals: Tyrone Guthrie Directs Hamlet* (Berkeley: University of California Press, 1970).
41. Guthrie, *Life*, p. 286.
42. See Shaughnessy, 'Shakespearean Utopias', pp. 233–7.
43. J.L. Styan, *Shakespeare in Performance: All's Well that Ends Well* (Manchester: Manchester University Press, 1984), pp. 4–5.
44. Susan Snyder (ed.), *All's Well that Ends Well*, The Oxford Shakespeare (Oxford: Oxford University Press, 1993), p. 31.
45. F.S. Boas, *Shakspere and his Predecessors* (London: John Murray, 1896), p. 347; John Masefield, *William Shakespeare* (London: Williams and Norgate, 1911), pp. 146–8.
46. Sir Arthur Quiller-Couch (ed.), *All's Well that Ends Well*, The New Shakespeare (Cambridge: Cambridge University Press, 1929), pp. xxxiv–xxxv, xxxi. Q's gustatory preoccupation echoes that of the first Arden editor, who had found the play 'revolting', leaving 'so unpleasant a flavour with some people that it is not tasted again'. Still, it was an 'acquired taste', and 'when the taste has been acquired, one wonders how the revolting side of the plot could ever have hidden the manifold, and in certain respects unique, interest of the play'. See W. Osborne Brigstocke, *All's Well that Ends Well*, The Arden Shakespeare (London: Methuen, 1904), p. xv.
47. Tyrone Guthrie, 'A Long View of the Stratford Festival', in Tyrone Guthrie, Robertson Davies and Grant McDonald, *Twice Have the Trumpets Sounded: a Record of the Stratford Festival in Canada 1954* (London: J. Garnett Millar, 1955), p. 165.
48. Styan, op. cit., p. 7.
49. Taylor, *Detroit Times*. The Shaw/Ibsen connections were obvious ones to make, given the 'problem play' tag which had been initiated by Boas and recently reiterated by Tillyard in *Shakespeare's Problem Plays* (London: Chatto and Windus, 1950), and in Shaw's own claim that Shakespeare anticipated *A Doll's House* by 'making the hero a perfectly ordinary young man, whose unimaginative prejudices and selfish conventionality make him cut a very mean figure in the atmosphere created by the nobler nature of his wife' (*Our Theatres in the Nineties*, vol.1 [London: Constable, 1932], p. 27).
50. Styan, op. cit., pp. 7–8.
51. Michel Foucault, *The History of Sexuality, Volume 1: an Introduction*, trans. Alan Sheridan (Harmondsworth: Penguin, 1979).
52. Steven Marcus, *The Other Victorians: a Study of Sexuality and Pornography in Mid-Nineteenth Century England* (London: Weidenfeld and Nicolson, 1966).
53. Michel Foucault, *Discipline and Punish: the Birth of the Prison*, trans. Alan Sheridan (Harmondsworth: Penguin, 1977), p. 25.
54. Ibid.
55. Promptbook for *All's Well that Ends Well*, Stratford Festival, 1953 (Festival Archive). I should emphasise that my reconstruction is conjectural, in that

it is based upon the evidence of the notation contained in this document (supplemented whenever possible by the observations of reviewers). Since it is, therefore, a reading of a performance-related text rather than a recon-struction of a performance, I have opted to write in the present tense.

56. I owe my account of this moment to the filmed record that is provided by the National Film Board of Canada documentary *The Stratford Adventure*, directed by Morten Parker (Canada, 1954; ISVN 9087–87–18).

5. Seeing through Shakespeare

1. Richard Allen Cave, *New British Drama in Performance on the London Stage: 1970–1985* (Gerrards Cross: Colin Smythe, 1987), p. 302; Colin Chambers and Mike Prior, *Playwright's Progress: Patterns of Postwar British Drama* (London: Amber Lane Press, 1987), p. 165.
2. See S. Schoenbaum, *Shakespeare's Lives*, 2nd edition (Oxford: Clarendon Press, 1991).
3. See E.K. Chambers, *William Shakespeare: a Study of Facts and Problems*, 2 vols (Oxford: Clarendon Press, 1930).
4. Edward Bond, 'Introduction', in *Bingo: Scenes of Money and Death* (London: Eyre Methuen, 1974), pp. vi–xii.
5. Alf Louvre and Jeffrey Walsh, 'Introduction', in *Tell Me Lies about Vietnam: Cultural Battles for the Meaning of the War*, ed. Louvre and Walsh (Milton Keynes and Philadelphia: Open University Press, 1988), p. 17.
6. James Aulich, 'Cartoon Representations of the Vietnam War in the British Press', in *Tell Me Lies*, p. 132.
7. 'Conversation with Howard Davies', in *Edward Bond: a Companion to the Plays*, ed. Malcolm Hay and Philip Roberts (London: TQ Publications, 1978), p. 62.
8. Quoted in Tony Coult, 'Creating What is Normal', *Plays and Players*, December 1975.
9. 'Conversation', p. 62.
10. Quoted in Michael Coveney, 'Space Odyssey: Three Leading Young Designers in Conversation', *Plays and Players*, June 1976.
11. Malcolm Hay and Philip Roberts, *Bond: a Study of His Plays* (London: Eyre Methuen, 1980), pp. 193–4.
12. Edward Bond, 'Beating Barbarism', *Sunday Times*, 25 November 1973.
13. Graham Holderness and Bryan Loughrey, 'Shakespearean Features', in *The Appropriation of Shakespeare: Post-Renaissance Reconstructions of the Works and Myth*, ed. Jean I. Marsden (Hemel Hempstead: Harvester Wheatsheaf, 1991), p. 186.
14. Bond, 'Beating Barbarism'.
15. Harold Hobson, 'Fringe Benefits', *Sunday Times*, 2 December 1973.
16. Coveney, 'Space Odyssey'.
17. Don D. Moore, '*Bingo*', *Educational Theatre Journal*, 27 (1975), 120.
18. Coult, 'Creating What is Normal'.
19. Quoted in David Hirst, *Edward Bond* (Basingstoke: Macmillan Press – now Palgrave Macmillan, 1985), p. 37.
20. Ronald Harwood (ed.), *The Ages of Gielgud: an Actor at Eighty* (London: Hodder and Stoughton, 1984), p. 4.

21. J.C. Trewin in *The Ages of Gielgud*, pp. 13–15.
22. Cave, *New British Drama*, p. 313.
23. Sigmund Freud, 'Recommendations to Physicians Practising Psycho-Analysis', in *The Standard Edition of the Complete Psychological Works of Sigmund Freud, Volume XII (1911–1913): the Case of Schreber, Papers on Technique and Other Works*, ed. James Strachey (London: Hogarth Press, 1958), p. 118.
24. Peter Hall, Diary entry dated Tuesday 20 August 1974, *Peter Hall's Diaries* ed. John Goodwin (London: Hamish Hamilton, 1984), p. 117. The entry continues, without apparent irony: 'Today I was handed one sheet of paper outlining a television commercial for an insurance company's pension fund which I could do. £1,000 for a day's directing work. Ridiculous . . .'
25. Raymond Goodlatte, 'The "Bingo" Shakespeare', *Listener*, 5 September 1974.
26. John Worthen, 'The "Bingo" Shakespeare', *Listener*, 26 September 1974.
27. Pam Gems, 'Bond Honoured', *Plays and Players*, November 1974.
28. Derek Paget, *True Stories? Documentary Drama on Radio, Screen and Stage* (Manchester: Manchester University Press, 1990), p. 147.
29. For accounts of the role of Buzz Goodbody and of the work of The Other Place, see Colin Chambers, *Other Spaces: New Theatre and the RSC* (London: Eyre Methuen, 1980); Peter Holland, 'The RSC and Studio Shakespeare', *Essays in Criticism*, 32 (1982), 205–18; Dympna Callaghan, 'Buzz Goodbody: Directing for Change', in *The Appropriation of Shakespeare*, ed. Marsden, pp. 163–81; Robert Shaughnessy, *Representing Shakespeare: England, History and the RSC* (Hemel Hempstead: Harvester Wheatsheaf, 1994), pp. 163–75.
30. Dennis Kennedy, *Looking at Shakespeare: a Visual History of Twentieth-Century Performance* (Cambridge: Cambridge University Press, 1993), p. 252.
31. Chambers, *Other Spaces*, pp. 36, 72.
32. Ibid., p. 34.
33. Alan Sinfield, 'Royal Shakespeare: Theatre and the Making of Ideology', in *Political Shakespeare: Essays in Cultural Materialism*, 2nd edition, ed. Jonathan Dollimore and Alan Sinfield (Manchester: Manchester University Press, 1994), p. 183.
34. Chambers, op. cit., p. 72.
35. On the politics of theatre subsidy in the 1970s, see Baz Kershaw, *The Politics of Performance: Radical Theatre as Cultural Intervention* (London: Routledge, 1992).
36. 'Conversation', pp. 57–60.
37. Chambers, op. cit., pp. 47–8, 39.
38. John Downie and Penny Gold, *I Was Shakespeare's Double*, RSC Promptbook, 1974, p. 56. The skit continues: 'We hear boos, Hitler Rallies etc. by mistake. Gielgud gives us a minute or so of to be or not to be, but with poor or anarchic lighting, and violent interruptions. Massive adulation. Music at wrong speed. Gielgud does not deign to notice anything is wrong and leaves unmolested, through increasing chaos.'
39. Howard Davies, interviewed by Peter Hulton, 6 January 1978, *Bingo and The Bundle*, ed. Peter Hulton, Dartington Theatre Papers, Second Series, no. 1 (1978), p. 9.

40. Ibid.
41. 'Conversation', pp. 10, 23–4.
42. Callaghan, op. cit., p. 171.
43. *Bingo and The Bundle*, p. 17.
44. Hay and Roberts, op. cit., pp. 188, 187.
45. David Marquand, 'Rule Britannia', *New Statesman and Society*, 22 June 1990.
46. Quoted in Ian Woodward, 'Suchet's Strange Faces', *Radio Times*, 30 June 1990.
47. *Bingo and The Bundle*, p. 13.
48. Stuart Hall, *The Hard Road to Renewal: Thatcherism and the Crisis of the Left* (London: Verso, 1988), p. 8.
49. Edward Bond, Letter to George Bas, in *Letters*, vol. 4, ed. Ian Stuart (Amsterdam: Harwood Academic Publishers, 1998), p. 86.
50. Other parts were doubled as follows: Antonio/William Combe: Daniel Flynn; Stephano/Son: Ian Driver; Adriana (this production's version of Adrian)/Joan: Romy Baskerville; Gonzalo/Old Man: Ken Farrington; Sebastian/Jerome: Stephen Hattersley; Trinculo/Wally: Jeremy Brook.

6. Ruined Lear

1. Tim Etchells, *Certain Fragments: Contemporary Performance and Forced Entertainment* (London: Routledge, 1999), p. 19.
2. Tim Etchells, 'Diverse Assembly: Some Trends in Recent Performance', in *Contemporary British Theatre*, ed. Theodore Shank (Basingstoke: Macmillan Press – now Palgrave Macmillan, 1996), p. 108.
3. Nick Kaye, *Art into Theatre: Performance Interviews and Documents* (Amsterdam: Harwood Academic Publishers, 1996), p. 244.
4. Etchells 'Diverse Assembly', p. 112.
5. Kaye, op. cit., p. 240.
6. Etchells, *Certain Fragments*, pp. 102, 221.
7. Andrew Quick, 'Searching for Redemption with Cardboard Wings: Forced Entertainment and the Sublime', *Contemporary Theatre Review*, 2, 2 (1994) 26.
8. Etchells, *Certain Fragments*, p. 77.
9. Tim Etchells, 'Nights in This City: Diverse Letters and Fragments Relating to a Performance Now Past', in Nick Kaye, *Site-Specific Art: Performance, Place and Documentation* (London: Routledge, 2000), p. 15.
10. Etchells, *Certain Fragments*, pp. 221, 179.
11. Quoted in Tim Etchells, 'Valuable Spaces: New Performance in the 1990s', *A Split Second of Paradise: Live Art, Installation and Performance*, ed. Nicky Childs and Jeni Walwin (London and New York: Rivers Oram Press, 1998), p. 35. For further discussion of the Wooster Group, see in particular David Savran, *Breaking the Rules: the Wooster Group* (New York: Theatre Communications Group, 1988), and John Russell Brown, 'Cross-Dressed Actors and their Audiences: Kate Valk's Emperor Jones and William Shakespeare's Juliet', *New Theatre Quarterly*, 15 (1999), 195–203.
12. Etchells, *Certain Fragments*, p. 52.
13. Ibid., p. 54.

14. Ibid., p. 53.
15. Carole Woddis, *What's On*, 18 December 1996, quoted in Steve Harper, 'Everytime You Go Away ... You Take a Piece of Me With You', *Contemporary Theatre Review*, 10, 3 (2000), 95.
16. Etchells, *Certain Fragments*, p. 63.
17. Email to the author, 16 November 2000. Unless otherwise stated, Etchells's comments on *Five Day Lear* are quoted from this and subsequent communications on 6 February and 6 June 2001.

Index

Printed in the United States
45898LVS00001B/153